Holocaust Literature and Representation

COMPARATIVE JEWISH LITERATURES

Bloomsbury's **Comparative Jewish Literatures** series creates a new venue for scholarship and debate both in Jewish Studies and Comparative Literature as it showcases the diversity of a nascent field with unique interdisciplinary footprints. It offers both a new way of looking at Jewish writing as well as insights into how Jewish literature is looked at by scholars indifferent to or sympathetic with these texts. Through its focus on the diversity of these groups' perspectives, the series suggests that disciplinary location informs how comparative Jewish literatures are understood theoretically, and it establishes new sectors that abut and intersect with the field in the twenty-first century.

Series Editor
Kitty Millet, San Francisco State University, USA

Advisory Board
Agata Bielik-Robson, University of Nottingham, UK
Sarah Phillips Casteel, Carleton University, Canada
Bryan Cheyette, University of Reading, UK
Nan Goodman, University of Colorado at Boulder, USA
Vivian Liska, University of Antwerp, Belgium
Orly Lubin, Tel Aviv University, Israel
Susan McReynolds, Northwestern University, USA
Paul Mendes-Flohr, University of Chicago, USA
Anna Parkinson, Northwestern University, USA
Na'ama Rokem, University of Chicago, USA
Maurice Samuels, Yale University, USA
Axel Stähler, University of Kent, UK
Ilan Stavans, Amherst College, USA

Volumes in the Series:
Jewish Imaginaries of the Spanish Civil War: In Search of Poetic Justice, edited by Cynthia Gabbay
Derrida's Marrano Passover: Exile, Survival, Betrayal, and the Metaphysics of Non-Identity, by Agata Bielik-Robson
Holocaust Literature and Representation: Their Lives, Our Words, edited by Phyllis Lassner and Judith Tydor Baumel-Schwartz
Kabbalah and Literature, by Kitty Millet (forthcoming)
Poesis in Extremis: Literature Witnessing the Holocaust, edited by Daniel Feldman and Efraim Sicher (forthcoming)

Holocaust Literature and Representation
Their Lives, Our Words

*Edited by Phyllis Lassner and
Judith Tydor Baumel-Schwartz*

BLOOMSBURY ACADEMIC
NEW YORK • LONDON • OXFORD • NEW DELHI • SYDNEY

BLOOMSBURY ACADEMIC
Bloomsbury Publishing Inc
1385 Broadway, New York, NY 10018, USA
50 Bedford Square, London, WC1B 3DP, UK
29 Earlsfort Terrace, Dublin 2, Ireland

BLOOMSBURY, BLOOMSBURY ACADEMIC and the Diana logo are trademarks of
Bloomsbury Publishing Plc

First published in the United States of America 2023
Paperback edition published 2024

Copyright © Phyllis Lassner and Judith Tydor Baumel-Schwartz, 2023
Each chapter © Contributors, 2023

Cover design by Eleanor Rose
Cover image: Helping Hand © Carol Troen

All rights reserved. No part of this publication may be reproduced or transmitted in any form or by any means, electronic or mechanical, including photocopying, recording, or any information storage or retrieval system, without prior permission in writing from the publishers.

Bloomsbury Publishing Inc does not have any control over, or responsibility for, any third-party websites referred to or in this book. All internet addresses given in this book were correct at the time of going to press. The author and publisher regret any inconvenience caused if addresses have changed or sites have ceased to exist, but can accept no responsibility for any such changes.

Library of Congress Cataloging-in-Publication Data

Names: Lassner, Phyllis, editor. | Baumel-Schwartz, Judith Tydor, 1959- editor.
Title: Holocaust literature and representation : their lives, our words / edited by Phyllis Lassner and Judith Tydor Baumel-Schwartz.
Description: New York : Bloomsbury Academic, 2023. | Series: Comparative Jewish literatures | Includes bibliographical references and index. | Summary: "The first volume to explore both the academic and personal journeys of scholars working in the field of Holocaust literature and representation"– Provided by publisher.
Identifiers: LCCN 2022028554 (print) | LCCN 2022028555 (ebook) | ISBN 9781501391590 (hardback) | ISBN 9781501391637 (paperback) | ISBN 9781501391606 (epub) | ISBN 9781501391613 (pdf) | ISBN 9781501391620 (ebook other)
Subjects: LCSH: Holocaust, Jewish (1939-1945)–Historiography. | Holocaust scholars–Biography. | College teachers–Biography. | Jewish historians–Biography. | Holocaust, Jewish (1939-1945)–Study and teaching.
Classification: LCC D804.348 .H648 2023 (print) | LCC D804.348 (ebook) | DDC 940.53/18072--dc23/eng/20220802
LC record available at https://lccn.loc.gov/2022028554
LC ebook record available at https://lccn.loc.gov/2022028555

ISBN: HB: 978-1-5013-9159-0
PB: 978-1-5013-9163-7
ePDF: 978-1-5013-9161-3
eBook: 978-1-5013-9160-6

Series: Comparative Jewish Literatures

Typeset by RefineCatch, Bungay, Suffolk NR35 1EF, UK

To find out more about our authors and books, visit www.bloomsbury.com and sign up for our newsletters.

Dedicated to the memory of Joan Ringelheim and Rachel Feldhay Brenner, dear friends, colleagues, and courageous pioneers who broadened and deepened our study of the Holocaust.

CONTENTS

Introduction 1
Phyllis Lassner and Judith Tydor Baumel-Schwartz

Part I: North America

1. Voices from the Past 13
   Victoria Aarons

2. Movies as Prosthetic Holocaust Memories 23
   Lawrence Baron

3. Personal and Professional Autobiographies: Reechoing Memories of the Holocaust 35
   Rachel Feldhay Brenner

4. A Winding Road 45
   Margarete Myers Feinstein

5. Biographia Literaria Feminista 57
   Sara R. Horowitz

6. My Journey into the Shoah 69
   David Patterson

7. My Holocaust Autobiography: *The Mortal Storm* 79
   Alexis Pogorelskin

8   Gendered Encounters; The Holocaust and Life Writing 91
    Ravenel Richardson

Part II: Great Britain

9   Before the Gate of Memory 105
    Joshua Lander

10 I Am Not Jewish 115
    Joanne Pettitt

11 Representing the Holocaust in Britain 125
    Sue Vice

Part III: Israel

12 Following in the Footsteps of Claude Vigée: From the Holocaust Trauma to a New Science of Judaism 139
    Thierry J. Alcoloumbre

13 Where Did Those People Go? 149
    Karen Alkalay-Gut

14 Untold Story, Indirect Course: My Path into the Field of Holocaust Literature and Representation 163
    Michal Ben-Horin

15 Too Much, Too Little: A Personal Journey through Holocaust Narratives 175
    Keren Goldfrad

16 "Why Don't You Move On?": A Sort of Play in Three Acts and Three Standing Ovations 187
    Roy Horovitz

17 Intersecting Narratives: When East Meets West 199
   Yvonne Kozlovsky-Golan

18 Voicing the Unvoiced 211
   Liliane Steiner

19 How Literature Chose Me 221
   Bela Ruth Samuel Tenenholtz

Notes on Contributors **231**

Index of People 237
Index of Places 243
Index of Organizations 245

Introduction

Phyllis Lassner and Judith Tydor Baumel-Schwartz

This book is what happens when a Holocaust historian (Judy) and a scholar of Holocaust representation (Phyllis) decide to collaborate, co-editing a collected volume of their colleagues' academic autobiographies. Actually, had it not been for a quirk of fate that caused Judy to major in history, both editors might have been scholars of Holocaust literature. At some point in high school, Judy had written a composition about Elie Wiesel's novel *The Oath* which, unknown to her, her father had sent to his old friend from Buchenwald. Wiesel answered immediately: "The composition is excellent and touching. Tell your daughter she should study Jewish literature: it is her subject, and the time will come when she will teach it to others with great ability, yours, Eliezer." Hearing the response, Judy laughed out loud. "Me? A university professor? Teaching Jewish Literature? Boy, do you have the wrong number!" Yet, in spite of becoming a Holocaust historian, she ended up collaborating in numerous scholarly endeavors that involved Jewish literature, such as the present volume.

Phyllis's encounter with Jewish literature and the Holocaust developed more gradually, with an accretion of revelations that began with no family or other connection or interest in the Holocaust. Instead, Phyllis's story developed from a passion for British fiction as an undergraduate that intensified in her graduate studies. However, her decision to focus on British women writers of the Second World War did not anticipate the shock she felt in response to the casual, unreflective antisemitism she encountered in the works of some of the most revered British modernists, including the avowed feminist anti-fascist Virginia Woolf. How, she kept repeating in her scholarly writing and at conferences, could writers who, during the height of Hitler's rise to power, not notice that their antisemitic depictions were complicit with the Fascism they were opposing? To this day, there has been no satisfactory answer to this conundrum or to how we should respond to so many other luminaries who failed to support endangered Jews. This silence remains a prime motivation for Phyllis's commitment to studying the representation of Jews and the Holocaust in British, American, and European culture.

Although we—Phyllis and Judy—were drawn to this project from different backgrounds, academic experiences, and disciplines, we began with questions we both found compelling: Why did a Holocaust historian and a scholar of Holocaust literature and representation feel that there was a need for another book on the Holocaust, particularly one that departed from the conventions of dispassionate academic discourse and which explored Holocaust history and representation through the personal narratives of scholars? What could such a book contribute to Holocaust scholarship, especially since our contributors represented so many different national, cultural, and generational identities, career paths, subjects, and approaches? How could personal narratives recounting divergent paths to careers in Holocaust Studies contribute to our knowledge of the Holocaust? Underlying these questions was our rationale for pursuing this project, the belief that a collection of academic autobiographical essays would address many questions to help us understand why Holocaust Studies occupies a separate, perhaps unique, and certainly contested place among the vast network of academic work.

We begin by contextualizing the essays in this volume with a reflection on the history of Holocaust Studies. Although scholars continue to debate various aspects of Holocaust history, there is little doubt that it was a watershed event of the twentieth century.[1] Even as it occurred, scholars were already studying its causes and various aspects of its development. During the first decades after the war's end, they focused upon what they felt were as its various major facets: Nazi policy towards the Jews, Jewish leadership, resistance, rescue attempts, and the Nazi camp universe. By the 1970s, academic scholarship about the Holocaust had expanded to include social and cultural topics such as daily life under Nazi rule, the plight of refugees, and the fate of children under the Nazis. It was only much later, however—and not without struggle—that the subject of women and the Holocaust was recognized as crucial to our knowledge. Today, these approaches are treated as worthy research topics that help us better understand the dynamics of this catastrophic period.

It was only at a second stage that scholars began to write about Holocaust Representation. First there was analysis of the Holocaust literature written during the Holocaust itself. This was followed by interpreting commemorative literature written by survivors, including memoirs and other forums of self-documentation. Eventually, there was analysis and interpretation of later Holocaust representations, among them memoirs and stories not necessarily written by survivors. The emergence of Holocaust fiction and feature films, as well as graphic, cartoon, animated representations, and even video games, has produced new analytical approaches as well as debates that developed from interest in trauma theory, memory, and its transmission to the second generation and onwards. All these are part of today's growing corpus of Holocaust scholarship throughout the world.

While the writing of survivors, refugees, and their families was quickly recognized as crucial testimony, scholars dealing with Holocaust representation confronted professional challenges. In both history and cultural studies, Holocaust representation in literature, film, and other media was often considered "parochial," "depressing," or as popular culture representations proliferated, offensive. With the exception of Jewish Studies and Holocaust Studies conferences, the subject was most often absent from conferences focusing on modern literature where the few presentations on Holocaust literature and film were received with silence. This absence discouraged the idea that this most cataclysmic event offered any illumination of twentieth-century cultural practice and production. What was particularly perplexing was the continuing lack of interest, even when the preeminent literary theorist Paul de Man was exposed as a contributor to a pro-Nazi periodical and his theory self-deconstructed. Although the event drove other scholars to confront the Holocaust and its ethical demands,[2] as a whole, the field of modern literature was not inspired to follow. This disconnect from mainstream interests in cultural studies persists, including in those fields where Holocaust Studies could make a difference to their historical and theoretical framing, such as critical race theory, postcolonial studies, multiculturalism, and gender and sexuality studies. Today, Holocaust representation in myriad forms constitutes a field of study unto itself but with recognition of the critical difference it makes to the politics of such canonical literary movements as modernism, postmodernism, or the new realism.

Ironically, the absence of Holocaust Studies intensified interest and commitment to the subject for a growing number of young scholars. Although young scholars in different places were warned against choosing Holocaust representation as their field of study, they persevered. Some advanced in rank; others became pivotal members of Holocaust research institutes and Holocaust memorial museums or chose to continue researching and writing on the topic as independent scholars while pursuing a different career. Today, younger scholars choosing this field no longer face the opposition that some members of the older generation had to combat. In fact, that same older generation is now mentoring and benefiting from the work of younger scholars. Whatever their professional status, each scholar working in the field of Holocaust Literature and Representation has a story to tell. Not only the scholarly story of the work they do, but their personal story, their journey to becoming a specialist in Holocaust Representation. With all their differences, their stories emphasize how the Holocaust is crucial to our exploration of twentieth-century culture, its production, and its reception.

Why do the personal stories of Holocaust scholars warrant a book of their own? What do these stories add to our knowledge of the Holocaust and even the work of scholars in other academic fields? Especially because the essays are personal narratives, there is the danger of sentimentalizing the lost past, its people and places, of creating nostalgic memories that belie the horrors research exposes. In their widely varied personal trajectories, the result contravenes such temptations by creating a hybrid form of academic work. Each essay demonstrates how the subject of the Holocaust, with its unfathomable horror and pain, provokes deeply subjective interpretive perspectives. Even as the passage of time creates critical distance, especially as scholars offer new knowledge from different disciplines, archival work, interviews, and the analysis of cultural artifacts, the extremes of Holocaust suffering and memory intervene. As our authors attest, the Holocaust past remains a haunting presence that cannot be researched or written away. It resounds throughout the twentieth century and beyond as its traumatic experiences, responses, and memories continue to shape political and cultural attitudes, and even public and social policies. Consequently, the subject of Holocaust representation, in all its documented history and emotional expression, continues to inspire inward looking, self-consciously self-questioning reflections on scholars' immersion in the subject, as well as on their critical approaches. To quote one of our contributors, Thierry Alcoloumbre, "the autobiographical discourse remains legitimate in order to retrace an intellectual itinerary, to signal the experiences and the encounters that raised questions or suggested the means to answer them."

The questions our contributors asked themselves reflect the lasting personal and professional concerns provoked by studying Holocaust representation. In turn, the depth and breadth of their questions and concerns became the inspiration for this book. In planning it, however, we did not request that contributors follow a particular theoretical framework. Instead, we wanted each essayist to develop their own stories to reflect their individual journeys in their own voices and styles. With a broad stroke to encourage this, we asked contributors to consider why and how their own stories intersect with or challenge their Holocaust scholarship and that of others. Read individually and collectively, the essays' varied approaches and answers to this question offer an original contribution to Holocaust and genocide studies that we hope will also inspire scholars and teachers in other fields. Instead of putting their own stories aside to assume or construct a position of scholarly objectivity or take objectivity for granted as intrinsic to analysis, our authors explore the ways their journeys to working on Holocaust representation involve affective and ethical responses and decisions. Reflexively, their essays raise further questions. Can academic forms of discourse reflect or be put in the service of analyzing experiences and responses that reflect realities we can never hope to fully understand? How do we assert or claim accuracy or authenticity in our responses to the silences or the reemergence of haunting memories? Unlike popular notions of trauma, how do we identify the language in which to interpret the lack of recognizable or even accessible narrative patterning and themes, the inability to heal, and the impossibility of closure? As so many have pondered, what are the criteria for assessing imaginative renderings of Holocaust experience? Is mimesis bound to fail the test of documented, detailed historical accuracy, or can imaginative creations offer emotional, psychological, or interpretive insights that facts and figures cannot?

Collectively, the essays suggest that interpreting Holocaust representation always involves ethical decisions that reflect our subjectivities—why we chose to study Holocaust representation and how that choice influences our interpretive practices. There is a powerful sense in all the essays that Holocaust scholarship demands the exercise of personal responsibility to the roles we assume of belated witnesses and agents on behalf of preserving and disseminating Holocaust stories and memory. We might even hope that collectively, our work represents a form of memorialization.

In their self-conscious, questioning responses, interweaving autobiographical and academic writing, our contributors explore hermeneutical and reflexive relationships between Holocaust research and its challenging meanings to the unfolding of their careers and reflections on their work. They ask themselves, what academic, political, cultural, and personal experiences led them to choose Holocaust representation as their subject of research and teaching? What academic, intellectual, and/or personal challenges did they face on their journey? How did their training as cultural critics affect their work on Holocaust representation? What approaches, genres, media, or other forms of Holocaust representation did they choose and why? Did that focus shift over time and if so, why and how? How and where did they find a scholarly "home" in which to share their work profitably? How did working on Holocaust Representation affect them as a scholar and in their thinking about themselves? How do they imagine their work moving forward, including new challenges, responses, and audiences?

Given their diverse experiences and stories, we could not expect any of our authors to tackle all these questions. Instead, following the remit of expressing individual experiences and responses, each author embeds responses that reflect their personal, often indirect or circuitous pathways, as well as their academic challenges and reflections. Contributors to this collection represent widely diverse cultural identities and backgrounds. Some authors are children of survivors or have family connections to the Holocaust, others are Jewish, but identify with different religious, social, or cultural communities and denominations. Those contributors who are not Jewish enlighten us about the inconsistent, unstable meanings of "outsider," especially as it relates to one's chosen field of study. This is of paramount importance today with debates about cultural appropriation, diversity, and inclusion. As though in response, the cultural diversity of our participants offers a lens on relationships between forms of representation and individual ethical commitment. We as co-editors, along with our contributors, have collaborated in our learning that as alien as the world of concentration and death camps, ghettos, and other sites of Holocaust suffering will always be, we are committed to its presence in our collective consciousness and academic work. All of our authors have devoted a significant part of their professional lives to writing about Holocaust Literature and Representation. We believe that this choice was not random, and in many cases was rooted in the personal history and professional experiences of each scholar which later affected the fruits of their scholarship.

Each author was asked to write an autobiographical-academic essay about their journey towards working on the topic and their experiences while conducting their research. Many of the essays take the form of a cultural history and address issues that may initially seem unconnected: their personal and family background, beginning with their home and early years up to and including their education, their first exposure to the Holocaust in history, in literature, and in film, as well as any personal or communal connection to the Holocaust.

While all our contributors reflect on the professional choices that brought them to study the Holocaust, some recount how their broader surroundings—friends, family, teachers—responded to their choice of topic, how and why they chose a particular aspect of Holocaust Literature and Representation as their specialty. To provide fuller personal context, many recall other research topics they have studied and the relationship of these, if any, to Holocaust Literature and Representation. A crucial revelation embedded in their narratives is the effect of their Holocaust work on their personal and professional lives. For many, issues of cultural and family identities, personal choice, religious, political, or cultural affiliation cohere with the focus of their research.

Despite family influences, after much deliberation about organizing the essays, we rejected a generational structure as only one of many focuses. We also considered but discarded such organizing principles as thematic structures as well as subject areas and disciplinary approaches because of the diverse departmental and programmatic settings for Holocaust Studies in different universities and regions. We recognized that the essays represented overlapping and intersecting generations and themes and that the interdisciplinary work of studying Holocaust representation could not be distilled into distinct fields of study or genres. Instead, the essays' interdisciplinary approaches combined with personal narrative created a hybrid genre: the academic autobiographical essay. Moreover, all of the contributors' work demonstrated that analyzing and interpreting Holocaust representation involved an ever-expanding spectrum of media, including written and graphic diaries, memoirs, and autobiographies as well as fiction, both written and graphic, creative non-fiction, poetry, film, photography, and the plastic arts. While all of these media and genres are expressed with distinct narrative and technical properties, there is also abundant borrowing among them which in turn produces hybrid forms of interpretation and analysis. Although each of our contributors works with close textual or visual readings, their analyses are informed by various avenues and forms of historical and cultural research and contexts. In turn, each essay is narrated in the particular vocal tones and rhetorical strategies as well as linear and non-linear styles and structures that contributors chose to represent their personal and professional odysseys.

Ultimately, we decided on a geographical division of essays, covering three locales: North America (eight contributors); the United Kingdom (three contributors); and Israel (eight contributors). Our rationale is that while each contributor's experience and interests are distinct, academic cultures in each region have been shaped by collective histories that have responded to Holocaust Studies with similar challenges to building careers in Holocaust representation. Avoiding any kind of hierarchy, essays in each section are listed alphabetically. For example, in the section on North America, Victoria Aarons focuses on the question, "Where was the Shoah in the midst of the literary attempts to reframe configurations and dispositions of American Jewish identity, community, and memory?" Lawrence Baron narrates his evolution as a historian of modern Germany to charting the changing focus of international Holocaust cinema. "Looking back at the Holocaust from a considerable historical distance," Rachel Brenner addresses her awareness "of the extent to which Holocaust consciousness informed vicariously [her] identity." Margarete Feinstein details the winding road from studying the history of Nazism to women's experiences as displaced persons (DPs) and a career in Holocaust scholarship. Sara Horowitz interweaves her own scholarly passions with an exploration of how personal experience shapes—and is shaped *by*—our cultures and communities of meaning. David Patterson explains how his journey into Judaism and eventually converting was interwoven with his journey into the Shoah. Alexis Pogorelskin details how the MGM film *The Mortal Storm* (1940) inspired her interest in representing the plight of Europe's Jews before the Holocaust and Hollywood's response. Ravenel Richardson's studies in Comparative Literature led to her doctoral work on women's diaries of the Second World War and the Holocaust.

In Britain, Joshua Lander outlines how his disconnection from Judaism and Jewishness shaped his interest in Jewish, and later, Holocaust literature. Joanne Pettitt writes about what it means to study the Holocaust as someone who is not Jewish, and Sue Vice uses her engagement with Holocaust representation to offer a way of reflecting on its history in Britain more broadly.

In Israel, Thierry J. Alcoloumbre reveals how his participation in a conference dedicated to the poet Claude Vigée opened up a new period in his career as a researcher, leading him to literature on the Holocaust. Karen Alkalay-Gut traces her fascination with German-Jewish actor Kurt Gerron from her quest for information about the slaughter of both her grandmothers and over thirty of her mother's family. Michal Ben-Horin analyzes her focus on aesthetics in dealing with issues of Holocaust representation. Keren Goldfrad reflects on her "realization that my thirst for knowledge in this field stemmed from the emotional impression left by my grandparents' stories." Roy Horovitz, director, actor, and dramaturg, explains the allure of the Holocaust in theater and revisits his various Holocaust-related projects to show their connection. Yvonne Kozlovsky-Golan posits how a woman of Mizrahi descent ultimately engaged in the academic study of film and the Holocaust. Liliane Steiner recounts her journey as a young immigrant girl from Fez, Morocco to ultimately becoming a teacher of Holocaust Studies, and Bela Ruth Samuel Tenenholtz gives a bird's-eye view of her life as a child of Holocaust survivors from Holland, and how her parents' decision not to speak about the Shoah became the moving force behind her research and writing.

As these summaries attest, this collection of essays can be considered a living laboratory that studies how Holocaust knowledge is produced in relation to the diverse identities, subjectivities, and pathways of scholars. As narrators and protagonists of their journeys to becoming Holocaust scholars, as participant observers and as interpreters of the knowledge they gained and constructed, the contributors to this volume create new perspectives on what it means to study Holocaust representation. In concert, these autobiographical academic narratives contribute to the knowledge, as Lawrence Langer so eloquently posited, that to study the Holocaust "is to regard the calamity as a summons to reconsider usual views of the self, its relation to time and memory, its portrayal in literature born of the Holocaust, its use and abuse by culture, and its role in reshaping our sense of history's legacies from the past and bequests to later generations."[3] In all their personal and cultural diversity, the writers in this collection reconsider the view of the scholarly self as enacting a necessary distance from the suffering wrought by the Holocaust. Instead, as their essays illuminate, to study Holocaust representation is to accept and embrace the responsibility of its legacies to create a bequest of self-searching, self-critical knowledge.

Notes

1 We do not ignore the phenomenon of continuing worldwide Holocaust denial. That subject has been explored in depth by Deborah Lipstadt and others. See, for example, Lipstadt's *History on Trial: My Day in Court With a Holocaust*

Denier (New York: Harper Perennial, 2006); *Denying the Holocaust: The Growing Assault on Truth and Memory* (New York: Free Press, 1993).

2 See, for example, Dominck LaCapra, *Representing the Holocaust: History, Theory, Trauma* (Ithaca: Cornell University Press, 1994); Dominick LaCapra, *Writing History, Writing Trauma* (Baltimore: Johns Hopkins University Press, 2001); J. Hillis Miller, *The Conflagration of Community: Fiction Before and After Auschwitz* (Chicago: University of Chicago Press, 2011); Jacques Derrida, *Cinders* (Minneapolis: University of Minnesota Press, 2014).

3 Lawrence Langer, *Admitting the Holocaust: Collected Essays* (Oxford: Oxford University Press, 1995), 3.

PART ONE

North America

1

Voices from the Past

Victoria Aarons

If I were able to draw, I would sketch my parents as I remember them best: My mother curled in a corner of the living-room couch with a book in her hands; and my father sitting at his writing table in his study, wall-to-ceiling bookshelves cocooning the room in words. My childhood home was filled with books, the presence of which formed an essential, immovable part of the landscape of my life. Everywhere I looked, there were books: On the shelves that lined virtually every room of our home, on tables, on chairs and couches, books that would spill over onto floors, books whose words provided a kind of solidity that would define my coming of age during the tumultuous period of middle to late-1960s America. When I think back to that time, an era of violence, upheaval, and uncertainty, I remember feeling that books buffered the world that circumscribed our family. Looking around me now, decades later, I find that I have recreated that world in my personal and professional lives, a link to the past in a material embodiment of memory.

I can't remember a time in which the texture of my days did not involve books. My earliest memories are of my mother reading to me and my father quoting aloud passages from texts; his speech, well into old age, was always dotted with remembered lines from his favorite books. Some of my most vivid, felt memories involve being read to, my mother reading to me award-winning children's books—the Caldecotts and the Newberys—my father, the short stories of Sholom Aleichem and the parables of the Rebbe Nachman of Breslov. As he would read, he would instinctively fall into the Yiddish-inflected English that, as the self-fashioned, formally educated son of immigrants, he had long since abandoned. These were the voices I grew up with: Those of my parents enjoined with a tradition of Jewish storytellers, the past entwined with the present.

Once I learned to read on my own, books were the physical and psychic place to which I would regularly go. I recall the tactile enjoyment of learning to read, the progressively heavy feel of the book in my hands as my reading became more sophisticated, the words mounting on the pages. Reading and talking about what we read was essential to the shared family project. The question at the dinner table was not "what did you do in school today?" but rather "what are you reading and what are you going to read next?" (To this day, if I don't know what I'm reading "next," I feel untethered.) Reading, very simply, was the family ethic. If you weren't reading, you weren't thinking. Books were openings for the expression of ideas and shared discourse that I associate with family, with distinct moments of memory. As I entered adolescence and was diverted by the seductions of increasing choices and possibilities of self-invention, my father would exert a cautionary reminder: "Jews are people of the book! Go read!"

In many ways, then, I associated reading with Jewishness, with a Jewish cultural ethos defining of self and place. My home was a world of talk, an arena for debate, for self-expression, and for the disciplined engagement of ideas. It was considered heresy in my family, especially in my teenage years, to respond to what seemed like the ambushes of parental inquiry by insisting, "I don't want to discuss it." That dismissive renunciation was sure to provoke a fury of parental recriminations. Unlike most of my peers, I was permitted to read and talk about anything, so long as I was reading and talking. The home of my childhood was filled with talk and with the freedom to express and reflect on possibilities for understanding and navigating the world. Words were openings, connecting links among those whose lives informed and were informed by one's own. Ideas shaped the self and defined one's place among others. After all, as one of Grace Paley's characters emphatically reminds another, "In the beginning [...] was the word!"[1] There was a kind of authority in the written word, an ethical guideline for the making of character and for living in the world among others, those "world-inventing words," as another of Paley's characters puts it.[2] Utterance, in my family, was always measured against thoughtfulness and the assumption that one was engaged in the contemplative life. Careless, sloppy thinking was considered something of a regressive impulse, never to be tolerated. Language in all its symbolic and referential forms was essential to identity-formation, bearing the weight of memory and possibility. As one of Bernard Malamud's beleaguered (if amazed) characters acknowledges, "If you said it, it was said. If you believed it, you must say it."[3] Thus, I grew up surrounded by books, by ideas, and by the conscientious, thoughtful expression of belief, in a way, of faith; these were the god-terms of my upbringing, central to a Jewish cultural and intellectual ethic. There was no doubt, then, that the life of the mind was the right profession for me, an extension of what I knew and trusted.

It was only natural when I left the domestic space of my family for university life that I would radiate toward literature as my field of study. In many ways, the university was an extension of my familial and familiar landscape. I grew up around a university. My father, a practicing psychoanalyst, regularly attended seminars at the University of California, Berkeley. Typically, from my pre-teens, I would accompany him to the university, where I would do my homework in Doe Library, in the Philosophy library in Moses Hall, or on one of the benches in Sproul Plaza. I would wander through the campus bookstores and the student commons, quietly sit through lectures that I could barely understand, and take in the campus's intellectual atmosphere with great and increasing anticipation. The fact is that I simply can't remember a time when the university was not a part of my identity and my daily activities. It's the safe, familiar space that I locate in any city to which I travel. My love for literature, for higher education, and for the life of the mind stems directly from my upbringing. I would eventually attend UC, Berkeley myself, entering the field of Jewish Studies.

But how did I get there? How did I move from a vague, if impassioned, interest in literature to Jewish writers, to a Ph.D. thesis on the late nineteenth- to early twentieth-century Eastern European Yiddish writer Sholom Aleichem, and eventually to Holocaust literary studies? As is so often the case, all it took was one class, one professor who opened the door, and my academic trajectory took hold. Scanning the course descriptions posted on the English Department walls of Wheeler Hall, I happened upon a class being offered by the young Renaissance scholar, Stephen Greenblatt. Greenblatt, for whatever reason at the time, was offering a Jewish literature survey course, and I, perhaps simply drawn to the two words that were most self-defining—Jewish and literature—signed up for it. I still remember the syllabus for the course. I still own the books I purchased for that class. The course began with Irving Howe and Eliezer Greenberg's classic collection *A Treasury of Yiddish Stories* and concluded with Robert Alter's 1975 edited volume of stories, *Modern Hebrew Literature*. In other words, we began with the influential modernist Yiddish writers and ended with modern Israeli writers. In between, we read primarily Ashkenazic American Jewish writers, from Henry Roth's masterpiece of immigrant literature *Call It Sleep* through the burgeoning voices of post-war Jews, such as Saul Bellow, Bernard Malamud, Philip Roth, and Grace Paley, to the contemporary writers of the late 1970s, landing, with apologies from Greenblatt about the omissions on the reading list, on the rich tradition of Hebrew writers. Collectively these were the voices I had been hearing all my life, melodies from long ago. These were narratives that spoke a language and sensibility that I recognized and that defined my experience of the world I knew. In other words, I found my place in these texts. These were voices that reflected a communal expression of Jewish history, identity, memory, midrash, and lamentation. And when I first entered the profession as a young, newly minted PhD, I fashioned my own course on Jewish literature on the same reading list that, all those many years ago, captivated my interest.

Thus, as I say, all it took was one class, and the direction of my academic and professional life was put into motion. But, of course, it's never that easy nor that un-bumpily charted. My initial focus when thinking about the direction of my dissertation was on the three major Yiddish writers, Mendele Mocher Sforim, I. L. Peretz, and Sholom Aleichem. Since I had read this literature only in translation, I needed to learn to read Yiddish, a language that I had been hearing all my life, but only in fragments, snippets of endearments, expletives, curses, and blessings—certainly not the literary language I needed to navigate the original texts. Thus, I set out to learn Yiddish, a language that was not formally taught at my university at that time (though it is now included in the course catalog). Finally, I found a tutor and a book, and my studies began. What I discovered was that the tenor of the language and the implied mannerisms, gesticulations, and ethos that it conveyed brought the literature to life and brought me back in memory. What I also found was that I had to limit the focus of my studies, and thus I ended up writing on Sholom Aleichem, whose voice carried over into what would become the golden age of American Jewish literature.

The response to my scholarly choice was not as I anticipated. While finding a thesis committee was not easy—very simply, there was no one in "the field"—nonetheless, my professors were all supportive, if bemusedly so. "Let the kid do it, and see where it takes her," seemed to be the avuncular attitude. But the real patriarchal response, the one that really mattered, was not as inspiring. It was my father, the rebellious, self-fashioned son of immigrants—who grew up speaking Yiddish to the customers in his father's butcher shop and who transferred the orthodoxy of the faith to Freudian psychoanalysis—whose reaction was ironically in keeping with my chosen scholarly direction. In words deeply familiar to me, he let loose a litany of Yiddish invectives, "Feh!" an ancient expression of guttural disgust. His response to my academic pursuits was glossed by his entreaty to study the "great writers," Shakespeare, Tolstoy, Dostoevsky. "What kind of a *fakakta* thing is that, studying Yiddish writers; where did that *meshugana* come from," he protested, even as he corrected my own flailing Yiddish. Our skirmish would have had the resonance of Borscht Belt shtick, had I not been the humorless dissertation student that I was. "The language of peasants!" my father insisted, "the language of persecution! the Holocaust!" Exactly.

Thus, I proceeded. My dissertation on this single Yiddish writer, Sholom Aleichem, a literary presence recognized immediately among Jews by the pseudonym, the most traditional of greetings, opened itself up to fluid and rich directions. From his ironic confluence of author and character and the characteristic first-person narrators who talk their way through their precariously self-invented worlds, my work veered in the direction of the American Jewish writer Bernard Malamud, whose *kleyne menshelekh mit kleyne hasoges* (little people with little ideas) mirrored Sholom Aleichem's flawed narrators and protagonists struggling to make sense of the worlds they inhabit. What I was primarily interested in was voice, the collective and individual voices of Jewish expression—from the voices of the Yiddish writers, who made a place for modern secular Jewish writing, to the voices of pre and post war American writers, who together established the place and influence of Jewish writing in American letters. There has never been *a* singular defining Jewish literary voice. And the trajectory of Jewish writing in American letters is a reflection of the range of structural, thematic, and rhetorical possibilities in the evolving expression of Jewish identities that might be said to characterize Jewish literature in America.

The post-war period has generally been considered something of a Golden Age of Jewish literature in America, characterized by a wide range of literary approaches: Grace Paley's first-person narrators who speak a colloquial urban melody; Cynthia Ozick's vivid and achingly descriptive prose; Bernard Malamud's tightly controlled chiastic structures that make emphatic the mutuality of suffering and also the necessity for *rachmones* (mercy, compassion); Saul Bellow's densely cerebral meditations on deeply flawed sensibilities; and Philip Roth's explosive voice of neurotically symptomatic libidinal compulsions. I was drawn to these voices—both collectively and individually. Together they spoke a language of the imagination with which I was intimately if often uncomfortably familiar. The post-war writers, in a general sense, brought Jews and Jewish sensibilities onto the literary scene. Together they spoke of what it meant or what it might have meant to be Jewish: a preoccupation with the strains of Jewish history—as Roth's recurring character Nathan Zuckerman would have it, "Jews ... are to history what Eskimos are to snow";[4] with the not-unhappy complications of the assimilated self that "shot like a surface-to-air missile right into the middle class";[5] with both the insidious and overt tides of antisemitism; with the anxieties of place and identity; and with storytelling as a structure for memory and continuity.

I devoted the first decade of my scholarly life primarily to the fiction of the post-war Jewish writers. Their works were openings into Jewish history, myth, tradition, and imagination. But I came to feel that, with few exceptions, these writers approached but never engaged with what seemed to me to be the defining moment of Jewish history. What was missing from the central concerns of those novelists in the initial decades following the war was a direct engagement with the Holocaust. Where was the Shoah in the midst of the literary attempts to reframe configurations and dispositions of Jewish identity, community, and memory, the three anchors of continuity and survival, the longstanding tradition well since Hebrew Scripture? The haunting presence of the Holocaust—the shattering fact of the Holocaust—had created a kind of background noise all my life. My parents spoke of the Holocaust in sotto voce asides, in pained utterances that, even to a young child, were the final measure of moral reckoning. My paternal grandfather's siblings, the nine brothers and sisters who did not "make it out"—relatives unknown to us—were lost in the enormity and confusion of the Nazi assault against the Jews. The Shoah was part of the fabric of Jewish history and catastrophe, an incomparable measure of loss. It was always *there* in the discourse—spoken and unspoken—of family life, a severed narrative.

But the absence of direct references to the Shoah in the literature of the post-war American Jewish writers in particular, became an increasingly absent presence, a noticeable and aching gap in those narratives written in the tumultuous period of post-war America. To be sure, the Holocaust hovered in the backdrop of some of the literature produced in the late 1940s and 50s by American Jewish writers. Bellow's slim novel *The Victim*, published in 1947, centers on Asa Leventhal, a man running from an indefinable sense of guilt and shame, who fears the antisemitic insinuations of those around him. The novel is a brilliant study of a fraught individual coming unhinged, a man running from others but avoiding, above all, himself and his responsibilities. Bellow's protagonist's implicit identification with the millions of murdered European Jews defines his experience of living in post-Holocaust America. Leventhal is a victim of the deceptive security and precarious protection offered Jews in America. But other than a desperately made reference to the "millions of us [who] have been killed," Leventhal avoids any direct confrontation with the menace of all-too-recent history.[6] I was struck the first time I read Bellow's novel, and in the many times since, by the ways in which the Holocaust—in both proximate and remote memory—shapes our consciousness of the precariousness of the lives we fashion and hold on to. It was a curious phenomenon to me then, and even now, that the Holocaust was approached with such caution, such indirection.

Indirect references to the Shoah emerge in other post-war literary works as well. Malamud's 1958 story "The Lady of the Lake," for example, focuses on a protagonist who, so desperate to shed his identity, changes his name and denies that he is a Jew just at the moment it matters most, when he is confronted by a survivor of Buchenwald. Roth's short story, "Eli, the Fanatic," published in 1959 in his debut collection of short stories, *Goodbye, Columbus*, evolves around the fearful and resentful attitudes of assimilated middle-class Jews toward the uninvited and looming presence of a *yeshiva* housing refugees from the war, those who have lost everything. The *yeshiva* is presided over by the tenacious Leo Tzuref, who calls upon the community of recalcitrant and apprehensive Jews to bend to the "law" of kinship and compassion for those who have suffered such irredeemable loss. "You have the word 'suffer' in English?" Tzuref demands of Eli Peck, legal spokesperson for the community, "Then try it. [. . .] You are us, we are you!"[7] Denying their identification and obligations is, for Roth, a *shanda*, a shame, a moral failure. There are other examples as well, but what is remarkable about the literature written by Jews in America in the immediate post war years is the hesitancy with which the Holocaust is approached. The Shoah, for the most part, seemed to have created a caesura in the literature of post-war American Jewish writers. As Nobel laureate Saul Bellow wrote as late as 1987, some four decades after the war, in a letter to the American Jewish novelist Cynthia Ozick:

Jewish Writers in America [...] missed what should have been for them the central event of their time, the destruction of European Jewry. I can't say how our responsibility can be assessed. We (I speak of Jews now and not merely of writers) should have reckoned more fully, more deeply with it. Nobody in America seriously took this on and only a few Jews elsewhere (like Primo Levi) were able to comprehend it all. [... E]very honest conscience feels the disgrace of it. [...] I can't even begin to say what responsibility any of us may bear [...] in a crime so vast that it brings all Being into Judgment.[8]

Arguably, it is not until 1961 and the publication of Edward Lewis Wallant's novel *The Pawnbroker*, that the Holocaust was more directly approached in American Jewish literature, not surprisingly corresponding to the Eichmann trial and the publicity it drew across the globe. I vividly remember reading *The Pawnbroker* for the first time in that class I took so many years ago, and feeling assaulted by the memory of the Shoah, a memory that, unlike Wallant's protagonist, was not mine, but one nonetheless that had silhouetted the world I experienced. In many ways, of course, the academy is a measure of the social, cultural, and political discourses of the times. It is not until the late 1970s that the cultural and political climate in the United States was prepared to recognize the extended imprint of the Shoah, especially on the survivor population. Indeed, works such as Bellow's *Mr. Sammler's Planet*, published in 1970, and *The Bellarosa Connection*, published in 1989, suggest the way in which the Holocaust emerged in the American literary consciousness in the decades following the war. In any event, such initial indirection in the literature might reflect America's position during and in the immediate aftermath of the war. But what was apparent to me, as I explored and wrote about the post-war literary period in American letters, was that the memory of the Holocaust, for the most part, had been set adrift. Thus, as a Jewish scholar who had been raised with a consciousness of the Holocaust, I seemed instinctively to move in the direction of Holocaust literary studies and those writers—survivors, descendants of first-hand witnesses, and others—whose writing, through a vast array of genres and approaches, bore witness to the memory of the Holocaust. As the Israeli novelist David Grossman rightly suggests, these are narratives "which have to be told again and again because that is the only way to reassemble the traces of identity and fuse the fragments of a crumbled world."[9]

Thus, I went on to develop the first course in Holocaust literature to be offered at my university, and, to my continuing surprise, it is a course that has continued to draw students throughout the years. The students who take the course are, by no means, exclusively or even primarily Jews. I teach at a small, private liberal arts institution in San Antonio, Texas, that does not have a significant Jewish student body. Nonetheless, our students are drawn to the course, perhaps because genocide is a reality of their own historical perspective of the global world they inhabit. But curiously, they are also drawn to what for them are voices of difference, perspectives and stories unfamiliar to them, whereas I, at their age, was drawn by familiarity and identification. Jewish history in a significant way has defined my own history, part of an ongoing narrative in which I locate myself. Not surprisingly, then, I am preoccupied with the intergenerational transmission of trauma and memory as these patterns and preoccupations emerge in the literature of the Holocaust. I am especially interested in the generational continuity of Holocaust representation, the ways in which successive generations of readers and writers approach the Holocaust.

My twin areas of emphasis, American Jewish and Holocaust literatures, have fortuitously intersected in provocative and vital ways. As a judge for the Edward Lewis Wallant Award, an award given annually in recognition of an emerging American Jewish writer whose work of fiction has significance for American Jews, I read every year a plethora of new material by contemporary American Jewish writers. What has become apparent to me and to the other judges of the award, especially in the years since the turn of the twenty-first century, is the number of writers who return to the Shoah, writers whose work reaches back in time to memorialize and keep alive the memory of those who perished and those who survived the catastrophic rupture of Jewish life. As the editors of the recent anthology of selected writings from Wallant Award recipients, *The New Diaspora*: *The Changing Landscape of American Jewish Fiction*, note, "the literary preoccupation with the Holocaust among Jewish writers, especially in the decades surrounding the turn of the twenty-first century, has taken on considerable momentum."[10] It is no surprise, I think, that American Jewish writers are returning to the Holocaust at this particular moment in history. This is an era that will see the end of direct survivor testimony, a moment in which Holocaust memory and representation are imperiled by the passage of time, the increasing remoteness of the events, and the competing pressures, preoccupations, and anxieties of our current age. As the editors of *The New Diaspora* suggest, "For post-Holocaust writers [. . .] the Holocaust has ineradicably shaped their lives, but as a kind of silhouette, for the memories of such defining events are 'borrowed' [. . .] 'second hand.'"[11] The specter of the Shoah continues to haunt the writings of contemporary American Jewish writers, particularly—but by no means exclusively—the second- and third-generation writers, the children and grandchildren of Holocaust survivors who have come of literary age and engage the traumatic events of history with an impassioned and obligatory reckoning. This current direction in Holocaust representation aligns with my own impassioned interest in the intergenerational transmission of trauma and memory and the complex ways in which the Shoah has come to inform the identity of post-Holocaust generations. The trajectory of my own work has followed the generational pattern from survivor writing to the second and third generation of writers whose literary attempts at representation have taken a wide array of genres, literary conceits, and rhetorical structures in an attempt to perform memory. I like to think that as the literature I study has evolved, so has my own thinking and scholarly work.

As a result, the direction of my work has taken turns I never would have predicted. And this is one of the most exciting aspects of Holocaust Studies, that the range of possibilities for scholarly work is continually expanding as new generations of writers generate new forms of representation. My most recent monograph was on the emerging genre of Holocaust graphic novels and memoirs, *Holocaust Graphic Narratives: Generation, Trauma, and Memory* (Rutgers University Press, 2020). In it, I argue for the ways in which the visual/verbal conventions of the genre create the conditions for the intersections and juxtapositions of time and space in locating memory. One of the very great pleasures of the work we all do in Holocaust literary studies is the evolving ways in which modes of representation change in order to recreate the traumatic past, the memory of the rupture of lives, communities, and worlds. Our field is always changing, enlivened by memory and by the active, ongoing attempts to preserve and reanimate the past. The process of doing so is ongoing, in large part because of the challenges inherent in recreating traumatic testimony and in the perceived dangers of historical amnesia. As the American Jewish novelist Joseph Skibell cautions, "If you don't tell that story, it disappears, and even if you do tell it, it might just disappear anyway.'"[12] Continuing to tell the story of the Holocaust is, for me, a kind of creed, a faith perhaps in Jewish survival, a faith in the future, as the poet Leonard Nathan once wrote, "as my foot every step of the way has believed in the ground."[13]

How do we talk about, write about, and remember the Holocaust now, in the third decade of the twenty-first century, over seventy five years since the end of the war, the liberation of the camps, and the relocation of lives and communities? As I write these concluding remarks, an anecdote comes to mind that perhaps answers one of the central questions posed by the editors of this volume in the introductory letter to the contributors, "How did working on Holocaust representation affect you as a scholar and in your thinking about yourself?" Sitting in the bar of our conference hotel, a colleague of mine, an early career faculty member just beginning in the field of Holocaust Studies, asked me a question that momentarily flummoxed me. And it did so, because I could not come up with what seemed to be an appropriately professional, academic response that might have been helpful in terms of his own emerging work. I had in fairly recent succession published two books on the Holocaust, one on third-generation Holocaust representation and the other on Holocaust graphic narratives. He asked, "How are you able to come up with ideas and write so quickly?" Of course, I had not written "quickly"; both books had taken countless hours of research, thinking, drafting, and revising. His question, as I reflect on it now, was meant to solicit advice on how to find a focus of investigation and follow through to the publication of a book beyond his dissertation. The more academic response might have been that the one topic on the third generation naturally evolved into the second on graphic novels. However, feeling even as I spoke that I was failing in my mentor/advisor capacity, I said, very simply, what was true: That I couldn't *not* write these books; that I felt such an urgency to get my thoughts on paper before they slipped away, before, that is, they were lost to the competing pressures, preoccupations, and inundations of time, lost, that is, to history. These were things that had to be said, and I felt that I had to say them—before it was too late. Over all these years spent thinking about the Holocaust, I have realized that there is precious little separating my professional and personal lives. Studying the Holocaust is, for me, a process of self-reckoning, an engagement with the limits of my understanding, and a reminder of my own obligations to memory.

How did I get here? I consider myself unbelievably lucky.

Notes

1 Grace Paley, "Faith in the Afternoon," in *Enormous Changes at the Last Minute* (New York: Farrar, Straus and Giroux, 1983), 41.

2 Grace Paley, "Ruthie and Edie," in *Later the Same Day* (New York: Farrar Straus and Giroux, 1985), 126.

3 Bernard Malamud, "Angel Levine," in *Bernard Malamud: The Complete Stories* (New York: Noonday Press/Farrar, Straus and Giroux, 1997), 166.

4 Philip Roth, *The Counterlife* (New York: Farrar, Straus and Giroux, 1988), 368.

5 Grace Paley, "Enormous Changes At the Last Minute," in *Enormous Changes at the Last Minute* (New York: Farrar, Straus and Giroux, 1983), 122.

6 Saul Bellow, *The Victim* (New York: Signet, 1965), 133.

7 Philip Roth, "Eli, the Fanatic," in *Goodbye, Columbus and Five Short Stories* (New York: The Modern Library/Random House, 1966), 265.

8 Saul Bellow, *Saul Bellow: Letters*, ed. Benjamin Taylor (New York: Viking, 2010), 438–9.

9 David Grossman, *Writing in the Dark*, trans. Jessica Cohen (New York: Farrar, Straus and Giroux, 2008), 13.

10 Victoria Aarons, Avinoan J. Patt, and Mark Shechner, eds., *The New Diaspora: The Changing Landscape of American Jewish Fiction* (Detroit: Wayne State University Press, 2015), 6.

11 Aarons, et al., *The New Diaspora*, 6.

12 Joseph Skibell, "Ten Faces," in *My Father's Guitar & Other Imaginary Things* (Chapel Hill, NC: Algonquin Books, 2015), 2015.

13 Leonard Nathan, "Creed," in *Dear Blood* (Pittsburgh: University of Pittsburgh Press, 1980), 18.

2

Movies as Prosthetic Holocaust Memories

Lawrence Baron

Film and Television as a Childhood Source of Holocaust Awareness

Attending the Lessons and Legacies Conference in November 2000, I listened intently to Peter Novick present an overview of his new book *The Holocaust in American Life* (1999).[1] When he asserted that the Holocaust generated little public discourse among American Gentiles or Jews between the end of the Second World War and the 1960s, it triggered a conflicting memory of when I first became aware of the Shoah, perhaps because his talk occurred in the same Evanston hotel where my bar mitzvah reception had been held in 1960.

Even though I had been teaching and writing about the Holocaust for twenty-five years then, I had never reflected on when it had first entered my consciousness. I was certain that I knew about it by the time I was thirteen. I recalled my father and me watching television documentaries about the Second World War which exposed me to images of corpses and catatonic skeletal survivors haunting the compounds of the liberated concentration and death camps. I remembered seeing *The Diary of Anne Frank* in 1959 and having nightmares in which the sounds of European police sirens augured the arrest of the Franks, their friends, and me.[2] Until I heard Novick's contention, I had never appreciated how much documentaries and movies had shaped my awareness of the Holocaust. This realization spurred me to spend the remainder of my career examining how mass media influenced public perceptions of the Shoah.

After I penned the above paragraphs, I experienced the pangs of a historian's conscience. Could my memory have deceived me about the origins of my interest in Holocaust cinema?

When I checked back to the Lessons and Legacies Program from 2000, I noticed that I presented a paper on Holocaust cinema there because I already had been doing research for a book on the subject and had published my first article on the topic a year earlier. Novick's remarks redirected me to trace the role the Holocaust played in American popular culture since 1945. My initial memory that his lecture spurred my study of Holocaust film reminded me that autobiographers often facilely impose coherence and meaning on what are the incoherent and messy trajectories of their own lives.

The Holocaust hardly was at the forefront of my thoughts as a child. Growing up in a predominantly Jewish neighborhoods in Chicago and Skokie, I was cognizant that parents of some of my friends were survivors, but kids my age weren't particularly interested in learning about the backgrounds of adults. Conversely, my relatives had immigrated to the United States from Eastern Europe before the First World War. That's probably why films became my default Holocaust education.

1961, the year of my bar mitzvah, coincided with the release of Otto Preminger's *Exodus*.[3] My congregation gifted my peers and me tickets to see it. It introduced me to how Hitler's lethal assault on European Jews motivated some survivors to fight for the emerging Jewish state. As a hormonal male adolescent, I naturally found Karen more attractive than Ari Ben-Canaan. My next Holocaust exposure came soon thereafter. Every Saturday night I watched a TV show which screened old horror movies, but footage from the Eichmann Trial preempted it during its proceedings. It rarely held my attention for very long. The gaunt, tall man with the crooked smile standing in a glass booth scared me less than Dracula, Frankenstein, and the Wolf Man. Indeed, the Cuban Missile Crisis, the assassination of President Kennedy, and the March on Washington for Jobs and Freedom dominate my high school memories more than the Holocaust.

My Path to German History

My undergraduate education at the University of Illinois piqued my interest in Europe during the interwar period. Like so many of my generation, I conflated the repressive backlash to the civil unrest, cultural experimentation, and political polarization of American society during the 1960s with the conditions that had thrust Hitler into power. Opposed to the Vietnam War and outraged by the assassinations of Martin Luther King, Jr. and Robert Kennedy, I found role models in the left-wing intellectuals who had fought in the Spanish Civil War and sympathized with the Soviet Union until it forged an alliance with Germany. I chose one of them, Stephen Spender, as the subject of my history honor's thesis.

My fascination with such activist intellectuals in the 1930s led me to study with George L. Mosse at the University of Wisconsin. Finally, I had a personal connection with an émigré from Nazi Germany. I had never intended to focus on Jewish history or the Holocaust, but Mosse's mentoring directed me to both. My dissertation about Erich Mühsam (1878–1934) dealt primarily with his anarchist activism and writings in Wilhelmine and Weimar Germany.[4] His Jewish origins and participation in the Munich Soviet Republic in 1919 led to his arrest following the Reichstag fire and his murder in Oranienburg concentration camp in 1934.

My year conducting research in Germany on Mühsam's life in East and West Germany heightened my awareness of the Holocaust and my own Jewish identity. My wife's aunt had fled Germany after Kristallnacht. She grew up in a village located near the archive where I was working. At her insistence, we visited it to see if her grandfather's grave remained intact. As we walked around her hometown, several locals inquired why were there. When we answered, one of them remembered my wife's aunt and retrieved a keepsake she had received as a present from her. Although everybody was cordial, I felt like a fossil of an extinct species. Hearing the story of the visit, our aunt bitterly recounted that her Gentile neighbors had failed to express any sympathy as her family was incrementally disenfranchised and ostracized by Hitler's regime. That prompted me to delve more deeply into modern European Jewish history.

From Esoteric Scholarship to Holocaust Research

The prospects for landing a tenure-track position were dismal in the mid-1970s. After receiving a raft of rejection letters, I secured a one-year job visiting position at St. Lawrence University in northern New York in 1975 to teach Western Civilization and modern Europe survey courses. Since I could introduce a new course each semester, I developed courses on modern German and modern Jewish history. Much to my surprise a tenure-track vacancy opened, and I was hired.

I remained at St. Lawrence for thirteen years. Since it was a predominantly Gentile school, I relished my role as the only Jewish Studies professor. In 1976, I offered a seminar on the Holocaust. The timing was propitious because Lucy Dawidowicz's *The War against The Jews* had been published the prior year, and Terrence Des Pres's *The Survivor* was released in 1976.[5] The debates generated by these books about the strategies of compliance, mutuality, and resistance pursued by the Jewish Councils, concentration camp inmates, and underground movements became the subject of my first article on the Holocaust, published in 1977.[6]

Despite my nascent attraction to Holocaust Studies, I decided to write a biography of the philosopher Theodor Lessing (1872–1933) who is primarily remembered for his book *Jewish Self-Hatred*.[7] What began as an exercise in intellectual history ended in chronicling how he was removed from his teaching position in response to nationalist students protesting his criticism of Hindenburg's presidency of Weimar Germany. This paved the way for his assassination in Czechoslovakia by Nazi gunmen in the summer of 1933. The Lessing research brought me back to Germany for archival work in 1979 following the broadcast of the miniseries *Holocaust* and its positive reception there.[8] The American Philosophical Society funded my trip, the purpose of which was to investigate Lessing's dispute with Edmund Husserl over the latter's charges of plagiarism. I found phenomenological concepts and terminology arcane.

I finished the Husserl/Lessing article in 1981 during a sabbatical.[9] I had come to view its subject as too esoteric. From that moment on, I selected research projects about the Holocaust which I deemed more relevant to ordinary people. In the same year, the United States conferred honorary American citizenship on Raoul Wallenberg. This influenced my decision to spend the rest of my sabbatical reading memoirs and biographies of "righteous Gentiles" to discern the factors that motivated them to risk their lives on behalf of Jews. Around the same time, I read a news item about the American Jewish Committee awarding Sam Oliner a major grant to interview rescuers of Jews to study the psychosocial roots of why they saved Jews. I contacted him and sent him the first draft of my rescuer article. He responded by inviting me to be the historian for the subsequent book *The Altruistic Personality: Rescuers of Jews in Nazi Europe* (1988).[10]

Since St. Lawrence University was located near Canada, most of the rescuers I interviewed were Dutch. Canada had liberated the Netherlands in 1945 and became a favored destination for Dutch immigrants escaping wartime memories. I quickly detected a recurring theme among those interviewees who identified themselves as fundamentalist Calvinists. They cited Paul in Romans 9:11 affirming that Jews remained God's Chosen People to explain why they protected Jews. Although members of their schismatic denominations constituted 8 percent of the Dutch population, they accounted for 25 percent of the rescuers. Historians before me had attributed this phenomenon to Calvin's philosemitism. What was apparent in the testimonies was that his theological legacy was transmitted by what Gospel passages pastors emphasized.[11] As was the case with all interviewed rescuers, the factors that prompted people to shield were influenced by their childhood experiences, empathy, ideology, personal traits, political affiliations, relationships with Jews, or significant role models. Rather than assess the impact of ideas as a top–down process as I had previously done, I recognized how subjective their reception was. This prepared me to appreciate the active role audiences play in how they filter the messages conveyed by films.

In 1988, I offered a course on Holocaust cinema for St. Lawrence's January term comprised of experimental courses that were not part of the school's curriculum. I did so for three reasons: 1) To co-teach with the chaplain Ted Linn, who shared my interest in the implications of the Holocaust for Christians; 2) to explore my growing attraction to Holocaust movies during a decade that witnessed the release of a spate of such films including Lanzmann's *Shoah*; and 3) to discuss the interpretations of significant Holocaust films articulated in the pioneering books by Annette Insdorf, Ilan Avisar, and Judith Doneson which were released in the 1980s.[12] Each student presented an oral review of one movie. I sensed that movies amplified student engagement with the issues raised by the Holocaust.

Becoming a Film Historian

The fall semester of 1988 marked the beginning of my tenure at San Diego State University as the director of the Lipinsky Institute for Judaic Studies. The next few years were a blur of fundraising, hosting visiting professors, organizing outreach programs, and recruiting faculty to teach courses. In 1992 my wife and I adopted our son. Caring for a baby rendered the best-intentioned efforts to budget time futile. Nevertheless, this period accelerated my shift to Holocaust cinema as my research area. As the Institute's director, I could choose the courses I taught. In my first year I developed a course on modern Jewish history in film, and in the second year, one on Holocaust cinema. In the Institute's newsletter I occasionally reviewed new Jewish films like *Schindler's List*.[13]

In retrospect I'm embarrassed by these reviews because I succumbed to the misconception that films should be judged by their factual accuracy rather than by how effectively they convey the circumstances, dilemmas, and issues they portray through acting, cinematography, dialogue, editing, images, *mise-n-scène*, music, set design, and sound. Academic history and filmed history should be subject to different criteria to gauge their cogency and impact on audiences. Feature films were never intended to be scholarly monographs. I would be disabused of my simplistic approach to film by two seminal figures who changed my thinking about movies: Judy Doneson and Robert Rosenstone. I met Judy in the 1990s at a Holocaust conference. We bonded over both of us having had George Mosse as our dissertation advisor but soon realized we were kindred spirits in our interest in Holocaust cinema, unlike most of our colleagues. We conversed at conferences and over the phone about the motion pictures we recently had watched. Judy taught me two significant things: 1) Historical films tell us as much about the time and place in which they were made as they do about the events they reenact; 2) artful popularization renders the past relevant to the present. Talking to Judy made me painfully aware that I lacked a formal background in film studies. I started spending my summers rectifying this deficiency which acquainted me with Robert Rosenstone's pioneering *Visions of the Past: The Challenge of Film to Our Idea of History* (1995).[14] Its first chapter critiqued the "Dragnet historian" who, like the lead detective on the eponymous 1950s television series, expected movies to present "just the facts, ma'am." Rosenstone posited film as an alternative form of history in a passage I would cite in *Projecting the Holocaust into the Present* (2005):

> This new historical past on film is potentially much more complex than any written text, for on the screen, several things can occur simultaneously—image, sound, language, even text—elements that support and work against each other to render a realm of meaning as different from written history as written was from oral history.[15]

With a medium as multifaceted as film, no cinematic style or genre should hold a monopoly on how the Holocaust can be depicted. The exacting verisimilitude historians expect from Holocaust films is a directorial choice and not a categorical imperative. I corresponded with Robert when I was writing my Holocaust film book, which benefited from his feedback. He reciprocated by referencing it in his book *History on Film/Film on History* (2006).[16]

The Emotional Impact of Holocaust Films

By the time I heard Novick speak, I had written an article on the portrayal of Jewish female resistance fighters in the movies *Hanna's War* (1988) and *A Woman at War* (1991).[17] While Doneson's influence on me was already discernible, I still felt obligated as a historian to point out factual discrepancies in both films. My reaction to Novick's assertion, however, reinforced my transition from a conventional intellectual historian to a film historian. What I had relegated to a teaching subject became the central object of my research.

Retooling to explicate movies compelled me to develop a radically different sensibility. I previously relied on oral and written texts which I analyzed as rational discourses. Acting, ambient sounds, background music, body language, facial expressions, and the interplay of color, light, and shadow on moving images involve audiences emotionally and viscerally as much as dialogue. When I presented my first papers on film at Holocaust conferences, I encountered the recurring criticism that most Holocaust films were emotionally manipulative and historically reductionist. I was defensive since this reproach discredited the academic value of studying films.

Yet the more I immersed myself in film studies, the more my appreciation of their emotive power and imposition of a comprehensible narrative on historical events grew. These qualities enabled viewers to feel they had vicariously shared this horrific past with characters and understood its dynamics. This capacity of the medium attracted millions of viewers compared to the thousands of students or readers most professors reach in their classes or through their books over a lifetime. I wondered if the hostility my colleagues manifested towards film masked an envy of movies as competitors in educating the public about the Holocaust.

Since the standard surveys of Holocaust cinema were published in the 1980s, I focused on feature films released between 1990 and 2003, the year I finished my book. Guided by Doneson's dictum that historical films are about the present, I examined how the genres and themes of Holocaust films changed according to when and where they were produced. To operationalize this approach, I compiled a database of Holocaust-themed movies from 1945 coded according to their countries, decades, and places of origin to detect chronological and geographical shifts in their genres and themes. I was astonished by the sheer magnitude of this corpus of films counting over 900 by the turn of the century. Although I failed to locate copies of all these movies, internet searches and reference works allowed me to gather filmographic information to categorize them.

The statistics gleaned from the database undermined Novick's contention that there was little public discussion of the Shoah in the immediate postwar period. Feeling obligated to counter his thesis bifurcated my writing into two tracks: the book and an article titled "The Holocaust in American Public Memory, 1945–1960," published in *Holocaust and Genocide Studies* in 2003.[18] In addition to citing the content from American documentaries, movies, and television from these years, I included the ways attention was paid to the Holocaust in fictional and historical books, magazine and newspaper articles, philosophy, the social sciences, and Christian and Jewish theology.

This research spawned several other articles and papers on the nascent Holocaust awareness manifested in advocacy, feature, and fundraising films that documented Nazi atrocities, combated domestic antisemitism, and highlighted the plight of Jewish displaced persons, the hunt for Nazi war criminals, their trials, and the adjustment of survivors to their lives in Israel or the United States. To be sure, it wasn't called the Holocaust during these years. How it was commemorated, conceptualized, and popularized morphed with the passage of time. Unbeknownst to me, other scholars like Hasia Diner, Kirsten Fermaglich, and David Cesarani were reaching similar conclusions about early Holocaust discourse challenging what they eventually dubbed "the myth of silence."[19]

My book, however, focused on more recent Holocaust films. I ascertained that the most popular Holocaust film genre in the 1990s was biographical films, which comprised a quarter of all films about the Shoah. Biopics individualize the impersonal forces shaping the past and furnish characters with whom the audience can identify or vilify. The antipathy or sympathy they engender for bystanders, perpetrators, resisters, rescuers, or victims function as "prosthetic memories," Alison Landsberg's term for how historical films cultivate a semblance of personally experiencing the quandaries of the characters portrayed in them.[20] Star-crossed love stories about mixed Gentile and Jewish couples constituted the second most common genre in these years. These melodramas similarly foster disdain or empathy for lovers whose bonds of affection are strengthened, strained or broken by the ostracism, persecution, or removal of their Jewish partner.

While both genres had long been staples of Holocaust cinema, films belonging to the other two top genres of the 1990s and early 2000s—comedies and children's films—had been rare until then. I surmised that the uptick in comedies represented a reaction to the somber realism that dominated Holocaust feature films and television docudramas the decade prior and reflected the transition from a generation of directors whose formative experiences were during or immediately after the war to younger ones more chronologically distant from it. Many of the directors of the comedies were children of survivors or perpetrators. Comedy served them as a way of engaging with the suffering their parents endured or inflicted while simultaneously buffering themselves from it with the balm of humor.

I ascribed the increase in children's movies to the incorporation of the Holocaust into educational curricula that began with the miniseries *Holocaust* in 1978 and culminated with the impact of *Schindler's List* and the opening of the US Holocaust Memorial Museum in 1993. Most of the films targeted at juveniles were adaptations of books frequently assigned for school units such as Disney's *Miracle at Midnight* (1998), whose plotline resembled Lois Lowry's *Number the Stars* or the Showtime dramatization of Jane Yolen's *The Devil's Arithmetic* (1999).[21] Such films conclude on a hopeful note to avoid traumatizing young viewers.

Although the majority of 1990s films revolved around common Holocaust film topics like Righteous Gentiles, ghetto life, Jews passing as Gentiles or in hiding, death camp survival, and the twisted mindset of perpetrators, they also dealt with hitherto neglected or underrepresented topics. *The Quarrel* (1991) revived a 1953 short story by Chaim Grade about two survivors debating whether they could still believe God exists after the Germans had murdered their families and the majority of European Jewry.[22] Movies like *Left Luggage* (1998) dramatized how the trauma of the Shoah haunted the postwar lives of survivors and their children.[23] This theme even served as the premise for a comic book movie like Bryan Singer's *X-Men* (2000), whose villain Magneto is a Holocaust survivor intent on averting humans from exterminating mutants like himself as the Nazis had done to his Jewish parents.[24] The upsurge of neo-Nazism in reunited Germany and post-Soviet Eastern Europe occasioned films portraying this phenomenon in movies like *Rosenzweig's Freedom* (1998).[25] Michael Verhoeven's *The Nasty Girl* (1990) commenced a cycle of films arising out of public debates over German collective guilt after reunification.[26]

I also discerned how trends in Holocaust films had been facilitated by changes in communication technologies, the funding of films, and screening venues. The advent of the VCR, premium cable channels, and Jewish film festivals opened opportunities to produce movies that found niche audiences among video renters, cable subscribers, and film festival-goers. These developments afforded Indie movies with alternative venues for reaching viewers without relying on expensive publicity campaigns. One cannot imagine a dialogue-heavy movie on theodicy like *The Quarrel* succeeding without its exposure at film festivals and art theaters. Similarly, would a children's cable movie like *The Devil's Arithmetic* ever be produced for theatrical distribution? The growth of multinational productions like *Left Luggage* minimized the distinctive national settings of Holocaust movies to broaden their global appeal.

Beyond Holocaust Cinema

After the book, I investigated the Holocaust's broader impact on movie genres not traditionally associated with it and on films about other genocides. The former led me to the works of Yoram Gross, a survivor and renowned Australian animator, who made the first feature-length cartoon about the Holocaust, *Sarah and the Squirrel* (1982). As I watched his other animated films and television series like *Blinky Bill: The Mischievous Koala* (1992), I realized he had transformed his experiences as a teenager hiding in wartime Poland into children's stories about animals separated from their parents and escaping humans who destroyed their habitats or hunted them.[27] In *Sarah and the Squirrel,* he recounted the story of a girl coded as Jewish finding herself alone after enemy soldiers discover her family's hideout in the forest. Befriended by animals, she sabotages the bridge enemy trains traverse by removing a brick daily from its base.[28]

The other direction my research took compared films about the Armenian Genocide with their Holocaust counterparts. Atom Egoyan's *Ararat* (2002) impressed me with its generational perspectives on the Genocide's history.[29] I was particularly interested in its references to the Holocaust. The few Genocide movies that had overcome Turkey's efforts to prevent their production typically mentioned Hitler's infamous quotation about no one remembering the Armenian Genocide and employed images and plots evoking the iconography and plotlines of Holocaust movies. I drew upon Michael Rothberg's concept of multidirectional memory to argue that these Holocaust references represented a strategy to legitimate the claim that what the Armenians endured was a genocide.[30] More recently, I have examined whether the earlier allusions to the Holocaust continued in Armenian genocide movies released during the Genocide's centennial and concluded they became less frequent as the Armenian Genocide garnered more international recognition.[31]

I also expanded the scope of my research to Jewish films *per se*. Nevertheless, the Holocaust loomed large in the anthology *The Modern Jewish Experience in World Cinema* (2011), which I edited.[32] Of the fifty-five movies discussed therein, 20 percent are primarily about the Holocaust, and another 20 percent feature it or its memory as a subplot affecting their characters. On the other hand, I had begun to write and lecture about more upbeat topics like the first generation of American Jewish women directors and the trope of Irish–Jewish love stories in American cinema.

After retiring in 2012, I have remained professionally active. Assessing my career, I am acutely aware of how film studies liberated me from the blinders of overspecialization. I once typified Isaiah Berlin's "hedgehog" burrowing into one subject that interested a small coterie of scholars in the same field. Analyzing movies transformed me into his "fox" by broadening my disciplinary and topical horizons.[33] While many Holocaust films distort or trivialize the event, others, "refract a vision of the past and the concerns of the present through a prism that has the potential to illuminate our hearts and minds, as well as the silver screen."

Notes

1 Peter Novick, *The Holocaust in American Life* (Boston: Houghton Mifflin Company, 1999).
2 *The Diary of Anne Frank* (1959) [Film] Dir. George Stevens, USA: George Stevens Productions.
3 *Exodus* (1960) [Film] Dir. Otto Preminger, USA: Otto Preminger Films.
4 Lawrence Baron, *The Eclectic Anarchism of Erich Mühsam* (New York: Revisionist Press, 1976).
5 Lucy S. Dawidowicz, *The War Against the Jews, 1933–1945* (New York: Holt, Rinehart and Winston, 1975); Terrence Des Pres. *The Survivor: An Anatomy of Life in the Death Camps* (New York: Oxford University Press, 1976).
6 Lawrence Baron, "Surviving the Holocaust," *Journal of Psychology and Judaism* 1, no.2 (Spring 1977): 25–37.
7 Theodor Lessing, *Der jüdische Selbsthass* (Berlin: Jüdischer Verlag, 1930).
8 *Holocaust* (1978) [Television Miniseries] Dir. Marvin J. Chomsky, USA: NBC, April 16–20.
9 Lawrence Baron, "Discipleship and Dissent: Theodor Lessing and Edmund Husserl," *Proceedings of the American Philosophical Society* 127, no.1 (February 1983): 32–49.
10 Samuel P. Oliner and Pearl M. Oliner, *The Altruistic Personality: Rescuers of Jews in Nazi Europe* (New York: The Free Press, 1988).

11 Lawrence Baron, "The Dutchness of Dutch Rescuers: The National Dimension of Altruism," in *Embracing the Other: Philosophical, Psychological, and Historical Perspectives on Altruism*, ed. Pearl M. Oliner, Samuel P. Oliner, Lawrence Baron, Lawrence A. Blum, Dennis L. Krebs, and M. Zusanna Smolenska (New York: New York University Press, 1992), 317–323.

12 *Shoah* (1985) [Film] Dir. Claude Lanzmann, France and United Kingdom: British Broadcasting Corporation, Historia, and Les Films Aleph; Ilan Avisar, *Screening the Holocaust: Cinema's Images of the Unimaginable* (Bloomington: Indiana University Press, 1988); Judith E. Doneson, *The Holocaust in American Film* (Philadelphia: Jewish Publication Society, 1987); Annette Insdorf, *Indelible Shadows: Film and the Holocaust* (New York: Random House, 1983).

13 *Schindler's List* (1993) [Film] Dir. Steven Spielberg, USA: Amblin Entertainment and Universal Pictures.

14 Robert A. Rosenstone, *Visions of the Past: The Challenge of Film to Our Idea of History* (Cambridge: Harvard University Press, 1995).

15 Lawrence Baron, *Projecting the Holocaust into the Present: The Changing Focus of Contemporary Holocaust Cinema* (Lanham: Roman and Little Publishers, 2005), 1.

16 Robert A. Rosenstone, *History on Film/Film on History* (New York: Longman/Pearson, 2006), 153–4.

17 Lawrence Baron, "Women as Resistance Fighters in Recent Popular Films: The Case of Hanna Senesh and Helen Moszkiewiez, in *Women and the Holocaust: Narrative and Representation*, ed. Esther Fuchs (Lanham: University Press of America, 1999), 89–96; *Hanna's War* (1988) [Film] Dir. Menahem Golan, USA: Golan-Globus Productions; *A Woman at War* (1991) [Film] Dir. Edward Bennett, France and United Kingdom: Canal + and Palace Pictures.

18 Lawrence Baron, "The Holocaust and American Public Memory, 1945–1960," *Holocaust and Genocide Studies* 17, no.1 (Spring 2003): 62–88.

19 See the following anthology of articles based on papers presented at the first conference on this topic: *After the Holocaust: Challenging the Myth of Silence*, ed. David Cesarani and Eric J. Sundquist (New York: Routledge, 2012).

20 Alison Landsberg, *Prosthetic Memory: The Transformation of American Remembrance in an Age of Mass Culture* (New York: Columbia University Press, 2004).

21 *Miracle at Midnight* (1998) [Television Film] Dir. Ken Cameron, USA: ABC, May 17; Lois Lowry, *Number the Stars* (Boston: Houghton Mifflin Company, 1989); *The Devil's Arithmetic* (1999) [Television Film] Dir. Donna Deitch, USA: Showtime, March 28; Jane Yolen, *The Devil's Arithmetic* (New York: Trumpet, 1988).

22 *The Quarrel* (1991) [Film] Dir. Eli Cohen, Canada: Apple and Honey Productions, Atlantis Films, and Cineplex Odeon Films; Chaim Grade, "My War with Hersh Rasseyner," trans. Milton Himmelfarb in *A Treasury of Yiddish Stories*, ed. Irving Howe and Eliezer Greenberg (New York: Viking Press, 1953), 579–606.

23 *Left Luggage* (1998) [Film] Dir. Jeroen Krabbé, Belgium, Netherlands, United Kingdom, USA: Favourite Films NV, Greystone Films, Left Luggage BV, Shooting Star Film Company BV, The Flying Dutchman Inc.

24 *X-Men* (2000) [Film] Dir: Bryan Singer, USA: Twentieth Century Fox, Marvel Enterprises, and Donners' Company.
25 *Rosenzweig's Children* (1998) [Film] Dir. Liliane Targownik, Germany: Südwestfunk.
26 *The Nasty Girl* (1990) [Film] Dir. Michael Verhoeven, West Germany: Filmverlag der Autoren, Sentana Filmproduktion, and Zweites Deutsches Fernsehen.
27 Lawrence Baron, "Jews, Kangaroos, and Koalas: The Animated Holocaust Films of Yoram Gross," *Post Script: Essays in Film and the Humanities* 32, no.2 (Winter/Spring 2013): 63–73.
28 *Sarah and the Squirrel* (1982) [Film] Dir. Yoram Gross, Australia, Sarah Films, and The Australian Film Commission.
29 *Ararat* (2002) [Film] Dir. Atom Egoyan, Canada and France: Alliance Atlantis Communications, Serendipity Point Films, Ego Film Arts, ARP Sélection, Téléfilm Canada, The Movie Network, Super Écran, and The Harold Greenberg Fund.
30 Lawrence Baron, "The Armenian-Jewish Connection: The Influence of Holocaust Cinema on Feature Films about the Armenian Genocide, in *The Holocaust: Memories and History*, ed. Victoria Khiterer, Ryan Barrick, and David Misal (Newcastle upon Tyne: Cambridge Scholars Publishing, 2014), 289–310; Michael Rothberg, *Multidirectional Memory: Remembering the Holocaust in the Age of Decolonization* (Stanford: Stanford University Press, 2009).
31 Lawrence Baron, "Persistent Parallels, Resistant Particularities: Holocaust Analogies and Avoidance in Armenian Genocide Centennial Cinema," in *Armenian and Jewish Experience between Expulsion and Destruction*, ed. Sarah M. Ross and Regina Randhofer, (Berlin: Walter de Gruyter, 2021), 269–98.
32 Lawrence Baron, *The Modern Jewish Experience in World Cinema* (Waltham: Brandeis University Press, 2011).
33 Isaiah Berlin, *The Hedgehog and the Fox: An Essay on Tolstoy's View of History* (London: Weidenfeld and Nicolson, 1953).

3

Personal and Professional Autobiographies: Reechoing Memories of the Holocaust

Rachel Feldhay Brenner

It would be hard to account for an autobiography of scholarly preoccupation with the Holocaust that has been motivated solely by an intellectual passion. The plethora of literary, cinematic, and theatrical representations of the Holocaust attests to the continuing need to comprehend and integrate the memory of the event and perhaps even the hope to redeem this watershed crime against humanity. Thus, the Holocaust presents the Holocaust scholar with a particular difficulty, precisely because it deals with a case of an event of a genocide, the moral transgression of which has not been resolved, nor has it been definitely understood and therefore, continues to haunt humanity.

While the producers of the representations of the Holocaust have the poetic license to imaginatively construct a morally uplifting closure to the story of horror—see for instance the blockbusters, such as *Schindler's List*, which reaffirms the power of human goodness and the possibility of redemption, or *Life is Beautiful*, which looks at the Holocaust horror through the redemptive lens of the fairy tale—such an option does not exist, at least not in theory, in the field of academic studies. In the case of the Holocaust, academic integrity cannot satisfy the natural human desire for a "happy ending," which would alleviate the terror. On the contrary, academic integrity requires that full attention be given to the analysis and study of the irredeemable tragic truths about unalleviated human evil that arise from the Holocaust as an event. The rationale for constructing a personal autobiography, therefore, requires that we go behind the academic façade to face the unacknowledged, to recognize the hitherto repressed echoes that demand recognition.

In the spring of 1991 during the First Iraq War (or Gulf War), I flew to Israel from Toronto, where I was living with my children at the time. I had been consumed by terrible guilt for having abandoned my parents to the widely predicted devastating attack of weapons of mass destruction in the form of scuds (ballistic missiles) filled with chemical substances and launched on Tel Aviv. Not surprisingly, the aircraft was quite empty; so was Ben Gurion airport where, upon landing, I was given a small portable box. It contained a gas mask and instructions to carry it with me everywhere. Upon my arrival, I found out that many of my friends had fled to Jerusalem on the assumption that Saddam Hussein would not attack the Holy City. My parents, however, were not particularly agitated. Though sick and frail, they were carrying on with their lives, which now also included the constant carrying of boxed gas masks. As they went about their usual business, they did not seem particularly concerned, having adjusted quite well to the new situation. That included sitting for hours at night (when the attacks were expected) in a suffocatingly hot room with duct-taped windows. We were wearing the heavy gas masks, which, as later turned out, were completely ineffective (and also smelled terribly). At one point I asked my mother how she could be so matter of fact in this quite disturbing (to say the least) situation. She responded with total composure: "My dear, I stood with my parents at the entrance of our apartment building when Hitler was bombarding and burning the Jewish Quarter [on Yom Kippur 1939], how can I be afraid now?"

This was one of my mother's very rare references to her Holocaust experience. Of course, I knew that my parents, who were married just before the war, in May 1939, in their native city of Warsaw, survived the Holocaust in the Soviet Union. I was also vaguely aware of their lifelong feelings of guilt for having left behind their parents, my grandparents, who, together with the rest of the family, perished in Treblinka. Once I even heard them telling the story how they tried unsuccessfully to re-cross the Bug River from the Soviet territory to return to Warsaw to rejoin their parents. I cannot help the realization that the eventual failure of this attempt in very real terms explains my existence. It would be, therefore, quite plausible to interpret my mother's response as an expression of my parents' continuing grief and remorse for having abandoned their parents to a fate that at the time nobody could have envisaged. But my mother's comment was also unusual because it associated the present moment with the past. While her recollection of the Holocaust experience informed her response to the present-day situation, it asserted the gravity of the imminent danger, while at the same time put it into a perspective that somehow minimized it.

Upon reflection, I realized that my mother was empowered by her Holocaust experience and felt quite capable of facing, together with my father, the looming threat. Similarly, my rushed journey across the Atlantic made me see that, paradoxically, it was *I* who could not let my parents confront the danger of the Iraqi scuds on their own. Clearly, *my* sense of guilt was powerful enough to brush away any concerns for my physical safety, not to mention the fact that I had left my children with baby-sitters, and undertaken a long journey at such a perilous time.

Looking back at the event from a considerable historical distance, I am aware of the extent to which Holocaust consciousness vicariously informed my identity. Could it be that my experience corroborated Dina Vardi's identification of the second generation as "memorial candles," which claims that the second generation represents and compensates for all that their parents had lost, while at the same time reversing the normal parent–child relationships by making the children assume the burden of the parental past?[1] Did my frantic response to the danger of another Holocaust signify a release of the deeper, hitherto unacknowledged (or perhaps only half-acknowledged) features of my identity, the "phantoms," as Abraham and Torok called them? Did these fearful fantasies emerge from the "crypt" of my psyche, revealing themselves in the harsh light of another war, another forthcoming atrocity to which my parents might be subjected?[2] Whatever scholarly categories it fits, my reaction to the Gulf War seems to have exposed the transference of my parents' perennial mourning and guilt for the horrendous circumstances of *their* parents' death. In that sense, my Gulf War trip to Israel can be read as my final realization of my inheritance of their trauma, which has been deferred by "the protective shield" of the Holocaust research.[3]

Considered from a psychoanalytical perspective, therefore, my professional autobiography rationalizes my emotional need as a second-generation individual to explore indirectly my Holocaust legacy. My research on the theme of the Holocaust in the fiction of the second generation reflects this subconscious need. Being a woman, my choice of female writers, daughters of Holocaust survivors, confirms the conjecture of a vicarious search for my "phantoms" in that literature. Thus, my work included literature produced by women writers, who, like me, did not experience the Holocaust directly, but who produced fictional representations of their traumatic responses to the catastrophe.

Rejecting the Zionist ideological stance which promoted the positive world picture encapsulated by the motto: From Catastrophe [the Holocaust] to Redemption [the State of Israel], these women writers insisted on the consciousness of the unspeakable losses in the reality of the State. Contending with the general trend to forget the diasporic past and to "move on" with molding the "new Jew" in the Jewish State, those women revealed their sense of guilt by transplanting themselves by means of their literary imagination from the sunny Land of Israel into the darkness of Europe which, as they all saw it, was transfigured horrifically by the Jewish genocide. To face the sun of Israel, the terrible guilt of survival must be expiated by a nightmarish return to the ghettos and the killing fields (Shulamit Hareven);

the encounter between the children of the survivors and the children of the perpetrators back in Europe is necessary to exorcise the ghosts and face the horrific connection between the parental generation of victims and victimizers (Ruth Almog); the loss of the European culture that linked the Jewish and Christian tradition of the Enlightenment cannot be compensated by the ideal of the pioneering "new Jew" (Leah Goldberg); the identity of memorial candles for lost family members must be recognized and properly mourned in the new Jewish reality of Israel (Michal Govrin).

I would explain my choice to study the elements of the fears, anxieties, and traumas associated with the catastrophe of the Holocaust which those women writers imported into Israeli literature as the displacement of the fears and inhibitions in my personal autobiography as a daughter of Holocaust survivors. The sense that the reality I was dealing with in an academic (and therefore intellectually detached) manner was coming true in the real world, as represented by the threat of the Gulf War, which confronted me directly with my guilt and my fears. It seems that my academic autobiography both emerged from and played an important part in putting me in touch with my personal life story in the circumstances of the historical crisis.

The traumatic experience of the Gulf War has also brought back distant specters of *my* personal autobiography. The sense of an imminent danger brought forth a palpable anxiety and fear of an unexpected and unpredictable catastrophe that could not be prevented, and which might happen any time. The Gulf War triggered recollections of *my* childhood and its traumas. As I see it now, my own formative experience of exile triggered a new academic trajectory.

A few more words about my parents' autobiography are in order here. When the Second World War ended, they repatriated from the Soviet Union back to Poland: Like many Polish educated Jews who grew up between the wars, my parents were indelibly connected with their native country, its language, and, above all, its culture. Furthermore, even though they were never members of the Communist Party, they naively believed that the extreme antisemitism that they had suffered before the war would disappear under the Communist regime, which promised equality regardless of religious and ethnic origins. And so, these two highly educated Polish-Jewish citizens—my father was a civil engineer and my mother a chemical engineer—set out to rebuild their lives in the completely destroyed city of Warsaw. Before long, they were disabused of their illusions, which came to a definitive end in 1956. Now in the post-Stalin era, antisemitic sentiments proved to be alive and well and, as a result of the Soviet rupture with Israel following the Sinai Campaign, many Polish Jews were "invited" to emigrate.

This time, however, the experience of dispossession, displacement, and loss of emotional anchor was mine as well. Despite my very young age at that time, I was quite aware of our new status; stripped of citizenship, we became—even if only for a short while—stateless refugees. Thus the trauma of adjustment to Israel, the new country which was ideologically designated to be our motherland, in addition to its foreign language, culture, and climate, was exacerbated immeasurably by the traumatic sense of having been betrayed by our place of birth. While my parents contended bravely with their second exile and with the new reality of Israel, I found adjusting to the new reality very difficult experience. The anxiety engendered by the abrupt departure from our old country was exacerbated by the constant state of war in the new one; the *modus vivendi* of perennial danger, which later on culminated in the Six Day War in 1967 and the October War in 1973, instilled a permanent sense of insecurity. In that sense the danger that the Gulf War posited for Israel reignited my own old fears and uncertainties; it reverberated with my experience of enforced exile, which, in turn, reechoed my parents' survival of the Holocaust as refugees. Looking back at those historical-personal vicissitudes, my personal autobiography looks very much like a catch-22 situation.

Thus, in an unexpected mindset—and one seemingly contrary to common sense—the need to understand the historical transformations which informed my life story moved me to write a new chapter in my academic autobiography. My intellectual interests were now leading me into the world of the victim and, more specifically, into lives of people whose world without previous warning transformed into an incomprehensible nightmare. How does one respond to the transformation of all accepted norms of human existence, where the right to live is taken for granted, into a life dominated by an irreversible, implacable death sentence?

This question initiated a new direction of study. I moved from attempting to *imagine* the Holocaust experience vicariously, by referring to works of writers who lived and died in the Holocaust experience and who communicated the direct, *real-time* experience of the victims in their diaristic recordings. I believe that my choice of subjects was determined by my completely secular—I would argue, atheistic—and rational upbringing. My being free of any religious preconceptions during my upbringing allowed me to focus on what I called (half-jokingly) "problematically Jewish women." I would thus like to believe that I have treated in a bias-free manner the unusual responses to the Final Solution of my subjects: Anne Frank, an assimilated young girl, who recognized that her Jewish origins made her the victim of historical circumstances, but who struggled to become a morally better person before she perished in a concentration camp; Etty Hillesum, a young Dutch-Jewish philosopher influenced by Christian mysticism, who volunteered to work in the deportation camp of Westerbork, and who, despite her distance from Judaism, chose to be with the Jews and died in Auschwitz; Edith Stein, the phenomenologist, who accepted Jesus and became a Carmelite nun, but never reneged on her Jewish roots, and who died in Auschwitz as a Jew; and the even more special case of Simone Weil, the philosopher who rejected Judaism and retained her antisemitic sentiments even when the Final Solution threatened her personally, and who starved herself to death in solidarity with the deprivations suffered by the French people. While comparisons between my experience and the experience of the subjects of my study are, of course, impossible, I believe that my engagement in this particular category of Holocaust victims was motivated by the desire to understand their responses in the world that betrayed them. Completely integrated in the culture of the Enlightenment, believers in human progress, ethics and reason, these women were discovering their Jewish origins as "catastrophe Jews," to paraphrase Jean Améry. While recognizing their Jewish origins as a reason for their sentence of death, they strove to maintain their faith in the world that betrayed them. Their quixotic struggle to hold on their ideals through writing—I titled the book *Writing as Resistance*—appealed to me on an academic level, but also in terms of my personal belief in humanistic ethics and moral progress.

But even as I was seeking some reassurance about the viability of the humanistic principles in the life stories of these women, their deaths ruled out such hopes. On the contrary, the consciousness of their horrific death stories confronted me with the need to face the world's moral turning point of the Holocaust. While, for instance, theatrical and filmic adaptations of Anne Frank's diary could evade the issue of her horrific, dehumanizing death in Bergen-Belsen by substituting it with spurious hopefulness, I could not ignore the fact that this young girl's death symbolized the human evil that took over the world.

My work on yet another diary revealed the total collapse of humanism during the Holocaust. The diary of the twenty-one-year-old Elisheva Binder from the Polish town of Stanisławów allowed me to gain insight into the relentless process of dehumanization of the victim, as attested by the victim herself. Writing until her death (the diary was found in the ruins of Stanisławów's ghetto), Elisheva detailed systematically—and with unsparing lucidity—the disintegration of her humanity, her dignity, and her self-respect. Starting with pages of quotations mainly from Polish fiction which she thought would guide her to become an strong moral person even during a war, Elisheva was eventually compelled to place at the center of her writing the degradations and deprivations of hunger, the horrible losses of her murdered friends, and her sister and parents beingtaken to their death. She ends up confessing, with terrible sense of guilt and shame, that she has turned into a hunted animal fleeing, for as long as she can, an inevitable death.

I believe that it was the discrepancy between the literature-inspired insistence on the rewards of becoming a morally better person and Elisheva's growing awareness of her inadequacy to live by those exhortations that initiated my latest research project. At a particularly personal level, I could identify with Elisheva's initial desire to test her moral mettle in the adversarial situation of the war and empathize with her horrible disappointment at the realization of her defeat. Paradoxical as it may sound, I felt we shared to a remarkable extent a cultural background that was so deeply entrenched in the ethos created by Polish culture and especially Polish literature, which I strongly believe was my formative intellectual and ideological experience. While the limits of this chapter do not permit me to elaborate on the extent to which the literary responses to the Polish history shaped the Polish *and* Jewish national identity, a few words of explanation are in order.

The ideal of a heroic, chivalrous, generous, and moral Polish character gained prominence during the historical period of Poland's partitions. It was fashioned and promoted by poets such as Adam Mickiewicz and Julian Słowacki, and it inspired the rebellions against the Russian empire in 1832 and 1863. The idea of Polish honor was taken up by the prominent Polish fiction writer and Nobel laureate, Henryk Sienkiewicz. The *modus vivendi* that these men of letters promoted—namely, that Poland had a special destiny and was an example to other nations—was cultivated by later writers in the interwar period. This worldview was corroborated by the reestablishment of the Polish state in the wake of the First World War. It also guided the decision to launch what would prove to be the futile defense of Warsaw in September 1939 and the tragic 1944 uprising in the city's ghetto. Perhaps it should be mentioned in passing that Polish Zionists drew upon the country's national concepts and were much influenced by its poetry.[4]

Thus, despite the fact that Polish national self-identity was indelibly connected with Polish Catholicism, many Polish Jews read this literature, identified with its ideals of honor and moral honesty, and considered themselves culturally Polish. And so my formative exposure to this particularly Polish *Weltanschauung* allowed me to comprehend fully Elisheva's initial desire to follow the literary prescriptions of moral self-improvement. It was, however, the terrible bankruptcy of these moral criteria in the horrific reality that she described in the final pages of her diary that informed the most recent part of my academic autobiography, which focuses on the Polish writers who were eye-witnesses to the Holocaust.

How did these Polish writers who adhered to the principles of the Enlightenment and, at the same time, believed in the particular role of Poland on the European stage, respond to the atrocity of the Holocaust? Looking back at this chapter, I note that my work on the Polish literary responses to the Jewish extermination marks the third stage in my professional preoccupation with the Holocaust. The first stage, motivated by my sense of dependency on *and* responsibility for my parents' Holocaust experience, focused on the responses of second-generation Jewish writers and their struggle to complete the always incomplete story of their parents' Holocaust legacy. The second stage, instigated by my experiences of unexpected, uncontrollable historical developments that wrote my personal autobiography of exile from my birthplace and adoption of Israel as a new home, sought a measure of understanding of the experience of the Jewish victims who struggled as long as they could, under the implacable tolls of dehumanization and physical destruction, to maintain their emotional and intellectual selves in the Holocaust situation.

The third part of my professional autobiography communicates a shift from the Jewish world of the Holocaust to the world of the witness. It is a well-known truth that the world abandoned the Jews. While the Allies refused to intervene, European countries, which collaborated with the Nazis, acquiesced for the most part with the decree of the Final Solution. The continuing controversy about Polish–Jewish relations during the Holocaust attests to Poland's spotty record of helping Jews. My studies of a small group of Polish writers who responded to the Holocaust either in their war diaries, or in their wartime or immediate-postwar autobiographical fiction, reveal a much more complex picture. The majority of these writers see the Holocaust as the collapse of their most cherished ideals. Whereas the implementation of the Final Solution decrees the end of their trust in the Enlightenment values of equality and justice, the mainstream's approval of the Jewish genocide and frequent assistance with capturing the hiding Jews communicated the end of their glamorization of the Polish-Catholic nation. Of particular interest is the extent to which witness-writers blame themselves for humanity's moral failure. The abomination of the Nazis' extermination of the Jews has tainted even those who witnessed the atrocity. Thus some reexamine their behavior, finding it morally inadequate, whereas others admit guilt for having escaped the Jewish fate just because of their non-Jewish identity. Ironically, the heroic ethos cultivated in Polish literature could not sustain the producers of this literature in the horrific ethical collapse precipitated by the Holocaust.

So how has the trajectory of my personal autobiography determined this particular evolution of my scholarly interests? Perhaps, just perhaps, the anxieties I felt as a child of survivors and my fears of the unpredictable and the unforeseen disaster notwithstanding, this research demonstrates my consciousness of my responsibility as a witness of the endless atrocities that beset the world. This conjecture makes sense if I consider the way I teach the Holocaust to my students. My emphasis on the Holocaust as a stepping stone to a larger view of the suffering and injustice in the world guides me in the way I structure my course. But that is another story.

Instead of a Conclusion

Recently, just before the COVID-19 pandemic took hold, my personal and professional autobiographies unexpectedly coalesced. At a Scholarly Workshop on Letters from the Holocaust, which took place in Paris in February 2020, I presented letters that my grandmother, Rahela Held, sent from the Warsaw Ghetto to my parents, Helena and Michał Feldhay, while they were in the labor camps in Arkhangelsk, one of the most northerly parts of the Soviet Union. The package of letters that was given to me by my parents included fourteen of the letters and postcards my grandmother sent them. The letters cover the period of October 1940 to May 1941, just before Hitler's Campaign Barbarossa (the invasion of the Soviet Union), which eliminated all possibility of communication.

As my scholarly presentation argued, the letters exhibit a remarkable interplay between speech and silence. They are almost completely silent about the life conditions in the Ghetto. Even though few random hints imply the scarceness of food and the increasing crowded spaces, the letters consistently speak of the pain of separation, the hope for reunion, worry about my parents, and yearning for news from "the distant north." My grandmother's constant reassurances that she, my grandfather, and the rest of the family are all doing well communicates a mental and emotional position of courage and resistance. My grandmother's exquisite, miniscule handwriting, her flawless Polish, and impeccably constructed sentences reveal self-control mirrored in the content that she chose to share with her children.

Trying hard to avoid sentimentality, I would like to believe that these messages—which insist on hope despite all evidence—my grandmother's personal correspondence with her children may be read as approval, and perhaps even a blessing of her granddaughter's professional choices.

Notes

1 Dina Vardi, *Memorial Candles* (Jerusalem: Keter Publishing House, 1990).
2 Nicolas Abraham and Maria Torok, *The Shell and the Kernel: Renewals of Psychoanalysis*, trans. Nicholas T. Rand (Chicago: The University of Chicago Press, 1994).
3 Freud quoted in Saul Friedlander, "Trauma, Memory, and Transference," in Geoffrey H. Hartman, ed., *Holocaust Remembrance: The Shapes of Memory* (Oxford: Blackwell, 1994).
4 Alina Molisak and Shoshana Ronen, eds., *Polish and Hebrew Literature and National Identity* (Warsaw: Elipsa, 2010).

4

A Winding Road

Margarete Myers Feinstein

"But . . . you don't look Jewish!" I can't count how many times I heard that growing up. I then had the pleasure of further disrupting their stereotypes by informing them that my blonde hair and blue eyes are from my mother's German-Jewish family, while my father's German-Protestant family is dark-haired. Yes, like everyone else in my mother's family, I am a blonde and blue-eyed descendant of Jewish refugees from Nazi Germany. My mother likes to say that there must be a haystack in our family tree. As a historian, I think it was more likely a predatory Crusader; however, I like my mother's version better. It was only later that I realized that my appearance may have played a role in my career. During a research trip to Munich, I was on a subway train, when I noticed that everyone had the same shade of blue eyes. At that moment, I realized that I was "passing." Although I had made a vow never to deny that I was Jewish should anyone ask, my appearance made it unlikely that anyone *would* ask. Would I be comfortable pursuing a career in German and Holocaust history had I "looked" Jewish? Even today, I am not certain that I would have.

My mother's parents fled Germany in 1936. My grandmother died when I was quite young, but my mother tells me that she often spoke of Germany, saying that she had dreamt that she'd taken my mother to some special place in or around Munich. My grandfather died the summer after my bat mitzvah, so I have some memories of him. I remember him as being very Germanic, Prussian even. He liked his oom-pah-pah music and Sunday constitutionals, and he never lost his thick German accent. Yet, he wanted nothing to do with Germany. I think that contradiction between his behaviors and his sentiments is what made me interested in German history and German-Jewish identity.

The Path to German History

My family history influenced my educational choices. In the spring of my freshman year at Reed College, the historian Fritz Stern came to speak about Einstein's Germany. Since my great-grandfather was the biochemist Richard Willstätter and a colleague of Einstein's, I attended. During his lecture, Stern mentioned that the chemist Fritz Haber had been his godfather. Knowing that Haber had been my great-grandfather's dearest friend, I introduced myself. Indeed, Stern remembered my grandmother from his childhood family vacations. Stern graciously made time for me during his weekend campus visit. We spoke at length. Although I knew him to be an eminent scholar, my excitement over meeting someone with a connection to my family from times in Germany overcame my normal shyness. Stern suggested that I consider becoming an historian. That endorsement came at a pivotal point. I was having difficulty deciding on my fall semester courses. Courses in my intended international relations major were not as enticing as were various history and German literature courses. Stern's suggestion validated my attraction to history and set me on my path.

Two events during my junior year foreshadowed the direction that my career would take. For the first time, a course on the Holocaust was offered by a visiting professor, Steven Aschheim. Aschheim's approach to teaching the Holocaust had a profound impact on me. Even today I use lessons that I learned from him: The importance of helping students navigate their emotional responses to the material, as well as the necessity of an interdisciplinary approach to study of the Holocaust. Later that year, my mother gave me a copy of a German bestseller: *Dies ist nicht mein Land* [*This is Not My Country*] by Lea Fleischmann. Fleischmann, the daughter of Polish Holocaust survivors, writes about her childhood in Germany and her decision to make Aliyah. What struck me was one line about having lived her first ten years in a displaced persons (DP) camp in Bavaria. Ten years! From the Leon Uris novel *Exodus*, I knew that many survivors had immigrated to Palestine/Israel and that the British had established detention camps on Cyprus, but it never occurred to me that Jews had remained in camps on German soil for years after liberation. Intrigued, I wrote my senior history thesis on Jewish DPs in the US occupation zone of Germany, focusing on Zionist politics and Jewish identity.

In graduate school I focused on Nazism and its legacies. My MA thesis at Columbia University examined the SS maternity home organization Lebensborn e.V., situating its pro-natalist policies within the context of eugenics and the Holocaust. When I began my PhD studies at the University of California at Davis, I was uncertain of what my dissertation topic would be. Fortunately, I received a German Academic Exchange Service scholarship to attend a summer seminar on postwar Germany at UC, Berkeley. This seminar not only led me to my dissertation topic (an analysis of state symbols as a means of understanding official efforts to shape national identity in the two postwar German states), but it also introduced me to a fellow graduate student in history, Doris L. Bergen, who, years later, would encourage me on my path to Holocaust Studies.

First Encounters with Holocaust Denial

My first job after graduate school was a tenure-track position as an assistant professor of modern European history at a small Lutheran college. I confess, I was rather naïve about the potential challenges of teaching at a faith-based school. Because my predecessor had taught a course on the Holocaust and had arranged for important Holocaust scholars to speak at the college, it never occurred to me that there would be pushback when a young, female, Jewish professor did the same thing.

My first year passed uneventfully. That first summer I sent out my dissertation to potential publishers. To pass the time, I decided to rewrite my college thesis into an article. I was delighted when the editors of the *Leo Baeck Institute Yearbook* expressed interest in publishing it. First, however, they suggested that I conduct oral histories of former DPs. That suggestion had an impact that I could not have foreseen. It just happened that the first survivors whom I interviewed were women. I was interested in politics, but the women told me about marriages, pregnancy, and the difficulties raising a child without extended family and on rationed food. After a few such interviews, I decided to stop thinking about what they *weren't* telling me and to focus on what they *were* telling me. With that, I realized that Jewish life was being reconstructed in the DP camps and that there was an entire social history that had been ignored. In two years, I would be doing more research on the role of women in the DP camps.

The first inkling of trouble, which I was too inexperienced to recognize, came in the spring of my second year. I had taught the historiography seminar for history majors. In the student evaluations, there was a comment from one student that I had unfairly criticized him and had been harder on him than on other students because he planned to become an ordained minister. At the time, I thought that it was an odd comment. First, I hadn't known that any of my students were planning to be ordained. Second, I have a great respect for people who are called to the clergy and certainly would not have targeted one of them. It was only later, when I learned about another female Jewish professor whose evaluations said that "someone with such a New York accent shouldn't be teaching at a Christian school," that I realized that I had been targeted as part of an antisemitic smear campaign against the handful of Jewish professors. The professor with the accent was denied tenure, ostensibly for faulty footnotes in her well-reviewed book and despite the strong support of her department chair, the only tenured Jewish faculty member. A year later, she was hired with tenure by a prestigious public university, confirming my belief that she had been wrongfully terminated. I still felt protected by my non-Jewish appearance and by the supportive attitude of administrators. I was a bit unsettled, however, when I told a colleague and former dean who was active in Habitat for Humanity that I would like to volunteer, and he responded that I wouldn't be comfortable because there was a lot of "God talk" on site. Even though I said that it wouldn't bother me, I was never invited to participate. I believe that he really meant that he would be uncomfortable with me there.

The following fall, I taught the Holocaust course for the first time. I'm very proud of the course that I created. The only problem was that one student insisted on bringing up Himmler and trying to exonerate Hitler. After a few weeks of tolerating these mostly off-topic comments and questions, I told the student that we had already discussed the issue and that he was welcome to talk with me further in office hours, but we would not spend any more class time on it. This student was the only one who did not accompany the class on a field trip to the newly opened United States Holocaust Memorial Museum (USHMM). In January, my department chair came to tell me that there had been an issue with my teaching evaluations and that the dean and the provost agreed that it was an antisemitic attack. I am grateful that they recognized it as such, because I would not have read between the lines on my own. Half of the evaluations made almost identical statements that I had not permitted a student to speak and that I did not permit alternate viewpoints. Clearly, the one student had lobbied his friends and convinced them that he was a victim of persecution.

The provost offered to write a letter to the class informing them that the student evaluation system had been abused through the collusion of the writers. I accepted and asked him to inform the students how they could properly report concerns about a professor's performance. As I told the provost, perhaps I had unwittingly done something that should be corrected, and I would welcome an opportunity to hear from the students. I hoped to demonstrate that I was open to other viewpoints and also to have an opportunity to defend myself.

The provost drafted a lovely letter. The college president, however, squelched it, saying that "students have a right to their opinions." I felt completely abandoned and vulnerable. The president made his decision without once speaking with me. He also had been pushing a business model for the university, and it seemed that the customer (the student) was always right. Immediately, I announced that I would be going on unpaid leave the following year to work on revising my dissertation into a book manuscript. While that was true, it was also my intent to find another teaching position.

The university did attempt to lure me back. The dean invited me to visit in the fall to introduce Lawrence Langer for a public lecture. In preparation

I read Langer's then-recent work,[1] which has enriched my analysis of videotaped survivor testimonies. The campus visit reminded me of the friendships that I had established with faculty and of the students I was mentoring. The president invited me to a private meeting and tried to persuade me that the university was actively investigating what needed to be done to recruit and retain Jewish students. His reasoning was that Jewish students would benefit the university by raising test scores and paying full tuition. I was taken aback by the stereotyping of Jewish students. That night for the first and only time in my life, I dreamt that I was packed in a cattle car on the way to a concentration camp. In the morning, I knew that I could not return. With hindsight, I realize that the school was in a struggle between its past as a Lutheran seminary and the efforts of the provost to raise its standing as a liberal arts college. I got caught in the crossfire. A few years later the president left, and the university today is supportive of its Jewish faculty and students.

First Steps into Holocaust Representation and Another Encounter with Denial

Historian Gerald Feldman had just taken over the directorship of the University of California's Center for German and European Studies, and he generously took me on as a research scholar, giving me library access and an intellectual home. During that fall, I revised my book manuscript and renewed my search for a publisher, ultimately publishing it with Brill Academic Publishers.

Once again, I turned my attention to survivors, this time examining the roles of women in the DP camps. I presented my initial findings that spring at the 27th Annual Scholars' Conference on the Holocaust and the Churches, where I first met other scholars working on women and the Holocaust. Pascale Bos impressed me with her insightful critique of historians' representations of women survivors. Her later article, "Women and the Holocaust," still informs my research on Holocaust survivors.[2] Attention to gender opened new avenues for me to understanding how Jewish men and women experienced and interpreted recovery differently as they rebuilt Jewish life in the DP camps.

At the same conference, I attended a panel about Holocaust denial. One presenter told of experiences that sounded like mine: A student who denied the Holocaust and a university administration that insisted that Holocaust denial was a legitimate position. Another presenter spoke about students trained by white supremacist groups to spread Holocaust denial and to harass faculty. I wondered how I could teach about the Holocaust again without fear. A new job would lead me to a solution.

Shortly after the conference, I accepted a position as assistant professor of European and world history at Indiana University South Bend (IUSB). My new teaching responsibilities included a topics course in twentieth-century world history. The course would be offered that fall, so I needed to choose a topic quickly. Since it was only a few years following the genocides in Bosnia and Rwanda, I decided to teach the History of the Holocaust and Genocide. I soon realized the advantage of beginning the semester with the Armenian Genocide. The students were blank slates when it came to this topic, so we read primary sources and scholarship that gave them a grounding in the history. When we then read about Turkish denial of the genocide, they were able to analyze that denial without falling for it themselves. Given my prior experience, I could not trust that there would not be a Holocaust denier among my students. By introducing the issue of denial early and in a context about which the students knew little, I hoped to ensure that later in the semester these students would be prepared to identify and refute Holocaust denial.

In the spring while I was still planning that course, I spent three months in Jerusalem, spending as much time as possible in the Yad Vashem archives, researching daily life in the DP camps. I told myself that this research was simply filling time until my book on German state symbols was published, but Doris Bergen would soon show me that I was only fooling myself. The move to South Bend reconnected me with Doris, who was across town at the University of Notre Dame. This friendship proved to be life altering. First, Doris played a significant role in my meeting my future husband, Rabbi Morley T. Feinstein. Second, she pointed out to me that in my research on DPs, I had the material for a book. Sitting across from her in my living room, I objected that the DPs were just a detour; I was a German historian. But Doris had planted a seed that would take root. I still published and gave conference papers about German national identity, but the Jewish DPs continued to call to me, insisting that I tell their stories.

Meanwhile, Holocaust denial once again rose its ugly head. The IUSB student paper published an advertisement from the revisionist Committee for Open Discussion of the Holocaust (CODOH) denying the Holocaust. Faculty members came to me as the university's historian of modern Europe, asking me to write a letter to the editors. Nervous after the experience at my prior school, I nevertheless wrote the letter, explaining that there is no debate about the occurrence of the Holocaust and informing students about reliable resources on campus where they could learn more. When I spoke about the matter in my class on modern European history, some students defended the student editors. I feared that I would be subjected to another hostile campaign by students. Fortunately, my fears were not realized.

The chancellor of IUSB was extremely supportive and called together faculty and local Jewish leaders for a meeting to discuss the incident. After a few additional meetings with concerned faculty, the advisor to the student paper, and the student editors, the chancellor paid for the student editors to travel to Washington, DC, to visit the USHMM. The assistant editor came back from the experience with a fuller appreciation of what the Holocaust meant and why the CODOH advertisement had been problematic. The editor remained defiant; however, she did not mobilize other students to her side. The alliance of faculty and administrators had succeeded in meeting the challenge of that teachable moment. I felt more secure; my confidence in myself and in the academy was being restored.

Serendipity continued to send me on the path of Holocaust Studies. My soon-to-be fiancé introduced me to his friend working at the Shoah Foundation Visual History Archive, who gave me a tour of the facility at Universal Studios. Later, I would do a lot of research at its new, permanent home at the University of Southern California. Morley also introduced me to one of his former congregants, a daughter of Holocaust survivors and an organizer of the USHMM's conference on DPs, "Life Reborn." The conversations that I had and the people whom I met at the conference helped me to recognize the depth of my commitment to the study of DPs and led to further invitations and collaborations.

Detours and Family Life

After our marriage, Morley and I decided to return to California, where he was called to a pulpit in Los Angeles. I was fortunate to find a one-year visiting position at Loyola Marymount University. That fall I was surprised to discover a sukkah at the center of campus, a clear sign that this faith-based school was inclusive and committed to interfaith dialogue. But the birth of our twin daughters, followed by the great recession, meant that, for the foreseeable future, there were no further teaching opportunities. Fortunately, I was invited to be a research scholar at the UCLA Center for the Study of Women, followed by a visiting scholar position at UCLA's Center for Jewish Studies. Then, historian Jonathan Petropoulos invited me to be a senior research scholar at what was then The Center for the Study of the Holocaust, Genocide, and Human Rights at Claremont McKenna College. I am grateful for the opportunities that these positions gave me to research and to write my book *Holocaust Survivors in Postwar Germany, 1945–1957*. While my young, twin daughters napped, I researched and wrote. After they went to bed for the night, I'd retreat to the home office to use the manual microfilm reader that I'd purchased, or I'd sit at the dining room table with my note cards and laptop, drafting another conference paper or book chapter. None of this would have been possible without the emotional and financial support of my husband. While the university affiliations gave me library access, I received no research or travel funds. Fortunately, my husband earned enough to pay for what I needed. The gift of being an independent scholar was that I could work at my own pace. I spent time with the girls at the playground, fingerpainting, reading stories. I also had a nanny and part-time housekeeper so that I didn't need to deal with laundry, dishes, or scrubbing toilets. These two marvelous women became members of our family, and I am greatly indebted to them for what they taught my daughters and for the time they gave me to do my work. At the time, I feared that I would never get another teaching opportunity and I worried that I would lose professional status. Now I can appreciate the time that I was able to be with my family and also to focus on my book project.

As I wrote the book, my interest in identity and daily life led me to oral histories and memoirs. My first article dealing directly with Holocaust representation arose from these sources. I had studied personal narratives by female survivors who referred to themselves or to other women as "mothers," often when they had no biological children or were even still children themselves. I became aware that although there were helpful, protective men, they were not referred to as "fathers." As I began to puzzle why this might be so, I read a memoir that seemed to contradict this observation. After liberation, a young female DP joined a group of survivors returning to Poland. She mentioned one of the men being like a father. So, I thought, it was simply a coincidence that I hadn't noticed surrogate father figures before. But a few pages later, the fatherly survivor was revealed to be an SS man attempting to evade capture by hiding among the group of survivors. Now I was completely intrigued. Did this fallen father figure represent a condemnation of Jewish fathers? Did the failure of Jewish men to protect their families result in a loss of paternal authority?

As I investigated those questions, I discovered that most survivors retained positive images of their own fathers, believing that they had been heroic in their efforts to protect their families; their paternal authority was not called into question. Instead, my readings in feminist analysis of autobiographical writing helped me to understand the gendered way in which memories are encoded, retrieved, and then narrated. The dearth of father figures in survivor narratives had more to do with gendered narrative construction, than with a crisis in paternal authority, which I argue in my article "Absent Fathers, Present Mothers." Feminist analysis helps to shape the questions that I ask and the methods that I use. In my current work on retribution, I have identified gendered forms of revenge as well as gendered definitions of perpetrators. Gender is a lens that leads to deeper understanding of Jewish communal life.

As the book neared completion, I presented related papers at the annual meetings of the American Historical Association and of the German Studies Association. At one GSA meeting I asked my *Doktorvater*, William W. Hagen, for advice about finding a publisher or book agent. Bill immediately whisked me to the Cambridge University Press table, introduced me to Lew Bateman, and told me to ask Bateman what I had asked him. I obediently and innocently complied. Bateman promptly assured me that I didn't want an agent (of course, I realized, that a publisher's representative might not want an author to get an agent) and then asked about my project. At the end of my elevator spiel, Bateman handed me his card and told me what I should send to him as a prospectus. And that is how my second book came to be published by Cambridge University Press. Had Bill not introduced me and prompted me, I might have shied away from approaching the inimitable Lew Bateman. Sometimes you just need the right person, at the right time, to give you a little push. Being a Cambridge author has led to invitations to review manuscripts and to participate in symposia. It also helped keep in check the imposter syndrome that has plagued me, especially when I was an independent scholar.

After the publication of the book, my friend and colleague Beth Cohen recommended me to teach a class at California State University at Northridge on the History of the Holocaust and Genocide. Then I was contacted by Holli Levitsky, director of Loyola Marymount University's Jewish Studies Program, to teach modern Jewish history there. This time when a student of mine was planning to become a priest, he thanked me for providing a space in which he could discuss theological issues. He is now a Jewish Studies minor and, on my invitation, participated in leading an interfaith service.

Holli encouraged me to create more courses, and I am now the first LMU faculty member teaching full-time in Jewish Studies. I revised my former course on the Holocaust and genocide and now teach it from the interdisciplinary perspective of history and social psychology. A course on Holocaust literature continues to bring me fresh ideas about Holocaust representation, leading me to write about the question of revenge in the writings of Elie Wiesel. Contrary to Naomi Seidler's position that Wiesel removed evidence of rage from *Night* in order to reach a non-Jewish audience,[3] I view the evolution of his writing on revenge as a sign that his feelings changed with the passage of time, a finding consistent with statements made by other survivors. At Holli's urging, I have joined the Jewish American and Holocaust Literature Association, where I have found a supportive and stimulating community of scholars.

Private life has had a major influence on my career path. My husband supported my research by serving as a rabbinic advisor, editor, and financier. Once the book on DPs was finished, I had thought to write about the return home of German victims of Nazism, both Jewish and non-Jewish. While the Jewish DPs left the land of their persecutors, most German victims of Nazism returned home to live among the perpetrators. I thought that studying this topic could give us insights into reconciliation and transitional justice.

To get a feel for the source material I spent a month at the Berlin branch of the Federal Archive. It was painstaking work. Unlike other archives, which permit photography or provide inexpensive photocopies, the Federal Archive charged a prohibitive amount for photocopies and forbade photography or scanning. Instead of collecting a cache of documents to study back at home, I slowly transcribed documents into my computer. I gathered enough material to write an article about the competition for housing among German victims of Nazism, DPs, and ethnic Germans expelled from Eastern Europe and the ways in which the groups represented themselves to Allied and regional authorities. I completed the article as part of a USHMM Summer Research Workshop—"Landscapes of the Uprooted: Refugees and Exiles in Postwar Europe"—organized by Adam Seipp and Andrea Sinn, who encouraged the examination of the entangled histories of different displaced populations. There is still much work left to be done in this area and on the return home of German victims of Nazism, but I realized that it would require at least a year of residence in Germany to collect enough documentation for a book manuscript. Since my family situation did not permit an extended stay in Germany, I looked for a new research project that I could do from Los Angeles with short research trips to archives elsewhere. Currently, I am working on the question of Jewish retribution after the Shoah, relying heavily on oral histories, although I hope to make short visits to some regional German archives.

Looking Back

My journey began with my grandparents' legacy and the path it took was shaped by the students, colleagues, and others whom I met along the way. When I encountered Holocaust denial and an unsupportive administration, I made an impulsive decision to take a leave of absence and to search for a new job. That choice had tremendous ramifications. It allowed me to research further the history of Jewish DPs and led me to South Bend, where I would teach about genocide for the first time, where I would work with a supportive faculty and administration to combat Holocaust denial, where a friend and colleague would encourage me to see myself as more than a German historian and would introduce me to my future husband, the father of my children.

Our decision to move to Los Angeles was also spontaneous. As a newlywed, I thought of the move as a new beginning for us as a couple and trusted that I would be able to pursue my career. While it took me longer to establish myself in Los Angeles than I had anticipated, I am grateful for the time that I had with my children while they were young, and the time that I had to write about the Jewish DPs; I felt a tremendous responsibility to tell the story of mourning and renewal in the DP camps. At LMU I found a mentor in Holocaust Studies and a community committed to interfaith dialogue. Looking back, I am surprised at how often I, an essentially cautious person, made choices based on instinct and emotion. Each of those choices led me to where I needed to be, even if I was unaware of it at the time.

Obstacles that seemed insurmountable led to a change of direction which brought me somewhere unexpected but welcome. I am grateful for the people I have met along the way: Students whose questions pushed me to learn more and to explain better; colleagues who shared their knowledge, challenged me, and befriended me; family who inspired me, encouraged me, and sustained me.

Notes

1 Lawrence L. Langer, *Holocaust Testimonies: The Ruins of Memory* (New Haven: Yale University Press, 1991).
2 Pascale Rachel Bos, "Women and the Holocaust: Analyzing Gender Difference," in *Experience and Expression: Women, the Nazis, and the Holocaust*, ed. Elizabeth R. Baer and Myrna Goldenberg (Detroit: Wayne State University Press, 2003), 23–50.
3 Naomi Seidman, "Elie Wiesel and the Scandal of Jewish Rage," *Jewish Social Studies* 3 (1996): 1–19.

5

Biographia Literaria Feminista

Sara R. Horowitz

Paths Not Taken

If my father had not died a few months before I was to begin my last year of high school, I would be a mathematician today, and not a literary scholar whose life work focuses on the Holocaust and its aftereffects. While my father was not a victim or a survivor of the Shoah, and had no close family members who were, his premature passing shifted the arc of my life trajectory in radical ways. Had he lived into old age, I would be researching imaginary numbers instead of imaginary people, striving for elegant proofs rather than elegant prose. But when I found myself orphaned suddenly and unexpectedly at the age of sixteen, it was the lens of literature and not the challenge of formulae that offered a portal to explore bereavement, absence, and cosmic cruelty.

I'm often asked what brings literary scholars to the study of the Holocaust—particularly scholars like me with no familial connection to the Nazi genocide. Retracing my own academic trail I recognize the web of unspoken impulses that impelled it. This brief literary autobiography reaches back decades to probe first the turn to literature, then to the Holocaust, then to gender. Tinged with childhood bereavement, my writing has woven the threads of the not-there with the unexpected lines that link nineteenth-century American literature, twentieth-century French literature, and the body of work we have come to call Holocaust literature. Literary theory tells us that meaning is created in the encounter between a text and a reader. Although it often goes unarticulated, engaged literary scholarship emerges from a fraught negotiation among the public and the private, the universal and the personal, the manifest and the hidden.

My penchant for both literature and mathematics bears my father's imprint. As far back as memory reaches, he entertained, stimulated, and soothed me with stories. I don't recollect my mother telling stories. A black-and-white snapshot on my desk shows me, at perhaps a year and half, sitting on her lap, rapt, as she reads to me from an ABC book. I sometimes point to the photo and say, half-jokingly, *this is where it all began— my love of reading, my career as a professor of literature. It's from my mother.* But the truth is, I don't remember my mother reading to me. Months after the photo was taken she was hospitalized, and within a year, she died of cancer.

My father's stories drew from an eclectic set of sources: the Talmud, Greek mythology, Hasidic masters, family lore, American history, and tales that sprang from his own imagination. I suspect that storytelling served unintendedly as the conduit for things he did not know how or could not bear to say to me. Even before I could articulate the thought, I understood that stories were a way to probe, and perhaps make shaky peace with, disturbance.

When I got a bit older, my father began to teach me mathematics. I hated the tedium of grade-school arithmetic, but adored the abstraction of math. My father taught math in an inner-city high school in New York. Evenings, I became his pupil. Sitting with him over geometry and calculus problems, I relished the universe of balance and order they invoked. Mathematics beckoned with beauty, perfection, elegance. Doing math together swaddled the two of us in a warm and protective bubble, inviting us to imagine a perfection that eluded us in the real. Things could be solved—if not now, then sometime in the future.

I never attended my final year of high school. After my father died, I persuaded several universities to offer me provisional admission without a high school diploma. Like my college peers, I became absorbed in courses, papers, exams, and social life. For two years I carried a double major— English and math. But my college years had a hidden undercurrent: contending with the death of my parents—each so premature and, it seemed to me, so undeserved. These losses affected me emotionally, of course, but also philosophically and theologically. More than I realized at the time, my engagement with literature connected with my inner life. Math and its promise of perfection did not. In college I was drawn to twentieth-century European writers, such as Kafka and Rilke, contending with a world whose certainties had been shattered. Yeats's line resonated: *Things fall apart; the center cannot hold.* Because the "immortality" of youth passed me by, I worried: What would make a life worth living? What would make it meaningful?

Ironically—given my subsequent professional path—I had no interest in doing coursework in Jewish studies. Studying the Holocaust never occurred to me. It was not a familial issue, as both sides of my family had come to the United States in the 1910s and 1920s. In the Jewish elementary school I attended, we saw films about the Holocaust and linked it historically and theologically to the long chain of Jewish catastrophe. Although I had gone to school with classmates whose parents spoke with Polish, German, French, Flemish, and other European accents, it did not occur to me (nor to any of my classmates with American parents) that they were survivors of atrocity and genocide. For the most part, the Holocaust was not on our radar, except, to use Primo Levi's poignant phrase, as something "distant, blurred, historical."

Still, the literature that most engaged me emerged from the multivalent crisis in faith, culture and ideology that emerged after the Second World War. I was particularly taken by French existentialist writers, especially Albert Camus. Camus's concept of the absurd touched the heart of my own inner compulsion: That we are hard-wired to desire meaningfulness in a universe with no a priori meaning.

After completing my BA in English, I slid into a doctoral program in English and Comparative Literature at Columbia University. For a graduate program, it was relatively large; I was one of over thirty students admitted that year. We were expected to complete a master's thesis in our first year; ideally, it would serve as the basis of a dissertation. I planned to deepen engagement with Camus and his cohorts. But my advisor pointed me in a different direction, nudging me towards American literature, his own area of expertise. I somehow landed on Mark Twain's later writing, much of it published posthumously, against the desires of his family. In these works, the raucous humor of his earlier writing had transformed into a sarcasm that barely masked the author's despair at what, decades later, would come to be called the human condition. Somber, despairing, irreverent and challenging, Twain took aim at prejudice and cruelty. He faulted the comforts of facile religious faith, and a God who witness human suffering but does nothing to alleviate it. In *The Mysterious Stranger*, Twain's darkest novel, the eponymous stranger repeatedly challenges the platitudes that, half a century later, the French existentialists would term *mauvaise foi*, bad faith. The stranger serves as the author's mouthpiece, as in this exchange with a poor but pious woman.

"The poor and God. God will provide . . ."

"What makes you think so?"

". . . Because I know it!" she said. "Not a sparrow falls to the ground without His seeing it."

"But it falls, just the same. What good is seeing it fall?"

Although they seemed disparate, the darkness of Twain's last novel connected philosophically with the darkness of the postwar era that compelled Camus's writing. Both writers struggled to construct an ethics in a world without sanctions. I did not yet know that their world views would seed my academic focus in years to come.

My advisor at Columbia encouraged me to work further on turn-of-the-century American literature. However, by the time I had finished writing my M.A. thesis, I experienced a *crise de conscience*. I loved probing literary texts. But what right had I to take pleasure in reading and writing and thinking while the world around me spun out of control? If Camus was right, and we each had to create our own meaning in the world, how was I creating mine? I requested a leave of absence from the doctoral program. I worked as a freelance writer while reassessing my direction. Literary scholarship was so . . . well, so intellectual, so cerebral, so ethereal. It seemed to me so disconnected from things that helped people concretely and palpably. Would it not be more meaningful, I asked myself, to study medicine and tend the sick? Or to study law and advocate for the powerless? Or to become a psychologist, or a social worker. Or, or, or. I began taking courses that were prerequisites to pursuing some of these fields. I applied (and was admitted) to several professional programs. But I could not settle on a direction. I wondered where I could do the most good. Mostly I wondered which path would allow me to say, when I reached the end of my days on earth, that I had led a live worth living.

At the time, I understood my career anxieties as part of the zeitgeist, an angst-ridden generational existential response to the aftermath of the war in Vietnam, the student revolution, rapid social change, and economic ease. Looking back, however, I see these anxieties also as imbricated in a grieving process.

Literary Encounters

During this break from academic work I continued to read widely, avidly. Someone gave me a copy of Elie Wiesel's novel, *A Beggar in Jerusalem*. While not entirely unknown, Wiesel's writing was not yet well known. It was my first encounter with his work. I reread and reread it, and then read some of his earlier novels. The books spoke powerfully to me: the catastrophe of the Holocaust, the bottomlessness of bereavement, the indelible aloneness of cosmic solitude. The strands I had teased out in Twain and Camus came together urgently in Wiesel's writing. In Wiesel's fiction, the events of the Holocaust moved out of the realm of history and into the present. The Nazi genocide shaped the world that my generation inherited. We lived its aftermath.

As an academic field of inquiry, Holocaust Studies was just developing. Historians and political scientists had carved out a robust area of research. Here and there, universities had begun offering courses on the subject. Few literary scholars were thinking about representations of the Shoah. Reading around in writing that engaged the Holocaust, mostly by European-born writers who had survived the Nazi genocide, deepened my sense of how my generation—the postwar generation in North America, seemingly so removed from the catastrophe "over there" had reaped the residue of that war: anomie, a collapse of faith, a crisis of ethics. Holocaust literature grounded the abstractions of literary study in an encounter between imagination and history, giving concrete and urgent context to issues of ethics and meaning.

I met some of the professors with whom I had studied at Columbia to discuss my intent to explore Holocaust literature. They did not encourage me; they did not deem my project viable or even literary. They reminded me that neither Hebrew nor Yiddish—both integral to the project—would count towards fulfilling the program's demanding language requirements. Some suggested that I consider programs in Jewish history or Judaic studies. But I did not see my project as either Jewish or historical, even though it engaged both Jews and history. I saw it as a project that challenged the foundations of western culture. It mapped onto the faultline my generation inherited. If I chose to be reinstated in the doctoral program after my leave of absence, I knew I would have to push hard against the prevailing authorities to pursue my interest. Or I could look elsewhere.

I applied to a small number of doctoral programs in comparative literature, making clear what I intended to work on. Of all the responses to my projected research, the faculty at the small and distinguished program in Literary Studies at Brandeis University were most intrigued. The study of Holocaust literature was then so new and so understudied that they were not certain where my project would lead. Not surprisingly, none of them worked even peripherally in the body of literature that engaged me. But—as I later learned—each of the professors who would later constitute my dissertation committee had a personal stake in the Holocaust and the issues raised in the literature. One, for example, had witnessed Kristallnacht as a child; another had an abiding interest in French antisemitism; another in Abraham Joshua Heschel.

I, too, had a personal stake in my project—something I barely acknowledged to myself. When I first came upon it, Wiesel's writing struck a deep but unlikely personal chord. Here I was, living out a privileged life in New York in the second half of the twentieth century, angsting over career options and graduate programs. And here was this tormented literary voice, orphaned by the Nazi genocide, thrust into a postwar world owning only the skin and bones of his own fleshless body. Captive to the *desiderium* of absent loved ones, an absent God, Wiesel's narrative voice conveyed the impossible push to express, even to restore, a shattered world, shattered faith. I remember feeling that these threads woven into his literary fabric were also the threads of my own struggle, monstrously magnified. And a wisp of a thought, barely registered: if Weisel, and the other writers that his work led me to read, could find the means to mourn such radical losses, to acknowledge and then move past the brutality that had wrenched their world, I could learn from them how to navigate my own much smaller bereavement.

Oddly, then, the plunge into that heart of darkness was driven by optimism. Immersing in that meaning-destroying world evoked by literary representations of the Holocaust was driven by my own thirst for meaningfulness. Looking back on this today, I cringe. I recognize my own hubris and my own naivete. Even then, of course, I understood the great gulf between my life and that of the shredded war refugees. I so little grasped the complicated inner state of people like Wiesel, and other writers whose books were piling up on my desk: Charlotte Delbo, Piotr Rawicz, Jakov Lindt, Jerzy Kosiński. Through them, through survivors whom I came to know and befriend over the years, I encountered the snarling of different emotional registers, the knotted tentacles of psychological, ethical, and theological crises.

As I read, I was overtaken by the enormity of my subject. The writers humbled me. Their world dwarfed my own. The literature I sought to address is fierce, welding together history, memory, and imagination. It suggested—suggests—the limits of knowledge, of ideology, of understanding. I saw these writers as balanced at the edge of a void to which they attempted to give expression—a concept that would later figure in the title of my first book, *Voicing the Void*. As a graduate student, I felt submerged in a literature born out of experiences I could not master.

Literary Mentors

Throughout my career, I benefitted from the generosity mentors—both scholars who modeled academic work and literary authors who discussed their own work and mine. Lawrence Langer's first book on Holocaust literature, *The Holocaust and the Literary Imagination,* appeared around the time I applied to the program at Brandeis. As he recounted in its introduction, the seeds of that book had germinated during a sabbatical in Germany. Looking at a pastoral landscape painting in an art museum in Munich titled "Dachau," he felt overwhelmed by the disparity between the beauty of the landscape and the atrocity that occurred at the same site. "I wondered for the first time," he recollected in his introduction to that book, "whether the artistic vision of the literary intelligence could ever devise a technique and form adequate to convey what the concentration camp experience implied for the contemporary mind." The book contained the first literary analyses I had come upon of many of the works I had been reading. I was struck by the rigor, clarity, and passion of his writing and the insistence that one face the implications of the Holocaust without romanticization, sanctification, or redemption. In truth, when I read his book, I worried that I had no dissertation topic—that he had said all that needed to be said about Holocaust literature. I could not know then that scholarship on literary representations of the Shoah would burgeon in the decades that followed.

Unlike the members of my doctoral committee, whose astute comments on my dissertation-in-progress relied on my own close readings of a growing body of fiction that they followed me into, Lawrence Langer was immersed in much of the literature I was writing about. His reading of my work would be more exacting, more critical. I wondered what he would make of my project. I learned that he was a professor in a college in Boston. Brandeis was located in a suburb of Boston, and I lived in Cambridge. I decided to seek him out.

We met one afternoon at his home. Sitting on the deck overlooking his backyard, we spoke for several hours. We snacked on a bowl of cherries, tossing the pits into the yard. As our conversation wound down, he offered to read and give feedback on my dissertation. His rigor, his sharp eye, and his honesty sharpened my thinking. His generosity of spirit nourished me as an emergent scholar. To this day, I admire his bold and lucid thinking and value his mentorly friendship.

Already then, I understood that my work fell into a crack between disciplines: literature, but sort of historical; broad-based, but Jewish-y. I often found myself explaining how literary scholarship contributed to the study of the Holocaust. The academic conferences where I presented were dominated by historians. Some—like the historian who served as external examiner at my doctoral defense—doubted that literature could contribute to understanding the Shoah. Some measured the worth of Holocaust literature solely by its factual accuracy.

Others applauded literary approaches as a way to engage people emotionally with history—where the real work was done. Behind this faint praise I discerned a presumption about the "softness" of literature as opposed to the rigor of history. To explain the insights of literary studies, I developed the extended metaphor. Historiography aspires to present a clear window onto the past. You focus on the vision of the past rather than on the glass pane through which you view it. Literary approaches notice not only on what lies beyond the window, but also on the texture and color of glass and the mullions that frame the panes. What matters is not only the story of the past, but the way that people choose to tell it. Whether by literary authors or simply people talking about their lives, the texture of the telling hints at how they experienced and interpret the past, what eludes expression, what they can bear to remember and what they cannot.

The literary imagination encourages a complexity of thinking that is different from the complexity of the historian—closer, perhaps, to the practice of midrash. A classical mode of Jewish biblical commentary that some scholars see as an early form of literary fiction, midrash responds to a disturbance in the readerly experience, generating a story to probe ethical, philosophical, and textual problems. In a similar way, literary responses to the Holocaust ask us to let go of a definitive master narrative of the past, and accept instead a fragmentary and shifting set of perspectives that may be contradictory. It challenges us to see memory as simultaneously flawed and accurate. It asks us to imagine our way into the stories that the murdered would tell if the dead could tell their own stories. Or to see in ourselves what

Joseph Conrad termed the "secret sharer"—with onlookers, bystanders, perpetrators. It invites our empathy while warning us of the perils of empathy; it pushes us to ask disturbing questions about our own connection with the past, our own ethical choices.

Central to the writers I focused on was an sense of the impossibility of what they had set out to do—to express what they felt was beyond expression. Literary critics would refer to this as a crisis of representation. The tension between the imperative to voice, and impossibility of doing so adequately found concrete expression in the presence of characters who were mute—that is, who could not or would not speak. These mute characters were at the heart of my dissertation work. In my first book, I built upon my dissertation work, complicating its rubric to encompass what I called textual muteness. I looked at ways that authors introduced pockets of silence, moments of unsaying, gaps in the narrative, in order to convey what remains unnarratable.

Larry Langer was the first of several generous mentors who nurtured my writing. Among the others was Geoffrey Hartman, the brilliant theorist whom I met at a small conference on Holocaust representation soon after I began my first academic post. Something I said about the different sensibilities of wartime and postwar writing caught his attention. He sought me out, inviting me to contribute an essay on ghetto writing to a book he was editing. The book was almost ready to go to press, but there was a gap that he hoped I would fill. In those pre-internet days, we had to rely on snailmail to exchange drafts. Because of the tight deadline, I would FedEx revisions to him. By the time the essay was complete, I had become acquainted with the FedEx pilot, who would grab the envelope from me at the airport.

That essay was my first extended pivot from fiction to lifewriting. I began to apply the lens of literary scholarship to material I thought of as historical, rather than literary—diaries, memoirs, testimonies, and other oral accounts—sources that historians treated with reluctance. Literary studies provided tools to understand them. Working on the essay for Geoffrey's book was prelude to my later work on gender, sexuality, and infanticide—work that integrates literary sources and literary tools with non-literary texts.

Not only literary scholars, but also some of the authors I treated became important mentors. Most significant among them was the Polish-born Israeli writer Ida Fink, whom I sought out in the summer of 1990, hoping she would agree to an interview. Coming upon her short stories, I was riveted by the quiet force of her luminous writing. Fink invited me to her home in Holon. After several hours of conversation, I began to request the interview. But I sensed that we were at a crossroads. I could take out my tape recorder and we would have a professional relationship. Or I could forgo the interview and develop a friendship. I opted for friendship.

Over the years, we corresponded often and intimately about our lives and our work. Whenever I came to Israel, I would visit her, often a day or so after arriving. Sometimes, lulled by jetlag and the unaccustomed heat of Holon, I would fall asleep on her sofa. When I awoke, she would say, "You looked like a Botticelli. I let you sleep." She would read book chapters and articles that I wrote—sometimes about her writing—and offer comments. I once accompanied her on a writers' retreat. She spoke of her protracted struggle to publish her stories. For years, potential publishers advised her to write in a different way—less quiet, less subdued, with more thundering outrage. Initially they did not get the subtlety and nuance of her powerful literary voice. When I began to think about issues of gender in relation to the Holocaust, she disagreed with its relevance. But as we continued to speak about it, even in relation to her own stories, she began to encourage me.

Thinking about Gender

In graduate school I found relief from reading and writing about catastrophe by reading around in feminist theory, a field just coming into its own. Like many young women then coming of age as scholars, I felt a direct connection to the issues that emerged. We all contended with cultural perspectives that diminished women's experiences and perceptions. We fought for entry into the boys' club that was then the academy. Women's studies developed into a separate stream of research and publication that I kept distinct from my work on the Holocaust. When I began my first academic position, I was nurtured by a small cadre of senior women professors who mentored newly minted female colleagues. About fifteen years older than me, they were stunningly accomplished—against the great odds faced by women of that generation. We formed women's studies reading groups and critiqued one another's work.

I did not think of Holocaust Studies as a "Jewish" subject *per se*, although there were certainly important Jewish components to it. But the university that hired me certainly did. When I first proposed a course on Holocaust literature, my department head shook his head. He thought it would be a great course but feared it would not attract sufficient enrollment because there were few Jewish students. I pushed; he relented. The course over-enrolled, and had a waiting list each time I taught it.

At first I bristled when asked about women and the Holocaust. Without consciously thinking about it, I had absorbed the prevailing wisdom in Holocaust Studies: the Shoah was about antisemitism and the oppression of Jews; gender was irrelevant. But the questions asked by my students and my working group got under my skin. I lifted the barrier between the two streams of my scholarly work, and began to look at Holocaust literature, testimony, and lifewriting through the lens of gender.

In a sense, as a literary scholar I was lucky to work on the fringes of Holocaust Studies and Jewish Studies, both of which resisted the insights of gender. Doubly marginalized, I felt oddly free to follow wherever my projects led. I became part of a core group of women in several disciplines who had begun to examine how issues of gender bore on our understanding of the Shoah. The established researchers in the field saw this focus as misguided, at best; at worst, driven by "trendy" but ideologically distorted thinking. Once after I spoke on women's memoirs at the U.S. Holocaust Memorial Museum in the mid-1990s, several historians in the audience objected to the very inclusion of gender as a category of analysis. A survivor declared that making scholarly distinctions based on gender offended the memory of the murdered men and women in his family. But several women survivors argued with him: their stories had yet to be told. After the event they sought me out. Over the years, many women survivors have brought me into their confidence—colleagues, literary authors, "ordinary" women. They share their journals, their poems, their untold stories. A few asked me to never to reveal what they told me. I have kept that promise. Their stories and their trust has fueled and deepened my work.

The immersion that this kind of scholarly work demands comes at a cost. It sears you, decenters you, sucks you into a netherworld. As I warn my students, plunging into Holocaust literature shatters complacency, certainties, and confidence in a benevolent world. I have learned to slow down the process of research and writing. I take breaks after each chapter or article to anchor myself to this world, not the one I write about, consciously reattaching to the world of the living. During a fellowship at the U.S. Holocaust Memorial Museum, I researched oral testimonies about what I considered gendered moments of memory. I spent months listening to testimonies about infanticide—not only witnessed by but also committed by Jewish women. As the archives closed at the end of each day, I would walk three miles back to my apartment, to clear my mind and my psyche. For two years, I could not bear to write up my findings. Recently the philosopher John Roth put into words what all of us working in this field understood: "You cannot visit hell with impunity. You must pay an entrance fee and an exit fee."

When I reflect back on the naivete that first drew me to Holocaust literature, and the entwining of my life and work, I am reminded of conversations with the Israeli writer Aharon Appelfeld. Although I had met him as a graduate student, our friendship took hold the first year I taught at York University. He was writer-in-residence for several months and I was his institutional host. My husband would drive him to speaking venues and to show him around town. We jokingly referred to my husband as *hanahag shel Appelfeld*—Appelfeld's driver. We often hosted Aharon and his wife for shabbat dinner. After that year, we would meet with him whenever we were in Israel—in the Jerusalem café where he wrote, at his favorite restaurant, at his home. Like Fink, he read and commented on my writing. In his later years, he often spoke of the difficult but necessary labor of owning one's roots and owning one's shame—as he owned the diminished self of his childhood, a feral and fearful boy navigating an unbearably hostile world.

That drive to own one's entire being I believe impels women survivors of the Shoah to reach back into what Fink calls "the ruins of memory" and talk about experiences that had been unnarrated for many years: stories of sexual violation, of infanticide. In a different way, it invites my own story of engagement with the genocide and gender. Today I teach Holocaust literature to a diverse group of students in Toronto, a city populated by families who bear their own stories of oppression and loss. Together we mediate diverse lived and remembered experiences, building shared cultures and communities of meaning.

6

My Journey into the Shoah

David Patterson

"You have to read this."

The lean, long-haired nineteen-year-old had just walked into my office at the University of Oregon, book in hand. He was one of the best students in my world literature class. His name was Matt.

It was 1979, a pleasant October afternoon. I had completed my PhD in comparative literature the previous year. I was excited about engaging the profound questions that shaped the great literary traditions. My students, too, were eager to learn: Their souls hungered for meaning the way their bodies hungered for bread. I cultivated that hunger at every turn: Go read Dostoevsky's "Dream of a Ridiculous Man." Read I. L. Peretz's "If Not Higher." This is Tolstoy's *Confession*: Take it. Read it.

So here was Matt placing a slim volume on my desk in the midst of the books that cluttered its surface. He was gentle with it, as if he were handling a treasure as fragile as memory. Now it was he who had something for *me* to read. With an unwavering intensity in his voice, just above a whisper, he softly repeated: "You have to read this."

I picked up the book: It was *Night* by Elie Wiesel.

"Who is Elie Wiesel?" I asked.

He smiled and said, "Just read it."

I ran my fingers over the word *Night*. The book felt warm to the touch, and my hands began to tremble. This young man, transformed into a messenger, had delivered his message; my task was to receive it. So it happened that someone who was hardly more than a child introduced me to a man whose writings are haunted by the screams and the silences of children.

He left me to my cloister, and I began reading. And rereading. Like Jacob at Peniel, I wrestled with a dark angel, with darkness itself, as I struggled to move from line to line, from page to page. From the opening page, some of it went over my head: Hasidic house of prayer? Shekhinah in exile? Kabbalah? What is this? What is that? One passage, however, penetrated my soul: "Where is God? Here He is: hanging on these gallows." But what could that mean? Questions and more questions. Professor Wiesel once said that the ultimate mystery of the Holocaust is that whatever happened took place in the soul. Something was now taking place in my soul.

So it happened that, just a year after completing a program of study for the PhD, I took upon myself another program of learning, one as vast as the sea. I read everything I could find about Jews and Judaism, Jewish history and the Holocaust, everything by and about Elie Wiesel. A critic once said that to read Wiesel is to burn with him, and so it was for me. And yet, the more I studied, the less I understood, and the more implicated I felt. There is no way to study the Holocaust *innocently*: To engage the Holocaust is to be undermined.

Two years later, in the fall of 1981, I wrote Professor Wiesel a letter in a faltering attempt to express my gratitude for his testimony. Without knowing exactly why, I begged his forgiveness, even though I knew that such a gesture was empty and absurd. He invited me to see him if I should ever be in Boston or New York.

Summer 1984: I set out for Harvard to spend two months in a seminar on Russian literature. As soon as I arrived, I contacted Professor Wiesel's office at Boston University. Yes, his assistant Martha Hauptman told me, it might be possible to see him: Professor Wiesel would be in and out of the country in June and July, but she would let me know if a visit could be arranged. Three weeks later I got the call: "Professor Wiesel will see you on Monday, July 16, 11:00 a.m., at his apartment in New York. This is the address . . ." It was the first of my many meetings with the Vizhnitzer Hasid.

From that meeting onward, I came to count Professor Wiesel among my teachers. He transformed me into a witness and a messenger. He led me to realize that when I stand before a classroom I must stand for something. He taught me how to answer to the living and listen to the dead. He taught me that, indeed, the dead are not only listening but also asking: "What will you make of us?"

And so my career was transformed before it really began. Instead of becoming a professor of Russian and comparative literature, I pursued a path that would lead me into Holocaust and Jewish studies. I would teach courses and write books on topics in which I had never taken a course. I would go on to hold an endowed chair in Judaic studies and direct the Judaic Studies Program at The University of Memphis; I now hold an endowed chair in Holocaust Studies at the Ackerman Center for Holocaust Studies of The University of Texas at Dallas.

But first I spent almost ten years studying the Holocaust and the sacred texts of the Jewish tradition. To be sure, I continue this study unto this day, this night. Even as I was writing and publishing books on Russian literature in the 1980s and into the 1990s, my studies were focused on the Shoah, antisemitism, and the never-ending range of Judaica, from Torah and Talmud to midrash and Jewish philosophy and even kabbalah. I studied Hebrew, Aramaic, and Yiddish. In 1991 I published a book based on the first conversation I had with Elie Wiesel, and since then I have had twenty-seven books on the Holocaust, antisemitism, and Jewish tradition published or accepted for publication, including several edited volumes, as well as a translation of *The Complete Black Book of Russian Jewry*.

For me, teaching has always entailed a process of learning. As one of the great sages of the Talmud once said, I learned much from my teachers and even more from my colleagues, but I have learned the most from my students. Whereas some professors take their teaching to interfere with their research, as if teaching were some sort of punishment, I have always regarded my teaching to be part of my research and my research to be part of my teaching. I regard my students as my children; the Hebrew word for "teacher," *moreh*, in fact, is a cognate of the word for "parent," *horeh*.

I taught my first course on the Holocaust in the fall of 1986 at Oklahoma State University. I was the first to teach such a course at Oklahoma State and the first to teach it at The University of Memphis, where I took a job in 1996. In both cases, however, my introduction of a course on the Holocaust met with some resistance.

When at Oklahoma State it was announced in a faculty meeting that I would be teaching a seminar on the Holocaust, a German-born colleague of mine stood up and announced that if I should teach a course on the Holocaust, he would never speak to me again. To which I replied, "Promise?" Other colleagues have put to me the question: "You're going to teach the Holocaust *again*? People are sick of it. It's all you hear about. It happened so long ago. Can't we get over it?" I have never heard one professor say to another, "What? You're going to teach the Civil War *again*? People are sick of it. It's all you hear about. It happened so long ago. Can't we get over it?"

Over the years, in the course of teaching courses on the Holocaust, I have come to a few realizations:

- Teaching the Holocaust, as the Final Solution to the *Jewish* Question, must be informed by a *Jewish* outlook. All of my teaching has been so informed. Certain critics of my books on the Holocaust have complained that they are "too Jewish." Those who deny or avoid the Holocaust live in a state of flight from a definitive Jewish presence in the Holocaust. Hence the phenomenon of de-Judaizing the Event. Turning away from the Jew, they turn away from the "Jewish question," which lies in the questions put to the first human and to his first-born: Where are you? Where is your brother? And what have you done? Going into hiding, as Adam hid, is the default position of many of us. And so we trivialize and relativize the systematic annihilation of the Jewish people by tossing the Jews into the category of "victims-in-general," self-righteously proclaiming, "Yes, but the Jews were not the only victims." True: The Jews were not the only victims. But if not every victim was a Jew, every Jew was a victim.

- The Western intellectual tradition has proven to be just as bankrupt in its response to the Holocaust as it was in preventing it. In fact, it contributed to the Event: if Christian antisemitism was necessary to paving the way to Auschwitz, so was the modern intellectual tradition. Many intellectuals hold dear the modern innovations in philosophy, music, literature, and the arts, not to mention modern ideological movements such as communism and socialism. And yet all of the communist and socialist ideologues of the nineteenth century wrote diatribes against the Jews, from Fourrier to Marx, from Proudhon to Toussenel. Kant and Hegel, Wagner and, yes, Nietzsche all vented their contempt for Judaism, which, according to Nazi ideologue Alfred Rosenberg, was the real target of the extermination project. For Jews *and Judaism*, he held, are the contagion that threaten humanity.

- A course on the Holocaust cannot be regarded as one among several on a class schedule, since it decides the whole matter of what is higher in higher learning. It addresses not only the horrors perpetrated by the Third Reich, but also what is at stake in undertaking such a daunting study: a deep understanding of the sanctity of human life and the infinite responsibility of each to all. Every teacher and student of the Holocaust is summoned to testify to that sanctity and responsibility and how very fragile both can be. That we are summoned to such a testimony is reason to rejoice—yes, to rejoice. This rejoicing alone can prevent us from slipping into the abyss of darkness that is the Kingdom of Night. And it is a very slippery slope indeed. I have had nightmares of being there, in the camps and the ghettos, on the trains and even in the gas chambers.

Thus my teaching and writing were transformed into testimony, which enabled me to keep from getting lost in the abyss of the Shoah. Which meant:

- I must attest to Judaism's unique teaching on the holiness of the other human being that the Nazis slated for annihilation. In my classes, where early on we read *Night*, this begins with an examination of several key terms that appear on the first page of my Teacher's memoir: Hasidic house of prayer, exile of the Shekhinah, the Divine suffering, the destruction of the Temple, the Talmud, the Kabbalah. Understanding the meaning and the history of these terms is essential to any understanding of the Holocaust and certainly of his memoir. Elie Wiesel once told me that the first line of a novel should contain the entire novel. Just so, this first page of his first book contains not only the foundation of his entire body of work but also the ground for any study of the Shoah.

- I must not forget that the Holocaust is not behind us; it is before us—and within us, just as the ashes of the dead are within us. I feel their presence in me. In an effort to grasp the graphic meaning of this *within*, recall the disaster that occurred in Chernobyl on April 26, 1986, when a cloud of radioactive material ascended into the atmosphere from one of the chimneys at a nuclear power plant. Two weeks later, radiation levels in Montana were elevated. In fact, earth scientists claim that one can determine air pollution levels over the years by taking a plug of snow and ice from Antarctica. *Antarctica!* In the time of the Shoah the remains of the Jewish people bellowed into the air in clouds of smoke, not for one day but for a thousand days; not from one chimney but from dozens. They reside in the earth from which we harvest our bread. In a grim Eucharistic reality, they abide in the bread we place in our mouths. *They are in us*: as the Torah is in us, so is the Shoah.

- The higher and human relationships central to Judaism are central to teaching and writing on the Holocaust. This intersection of the vertical and the horizontal, of the bonds between the holy and the human, is central to my writing and my teaching. I have had high-school teachers in workshops tell me that they are not permitted to speak about God when they teach the Holocaust. And I answer: How can you delve into the hanging of the child as a hanging of God in *Night*, which is pivotal to any understanding of Wiesel, without speaking of God? How can we speak of the Shoah without speaking of God? As Professor Wiesel once said, you can affirm God or deny God, but you cannot ignore God if you want to deal with the Holocaust.

With these realizations born of my engagement with the Holocaust came another realization: My soul is Jewish. Perhaps it was the dreams, the nightmares, of being there among the Jews. And so I was led to convert to Judaism in 1989. My first trip abroad as a Jew was to Treblinka, Majdanek, and Auschwitz in 1991. I wrote a book about it called *Pilgrimage of a Proselyte*. From Poland I traveled to Israel, my first trip to the Holy Land as a Jew. And my first visit was to Yehiel De-Nur, the Holocaust survivor and author known as Ka-tzetnik 135633, whom I had already befriended in previous trips, thanks to Israeli author Haim Gouri, the writer who translated *Night* from French into Hebrew. I had traveled to Israel by way of the murder camp sites, where the Jewish people had been systematically slaughtered. When Yehiel greeted me at the door, he was taken aback for a moment, a bit puzzled: He did not recognize me at first.

"David, you are so different," he said.

He could not put his finger on it, but he insisted that I had changed dramatically. I could not imagine what he was talking about. But then I realized: The mountain of ashes at Majdanek and the ashen earth that I had trod at Auschwitz had left their mark on me; my eyes had been transformed by what they had seen. And so had my soul.

But his beautiful wife Eliyah, who had translated his works into English, insisted that I had not changed a bit. Eliyah had a way of seeing through the ashes. But she had changed. It was only a year or so since I had last seen her, but she looked ten years older. Her face was marked with the pain and the sickness of her third bout with cancer. She apologetically said that she would hug me, but it hurt too much.

"This always happens to me when I start to love someone," she said to me. Then, after a moment of silence, she look into my eyes and said, "You know I love you, don't you?" And she went off to her room. We exchanged a last look. And she sang, "We'll meet again, don't know where, don't know when . . ." When she excused herself to go rest, her eyes had the look of a last look. She knew. And so did I.

Yehiel asked me about my visits to the sites of the murder camps in Poland. There was a strange desperation in his voice. He wanted to know whether the wooden blocks are still standing in Birkenau, whether they were as he has described them in his books. It was as if he were not quite sure that they had ever existed, as if he were trying to confirm for himself that he had not gone insane and invented it all.

Yes, Yehiel, I assured him, the plank beds are there in the blocks, just as you describe them. Yes, the cold stone oven runs down the middle of the four remaining blocks. Yes, opposite the tracks where the Jews were unloaded and selected for the gas chambers stand the barracks made from the bricks of the village of Birkenau, the women's camp. You did not make it up, Yehiel. You have not gone mad. (Or have you? How have you kept from going mad? How shall I keep from going mad?)

Yehiel De-Nur died in July 2001. But I wonder whether Ka-tzetnik 135633 does not live in us all, curled up in the nagging ashes of the dead that invade our soul. Yes: I wonder . . . I teach, I study, I write, and I wonder.

I wonder and I wander, never ceasing to study, teach, and write, each endeavor informing the other. From the late 1980s and into the early 2000s my research was shifting more and more from literary studies to philosophical and religious studies. I became the friend and student of the greatest of the Jewish thinkers to undertake a sustained philosophical response to the Holocaust, spanning more than thirty years: Emil Fackenheim. Very few Jewish thinkers could fathom and articulate the singularity of the Shoah and it implications for humanity and the Jews as Fackenheim could. Where others turned to Auschwitz and encountered only an empty, abysmal silence,

Fackenheim turned and heard a Commanding Voice, akin to the Voice that broke the absolute, pervading silence at Mount Sinai. It is the Voice of the 614th Commandment, the commandment to Jews that they must refuse the Nazis a posthumous victory through an embrace of the millennial teaching and testimony of the tradition.

One thinker who has most profoundly informed and influenced my engagement with the Holocaust is, in my view, the most important Jewish thinker of the twentieth century: Emmanuel Levinas. As a quintessentially Jewish thinker, Levinas restored the primacy of the ethical, what he calls "ethics as first philosophy," in the aftermath of the debacle of the German philosophy, which culminated in the unrepentant, card-carrying Nazi Martin Heidegger. Levinas articulated the truth that antisemitism is not a form of racism, but rather racism is a form of antisemitism. He, like Fackenheim, demonstrated that the Nazis were not antisemites because they were racists, but that they were racists because they were antisemites. He explained how and why the divine prohibition against murder, which the Nazis systematically obliterated, emanates from the human face, from the human soul, that came under a radical assault in the time of the Third Germany. Above all, he drove home the ethical demand and the effort to answer, "*Hineni!*—Here I am for you!" to the outcry of the living and the dead.

Without such an ethical engagement with the Holocaust, there is no engagement with the Holocaust. And yet most of us flee precisely from the decisive ethical engagement. Why? Because from such a reckoning we always emerge in arrears: We have never done enough or testified enough, learned enough or listened enough, helped enough or answered enough. Therefore one thread that runs through my teaching and study and writing about the Holocaust is that it is never enough: The debt increases in the measure that it is paid. With each response, I grow more responsible. Ethics opens up this infinity. And, for me, Levinas opens up ethics, the ethical dimension of Holocaust Studies, which is the Jewish dimension, the human dimension. This singularity that defines the Event also defines its universality.

I once attended a conference on the Holocaust with a good friend who is a survivor. As we were leaving a plenary session, she announced that she had come to a horrifying realization about the relation between Holocaust scholars and Holocaust survivors. Speaking in a whisper, as though afraid of her own words, she said to me, "I know now what they want us to do: They want us to die." I was shocked. And then it hit me: We scholars, heirs to the witnesses, who pretend to deal with the Shoah, do not want to deal with the surviving Jews because we do not want to deal with the flesh and blood of Jewish life, which is rooted in Torah. We do not want to look into the faces that announce our ethical obligation and put to us the question of what is ultimate in life, from beyond life. Entrenched in our vanity, we are too ambitious, too arrogant, to deal with them, as we take ourselves to be more sophisticated, more "nuanced," than the survivors. In the presence of the survivors, the scholars collide with the cry of an absolute commandment that, like the shofar of Mount Sinai, shakes us from our solipsistic slumber. That is why we want them to go away.

Thus my friend's words shook me from my own shameful slumber. She opened my eyes to a pervasive pattern in Holocaust Studies, both in teaching and in scholarship, a pattern characterized by the elimination of the Jews and, by implication, of the Torah from a consideration of the Shoah. It is tied to the phenomenon that Alvin Rosenfeld describes in his book *The End of the Holocaust*, something that can be found not only in the popular culture that would trivialize it but also in the halls of the academy and the exhibits of the museums that would relativize it. As the mass murder of millions of the Jews is trivialized and vulgarized, a less taxing version of a tragic history begins to emerge—still full of suffering, to be sure, but a suffering relieved of its weightiest ethical and intellectual demands. Relieved of such demands, the Shoah is relieved of the demands of Torah. The Nazis' victory turns out to be more pervasive than we think. More and more—in academia and in the public mainstream, on museum boards and Holocaust commissions—we do not speak of Jews at all. If we happen to comment on the Jews, we generally say nothing of what it means to be a Jew. But what can it mean to speak of the murder of the Jews without addressing the Torah that makes them who they are?

I see this flight from the millennial testimony of the Jewish people at work in my interactions with other Holocaust scholars and institutions, from my encounter with the professors who proclaim that the Jews were not the only victims, to my consultations with museums and state "Holocaust" commissions (I served on one in Tennessee and on the Texas commission) that want to include genocide and human rights in their missions.

For me, what has emerged from all of this is another, more subtle, more dangerous form of Holocaust denial, what I call "Holocaust Studies without the Holocaust," which lies in de-Judaizing the Holocaust, as I have already suggested. Why de-Judaize the Holocaust? So that we do not have to contend with the Commanding Voice of Mount Sinai or, God forbid, the Commanding Voice of Auschwitz. We can go on with the pretense of Holocaust and genocide and human rights studies, feeling good in the self-righteous illusion that, in dealing with bullying and creating "safe spaces," we are dealing with the Holocaust, the Shoah, the Churban, the Final Solution to the *Jewish* Question.

Realizing that this subtle, fashionable form of Holocaust denial is a form of the antisemitism that went into the happening of the Holocaust, in around 2002 I turned to the study of antisemitism. The first thing that struck me was how few scholars of the Holocaust were also scholars of this specific prejudice. Yes, both fields are immense, but an understanding of each is essential to an understanding of the other. In my study of antisemitism and its history, I came to understand more about the essence and the singularity of the Holocaust. I wrote a book called *A Genealogy of Evil: Anti-Semitism from Nazism to Islamic Jihad* (2010), to explore the extent of the Nazi influence on today's Jihadist movements that have most thoroughly heeded Hitler's last words, his injunction to carry on the war against the Jews. This was followed by my book *Anti-Semitism and Its Metaphysical Origins* (2015) and most recently by my book *Judaism, Antisemitism, and the Holocaust: Making the Connections* (2022). In the end I came to understand that the singular horror of the Holocaust, as well as other contemporary manifestations of antisemitism, lies in a radical assault on the very principle that makes other horrors horrific, and not just matters of academic curiosity.

So where do I go from here?

Today is another Holocaust in the works. It arises not only from the imams of Iran but also from what has become what I call in the title of the book I am writing now *Morally Required Antisemitism*. It assumes a variety of forms, but what they all have in common is anti-Zionism, conceived as an opposition not to the policies of the Jewish state but to the very presence of a Jewish state. It can be found in all the current fashions and fads of the intelligentsia, on college campuses and in social media, in Critical Race Theory and Black Lives Matter, in the Boycott-Divest-Sanction movement and the Woke cancel culture. Many people have grown fearful of not being part of such movements. And for good reason: I have colleagues who have been censured and have even lost their jobs over their support of the Jewish state.

The book I am writing is the product of years of engagement with the perennial, eternal phenomenon of antisemitism. My aim is to sound the depths of the current, most insidious manifestation of this form of prejudice, of the antisemitism that is demanded of anyone who wishes to be considered a good person. And who does not want to be considered a good person? Who does not want to be counted among the righteous and the redeemed? It is, indeed, a redemptive antisemitism steeped in the stink of self-righteousness. The antisemitism that led to the Holocaust is the longest hatred, a perennial hatred, that morphs into all the ingenious ways that we have of justifying it: It has become essential to the entry into paradise, whether it be the heavenly paradise above or the earthly utopia below, whether religious or political, whether spiritual or social. This redemptive antisemitism has always been there: The Holocaust was, above all, a project of purification, bent on rendering the world *Judenrein*. And so it continues.

Matt, the young man who placed in my hands Professor Wiesel's memoir that day long ago, must be in his early sixties by now. On that October afternoon in 1979 he summoned me to the witness stand, as a teacher, a scholar, and a human being—and now as a Jew. I have never left the stand. I continue to testify before God and humanity, in spite of myself. As it is written in Paul Simon's song "Silent Eyes,"

Halfway to Jerusalem
We shall all be called as witnesses
Each and everyone
To stand before the eyes of God
And speak what was done.
What, now, will my testimony be? What, now, shall I speak?

7

My Holocaust Autobiography: *The Mortal Storm*

Alexis Pogorelskin

Discoveries

I was sixteen and had an important announcement to make. I walked into the kitchen where my parents prepared dinner and shared their workday with each other. "I want to change my name to Freya," I informed them. My mother did not miss a beat. She turned to my father as though I were not even in the room: "Milt, she stayed up last night and watched *The Mortal Storm*."

Her statement was loaded with meaning. I had been found out. For months I had evaded the stricture on my bedtime and snuck downstairs to watch mesmerizing movies of the Second World War that had by now become the source of a secret life that constituted my own private world of adolescent romanticism and anti-Japanese/anti-Nazi heroism. My parents, on the other hand, had just risen in my esteem for their immediate recognition of my treasured, heart-felt reference. It was a draw. I would go unpunished but drop a complicating request in the midst of college applications.

There was still more to the situation. Even at sixteen, I had perceived a common thread that ran through the movies that mattered most to me: *Good-bye, Mr. Chips* (1939), *Random Harvest* (1942), *Mrs. Miniver* (1942), *The White Cliffs of Dover* (1944), and of course *The Mortal Storm* (1940). They all bore a common stamp. They were produced by Sidney Franklin and employed the same team of writers. But *The Mortal Storm* mattered most of all. As I would learn decades later, it was the first feature film by a major American studio (MGM, in this case) to depict the plight of Europe's Jews before the Holocaust. Little did I know that in comprehending among those MGM films the common qualities of literate dialogue, emotional integrity on the part of strong female characters, and the inherent heroism of those who fought the Nazis, that I had already found the seeds of the book I would write devoted to that one film. What counted for me then was that I could see myself in the ardent, determined heroism of the half-Jewish Freya Roth, with whom I shared a common identity. I had already begun to ask, to what degree was I Jewish? Could I be Protestant like my mother without betraying the Jewish identity I observed in my father? By the same token, could I be Jewish without abnegating all that I had received from my mother? The character of Freya, my secret role model, had raised the question of Jewish identity for me in the context of the Holocaust. I never forgot her or the Second World War. I carried both, along with so many unresolved questions about identity, into maturity.

But to return to my fascination with the Second World War that had impelled me to sneak downstairs and watch *The Late Show* in secret. That fascination had begun early in my life. My parents and their friends often spoke about the war, investing the two words, "the war," with a breadth of meaning that was almost mythic. They were speaking of their youth, a cause to which they had all contributed, a defining period of liberation from the Great Depression, and other associations that as a child I was not yet ready to imagine. That the war still lived for them helped me understand who they were.

I went in search of my parents and their generation from a source available in plain sight. I would go around the neighborhood visiting my friends while stealing a few moments to check out what the grown-ups read. I discovered that most of the adults had the same books on their shelves. All the fathers had served in World War II and so books on that subject predominated. Nearly everyone had copies of Ernie Pyle's dispatches: *Here Is Your War: The Story of G.I. Joe* and *Brave Men*. Some had Churchill's six-volume history of the war. Roosevelt was my parents' hero. Arthur Schlesinger's three-volume *The Age of Roosevelt* figured in our collection.

Curiously, mixed among the books of the neighborhood about the Second World War were ones devoted to the American Civil War as though the two conflicts were almost one and the same. My mother read Margaret Leech's *Reveille in Washington* (1942), she explained to me, for the second time, because she had liked it so much. Leech had won a Pulitzer Prize for describing how, in the 1860s, a provincial backwater had become the capital of a nation at war. I asked what drew her to it. She said that it reminded her so much of the Washington at war she had known. Once again, a great president was in office but by the 1940s, the streets had been paved. Little did I know that in what she said about Leech's book lay another theme of my book on *The Mortal Storm*. When it is too frightening to speak of a war threatening on the horizon, another one safely in the past could provide an alternative discourse.

When I entered Bryn Mawr College at age seventeen, I was determined to study subjects that I had not already exhausted. My hometown, originally a

New Deal project, had a public library that boasted nearly all the secondary literature on Roosevelt's presidency. I had devoured all of it. The ancient world also fascinated me, and I was good at math. I intended to study both. I had a schedule conflict between first-year Ancient Greek and Calculus. As a freshman math major, I could not forego Calculus. And so, to meet the foreign language requirement, I signed up for Russian, yet another passion. After two weeks, I discovered a wonderful truth. I would major in Russian. I could hardly then imagine that the language would for a time replace my native tongue as my first language, but that is the subject for another essay.

At Yale to begin my quest for a doctorate in Russian history, I found myself in a similar situation to the one in which I had begun my undergraduate studies at Bryn Mawr: a veritable feast lay before me. I would certainly not waste my time studying the New Deal and the Second World War with John Morton Blum. I already knew all about that. But World War II was in my blood, and its pull would not be denied. I'll study modern Japan, I thought, adding a perfectly reasonable explanation: it was the country both my father and my grandfather (in the army of the Tsar) had fought. But once again a schedule conflict intervened. I could not take both Modern Japan and the seminar on Russian history that year. Henry Turner's seminar on Fascism was perfect for my schedule. I had arrived back at World War II and its prelude. It seemed once more that fate had intervened, to paraphrase a line from *Casablanca*. Before I was done, I had also taken a Minor Field from Professor Turner on Interwar Europe, carefully balancing among France, Britain, and Germany.

Turning Point

In 1987 I was hired by the University of Minnesota-Duluth to teach Russian history, all periods. It was a good time for a Russian historian. The students and the community clamored to know more about Russia and the new era that Gorbachev had inaugurated. But interest in that country—impoverished, dysfunctional, so desperate to be like us—waned with the decade. *The New Yorker* summed it up with one cartoon: A man wearing glasses sits on the sidewalk, a seemingly empty bottle of vodka before him. Around his neck is a sign, "Russian expert for hire." To the end of the 1990s, I could still fill a large lecture hall with 125 students. But I felt that for both my students and myself, I needed to offer a subject that challenged them in a new way.

Sometime in the summer of 2000, I dashed off to Target, the local department store, for a last-minute item. There I ran into a friend, also a Bryn Mawr graduate, whose husband taught at one of the local universities. "Alexis," she said with excitement, "Joel's department just hired a guy to teach the History of the Holocaust. He prepared for it in a special program at Northwestern. Call him up and find out about it." I did so that very afternoon. How ready I was to make such a phone call. My academic life has never been the same.

[The] Holocaust Education Foundation

There were many reasons why I hastened to call someone I had never met and inquire about a university program devoted to Holocaust education. As noted, I had begun to feel a certain academic restlessness from being focused on Russia for so many years. As a step in a new direction, I had recently taken over the course on Interwar Europe from a colleague who had retired. I began teaching it much the way I had first explored the subject years earlier with Professor Turner at Yale; that is, balancing France, Britain, and Germany. That approach no longer worked. The center of gravity of the subject matter lay with Germany. After the First World War, antisemitism began to consume the course, and all roads led to the Holocaust. I was not prepared for those terrible truths. I might have been as surprised by them as the students. It was not as though the course taught itself, but the scholarship had moved on and expanded dramatically since I was in graduate school. The field of Holocaust Studies now existed as a distinctive, even disruptive academic discipline that forced me to ask new questions about the twentieth century and its relationship to the one that preceded it. Where did motivation and causality lie in explaining cataclysmic events that now appeared to be interconnected in ways that I had not considered before. I needed help to continue to teach the course with integrity. Should I at least be teaching a complementary course on Modern Germany? Fate again was about to intervene.

The new person among the academics in town directed me to call Zev Weiss of the Holocaust Education Foundation in Evanston, Illinois. With the number in hand, I promptly did so. The conversation was part academic interview, part something else, but just what Zev tried to elicit I could not be certain. I managed to tell him that I taught a twentieth-century Europe course without the Holocaust and what led up to it. My students were therefore bereft of what I had come to see should be the heart of the subject matter. He asked me to explain in writing why I wanted to attend the Foundation's forthcoming Lessons and Legacies conference, due to take place in November; and be sure to include a $40 non-refundable check, he added. I did not know whether I had spoken with an usher or a gatekeeper. He was brusque and to the point. I liked him, but now I waited anxiously to learn whether I would enter the precincts of Holocaust Studies or not.

Several months later, as the crisis over the Florida recount deepened and uncertainty mounted over whether Bush or Gore had won the state's twenty-nine electoral votes and would become President, I sat for two days in the auditorium of the Kellogg School of Northwestern University, determined to remain quiet and go unnoticed if I could. After all, I had only my ignorance to share. Most vividly, I remember one confrontation at that conference. Zev and a participant named Christopher Browning took Peter Novick to task for his book *The Holocaust in American Life*, which had been published the year before.[1] Zev clearly respected Browning, referring to him with a hint of deference in his voice. I made a mental note to check out what Browning had written. Novick termed the academic embrace of the Holocaust "moral aggrandizement," and merely "a recent discovery in terms of acknowledgement and commemoration." He condemned what he termed "the competition for primacy in suffering." He also denied the idea that the Holocaust was "unique," rather as a catastrophe, he termed it "ordinary."

Zev and Browning went to work on Novick and his book. Why had Novick not addressed such and such, they challenged him. Why had he failed to treat such and such? Didn't he know that such and such had occurred? Novick left the conference early in disgrace. The debate was fascinating, if a little unnerving in its vehemence. I surmised that it was a product of the fact that Holocaust Studies were emergent: where Russian Studies had been fifty years earlier. Perhaps it would not be so difficult to catch up after all, I concluded.

With one Holocaust conference under my belt, I applied for Northwestern's intensive Summer Program in Holocaust Studies for 2001. I got in. The program was to change how I understood European history and my own identity. Each night I studied in the library with my new friend Petra. She was German, from Alsace, and so ashamed of what her compatriots had done that she converted to Judaism. Her parents disowned her. I was struck then by the large number of Germanists in the program. We Slavicists have been asleep at the switch, it seemed; yet we have the linguistic tools so many in the field lack. This is an area that cries out for research in Polish and Russian archives, my bailiwick.

Christopher Browning, now one of our instructors, admitted his linguistic deficiencies ruefully: German at times defeated his best efforts; and although he had written extensively about Poland, he knew no Polish, despite his pioneering work on what the Nazis called the General Government. He introduced us to the research and psychological studies behind his *Ordinary Men*.[2] The material mesmerized me, and initially I fell under the spell of his arguments. He told us of his war with Daniel Goldhagen over Goldhagen's book *Hitler's Willing Executioners: Ordinary Germans and the Holocaust*.[3] "We cannot stand to be in the same room," Browning acknowledged. Goldhagen's weaknesses seemed obvious, yet a small error in *Ordinary Men* nagged at me. I was sensitive to the misspelling of "Kremenchug," located within the Tsarist Pale of Settlement in Eastern Ukraine, Poltava *guberniia*. My grandfather had been born there. His brother and three generations of that family died in the town on July 30, 1941 when the Germans entered and massacred all the Jews in one day.

When I came to teach my own Holocaust course, I certainly assigned *Ordinary Men*, but I did not use it as Browning had intended. If the German order police were "ordinary," the culture and society that had formed them, I argued, certainly was not. Germany was no ordinary country. To develop that idea, I used George Mosse's *The Crisis of German Ideology* regarding the malevolent Volkish thought of the nineteenth century which grew lethal after the First World War.[4] I complemented it with Modris Ekstein's *Rites of Spring: The Great War and the Birth of the Modern Age*.[5] Eksteins argued just how unordinary (in the sense of exceptional) the newly unified German state regarded itself *vis à vis* France and Great Britain. His idea of German exceptionalism, along with Browning's insistence on the "ordinary" in the Holocaust, in contrast to Novick's or Goldhagen's use of the term, provided an important stimulus to my own understanding of the subject.

Another instructor on the program who taught the Literature of the Holocaust course proved to be the most important intellectual influence I encountered that summer. We did not have Phyllis Lassner as an instructor until the second week. The gift she gave lay not so much in the subject matter itself as in the openness of her classroom, the sheer empowerment that her warmth and reception to our contributions encouraged. I thrived in the atmosphere, discovering that I did indeed have ideas of my own and had begun to make connections within this new field. I no longer sat quietly, hoping to go unnoticed as I had back in November at the Lessons and Legacies conference.

The students in the course flocked to Phyllis, surrounding her in the faculty dining room to continue what had begun in the classroom. I held back. At times I feared that I spoke too much in class unable to contain myself. I did not want to be intrusive during lunch either. I also sensed that I would come to know Phyllis, that our paths would cross again, and she would have a profound influence not only on my thinking but on my life as well. The Celtic side of me, with its sixth sense, urged the Jewish half to be patient in getting to know her.

Rediscoveries

My instincts were rewarded thanks to a curricular innovation at the University of Minnesota-Duluth, where I taught. In 2002 Mark Yudof, President of the university system, introduced a program of "freshman seminars" devoted to innovative topics outside the regular curriculum and designed to catch students' attention at the very beginning of their undergraduate careers. Departments that agreed to offer at least three such seminars would get a new faculty line. As department chair, I convinced my colleagues to join the program for the sake of the position in East Asian history we had long sought. Having roped others into extra work, I knew I had to participate. I titled my freshman seminar "World War II: War of Technologies." I would address four technological innovations: Bletchley Park, the aircraft carrier, the Bomb, but first—the movie camera. What Americans knew of the war and its prelude, they learned from the movies. But how to capture the essence of that proposition? Somehow, for reasons probably lost in my subconscious, I decided to screen the film I had not seen in over forty years: *The Mortal Storm*. Viewed for a second time, it astounded me. This time I experienced the film not as an adolescent in search of identity, but as a professionally trained historian. The film cried out for closer examination. The students appeared less enthusiastic. What was a "non-Aryan" anyway, they asked, why not just say "Jew"? Little did I know then, their frustration mirrored the debate over use of the word "Jew" in the film at the time MGM produced it.

Shortly after that classroom screening, *The Mortal Storm* again unexpectedly came to my attention. The *Tablet Magazine*, an online publication devoted to Jewish arts and culture, had a regular feature in each issue that paid homage to "the book of the day." At the time I taught the freshman seminar, the *Tablet* wrote a glowing review of a republication of Phyllis Bottome's 1938 bestseller *The Mortal Storm* with an introduction by Phyllis Lassner and Marilyn Hoder-Salmon.[6] Our paths, as I had believed they would, had crossed again. I ordered a copy and quickly read the nearly twenty-page foreword. "Brilliant," I thought. Nothing more to say about that. But wait. The authors of the foreword made a passing reference to congressional hearings directed against so-called "propaganda films" made shortly before the United States entered the Second World War. If I could obtain information on the hearings, perhaps I would find something of my own to say about *The Mortal Storm* as novel and film.

Opportunity again presented itself. When a colleague invited me to participate on a panel devoted to Holocaust film, I tracked down a 1942 reprint of the transcript of the Senate hearings on "Propaganda [for war] in Motion Pictures," September 1941.[7] About 500 pages in length, it reminded me of the typescripts or *stenograficheskie otchëty* of the party congresses of the 1920s which I used in my research on the opposition to Stalin. Such sources carry the voices of my subjects. They are golden.

I sat and read at my dining room table. I had reached the third and final week of the hearings, having gone through more than 300 pages of text. Chairman D. Worth Clark (D-ID) grilled Nicholas Schenck, President of Loew's, Inc., the parent company of MGM, the studio that had produced *The Mortal Storm*. "There is one picture *particularly* [italics mine] that people say propagandizes for war . . ." I stopped reading and looked at the crowded bird feeder just outside the window. I told myself that if the film Clark referred to was *The Mortal Storm*, then I have a book. I looked back at the page certain of the film Clark was about to accuse Schenck of using to propagandize for war. "*The Mortal Storm*." I knew at that moment a book lay hidden in those words.

The next Lessons and Legacies conference was to take place again at Northwestern. I went determined to reintroduce myself to Professor Lassner. "But what if she doesn't remember me?" I asked my friends. Scared, shy, and filled with trepidation, I walked up to her before the opening dinner and said, "Professor Lassner, you probably don't remember me, but I was in your Holocaust Literature class in the summer program of 2001. I want to congratulate you on the excellent write-up the *Tablet* gave you for your introduction to the republication of *The Mortal Storm*. I hope to write something on the work myself." She stared hard, looking at me directly. "Yes, I do remember you. I remember your face. You know Bottome's papers are now available in the British Library." Phyllis modestly refrained from mentioning that she had helped negotiate the library's purchase of those papers. "Come join Ava [gifted artist and hidden child survivor] and me at our table. Let's talk." Dinner was about to make up for all the lunches I had missed with Phyllis a few years earlier. My Celtic patience had paid off. Our friendship had begun.

The Mortal Storm

Ironically, my work in Russian history contributed to my decision to write a book on *The Mortal Storm*. A colleague at Northwestern invited me to present my research on the opposition to Stalin. I had just spent three months in the former party archive in Moscow as a Fulbright Scholar. Phyllis attended with her husband Jacob, an esteemed scholar of medieval Islam. The lecture, I thought, went well. The next morning as I packed to leave, Phyllis called. "Write a book on *The Mortal Storm*," she said, confirming my instinct about the film's significance. She knew I had a basis from which to work. I had attended the conference of an organization in which she was active: the Space Between: Literature and Culture, 1914–1945. I gave a paper on *The Mortal Storm* which shared the prize for best conference paper. It would go on to appear in the society's journal.[8]

I began a journey of research and writing that has taken a decade to complete. I worked first in the Academy of Motion Picture Arts and Sciences' Margaret Herrick Library, where I read twenty scripts, carefully following the penciled revisions of Claudine West, primary scriptwriter for *The Mortal Storm* as she fought through the spring of 1940 to save the word "Jew" and avoid its replacement with "non-Aryan," insisted on by studio head L. B. Mayer.[9] While formally listed as one scriptwriter on a team of three, West in fact provided not only the original shooting script for *The Mortal Storm* in 1939, but all the subsequent versions of 1940 on which the studio based the completed film. In addition, the archival record confirmed what had first occurred to me as a star-struck sixteen-year-old. I now knew that a single creative vision—namely that of Claudine West—provided the heroic, upright image of Britain in *Random Harvest* and *Mrs. Miniver* as well as the screen adaptation of Phyllis Bottome's novel.

A research trip to London proved invaluable. I read Bottome's extensive correspondence in the British Library regarding her difficulties in selling *The Mortal Storm* to a major studio, although a bestseller on both sides of the Atlantic. In Britain, she had been labeled "a premature anti-Nazi."[10] In the US, she found the Hollywood moguls to be "cowardly."[11] Outside the British Library, I encountered by chance an equally important resource. On that first London trip, I met a renowned British film scholar who assisted me in gaining access to what remains of the MGM archives. I spent an intense weekend immersed in documents and correspondence devoted to production decisions regarding *The Mortal Storm*.[12]

Another cache of source material proved almost as significant. Increasingly I became aware of how disturbing *The Mortal Storm* had been for an antisemitic cabal in the US Senate, led and encouraged by Charles Lindbergh. The film embodied the antisemites' fear lest Hollywood produce films in defense of Europe's Jews. Reeve Lindbergh generously gave me permission to work in her parents' archive at Yale.[13] I discovered from his unpublished diaries that Lindbergh, the moving spirit behind the Senate hearings of 1941 directed against Hollywood, had been far more antisemitic than his biographer, Scott Berg, had allowed.[14] That consuming prejudice infected the aviator's Senate allies, encouraging them to make *The Mortal Storm* their primary target in the congressional hearings of 1941.

Even at sixteen, I readily perceived the film's obfuscated references to Jewish identity despite use of the word "non-Aryan" in place of "Jew." I knew then that I proudly shared with Freya the same identity, but as noted above, I was not yet ready to claim it. Nor was MGM at the time the studio made the film. In the original script, Claudine West has a character anxiously ask, "Doesn't Hitler mean to kill every Jew?"[15] On screen the woman tepidly queries, "What about those who are non-Aryan?" Censorship lay with L.B. Mayer, who shrank in fear from his own Jewish identity, the identity I have pondered since I first saw *The Mortal Storm* just twenty years after its release. One can only speculate what it might have meant for the American public to hear the word "Jew" in the film, along with issues of Jewish achievement and vulnerability, proclaimed unequivocally as the US found itself on the eve of war. West fought valiantly not only for the word "Jew," but also for a scene in which one of the protagonists lists the many contributions to Western civilization made by Jews. She lost on both counts. The film nonetheless remains one of the first attempts in American popular culture to reveal what the Nazis intended to do to the Jews of Europe before the Holocaust occurred. It also remains a source of Jewish pride and identity which Mayer's long-ago cowardice failed to hide from me or anyone else who perceived what Bottome and West made of the character Freya Roth.

My decision to pursue the Holocaust did indeed change my teaching. Some students told me the course changed their lives. My student evaluations for the course were the highest in the department. I taught from a safe space: Nazism and Fascism were European phenomena that never reached American shores. How comforting that proved for my student audience. Then I read Leonard Dinnerstein's *Antisemitism in America*.[16] We invited him to speak. I revamped the course incorporating America's vibrant homegrown fascism of the 1920s and thirties. At one point, I received death threats.[17] Mercifully, that phase passed quickly. But how could I do otherwise than teach what really happened? For the first half of the twentieth century that meant the Holocaust and the events that led to it.

Notes

1 Peter Novick, *The Holocaust in American Life* (New York: Houghton Mifflin Co., 1999).
2 Christopher Browning, *Ordinary Men. Reserve Police Battalion 101 and the Final Solution in Poland* (New York: Harper Perennial, 1998).
3 Daniel Goldhagen, *Hitler's Willing Executioners: Ordinary Germans and the Holocaust* (New York: Alfred A. Knopf, 1996).
4 George L. Mosse, *The Crisis of German Ideology. Intellectual Origins of the Third Reich* (New York: Grosset & Dunlap, 1964).
5 Modris Eksteins, *Rites of Spring: The Great War and the Birth of the Modern Age* (New York, Houghton Mifflin Co., 1989).
6 Phyllis Lassner and Marilyn Hoder-Salmon, "Forward," in Phyllis Bottome, *The Mortal Storm* (Evanston: Northwestern University Press, 1998), vii–xxv.
7 Senate Subcommittee on Interstate Commerce, *Propaganda in Motion Pictures*, 77th Cong., 1st sess., 1941 (Washington: U.S. Government Printing Office, 1942), 1–449.
8 Alexis Pogorelskin, "Phyllis Bottome's *The Mortal Storm*: Film and Controversy," *The Space Between. Literature and Culture, 1914–1945* 6 (2010): 39–58.
9 All scripts for *The Mortal Storm,* except for the copyright script in the US Library of Congress, can be found in the Margaret Herrick Library (Los Angeles), Department of Special Collections, Turner/MGM Scripts, starting with Box 2170.
10 Phyllis Bottome, *The Goal* (London: Faber and Faber, 1962), 258.
11 Phyllis Bottome to Professor Potter, British Library (London). Bottome Papers. Add. Mss. 88921/2/2. March 3, 1939.
12 The Margaret Herrick Library is currently in negotiation for purchase of these papers, which are held in private hands.

13 Yale University, Sterling Memorial Library, Manuscript Collections, Lindbergh Papers, Collection 325.
14 A. Scott Berg, *Lindbergh* (New York: G.P. Putnam's Sons, 1998).
15 Margaret Herrick Library, Turner/MGM Scripts, Box 2176, f. 1647.
16 Leonard Dinnerstein, *Antisemitism in America* (Oxford; Oxford University Press, 1994).
17 Alexis Pogorelskin, "I'm Not Sure What George Bush Has To Do With Hitler," *Thought and Action* (Fall 2005), 138–45.

8

Gendered Encounters: The Holocaust and Life Writing

Ravenel Richardson

Holocaust Encounters

In 1994, my cousin invited me visit him in Washington, DC. One of his interns took me on an outing to DC's newest museum: the United States Holocaust Memorial Museum (USHMM). I remember aspects of that tour vividly: choosing the card of the child whose fate you learn at the end of the tour, the pile of shoes, the films of Nazi medical experimentation, and walking through the cattle car that transported countless Jews to death camps in Poland. My visceral response was to vomit in the museum bathroom. No one can prepare for such confrontations with human brutality, but my encounter, as a thirteen-year-old accompanied only by an uninformed twenty-year old was damaging. I could not assimilate what I saw and learned at the museum. As a result of this experience, I did not voluntarily read anything else to do with the Holocaust for nearly a decade. Nor did I, despite attending boarding school in the US capital, return to the US Holocaust Memorial Museum until I was a doctoral researcher in 2007.

I have no Jewish heritage. I have no direct connection to the Holocaust that I am aware of. My family arrived in America in the seventeenth century; and my family history is one of privilege, and at times oppression, not of privation and destruction. How then, I have been asked countless times, did an Episcopalian from the Lowcountry of South Carolina become a Holocaust scholar? The short answer is that it was not a direct route.

What we talk about when we talk about war

Speaking with my Jewish and particularly my Israeli friends about Holocaust education, I learned how early they study it, how much it is emphasized in school, in synagogue, and at home. My Israeli friends all have a fairly comprehensive understanding of Holocaust history and how it affected their families from a very young age. This couldn't have been further from the truth for me. I grew up in Hilton Head, SC, where my Holocaust education consisted of watching the film of *The Diary of Anne Frank* (where she says she believes humans are all really good at heart) and reading Elie Wiesel's *Night* in eighth grade. No comprehensive explanation of the Holocaust was provided in either case.

One of my grandfathers was a fighter pilot in United States 15th Air Force based in Italy during the Second World War, and the other was part of the United States Army's occupying force in Germany in the 1950s. This was the family history that was shared with me regarding WWII: heavy on the narrative of Americans winning the war, nothing about the Holocaust. Almost astounding, really, considering that I traveled with my grandparents to Russia and Germany in 1991 (I was ten), listening to war and occupation stories along the way. I returned with a piece of the Berlin wall, but little understanding of why it was erected.

If there were a war narrative that was central to my family's identity, it was that of the Civil War. This was the conflict my ancestors fought in to preserve their human property and land, yet the narratives passed down never mentioned enslavement, only loss and tribulation. My family's role in the Confederacy, as you might imagine, was not one I had any interest in exploring as a teenager. I left the South for boarding school in Washington, DC in 1996, a choice that provided as much of a welcome cultural education as an academic one, and I didn't return to the Deep South for almost a decade.

University, or Accidental Exposure to Comparative Literature

I arrived as a new junior to the University of Georgia in 2003, having begun my academic career at the University of Virginia. I was an English major but was fulfilling the university's multicultural requirement with a survey course in a field I had never heard of: Comparative Literature. My professor, Dr. Linda Brooks, punctuated her lectures with personal stories of academic café life across Europe. Two weeks later I was sitting in her office begging her to help me switch majors to Comparative Literature. Within an hour she had convinced two professors to let me in their classes: Katarzyna Jerzak into Modern European Poetry and Katharina Wilson into Medieval Women

Writers. Their generosity has remained with me. Years later, I learned that Dr. Wilson was the English translator of *Kaddish for a Child Not Born*. Dr. Jerzak, who fled Communist Poland as a university student, and her mother would help me translate a Jewish woman's diary from the Warsaw Ghetto a decade later.

Comparative Literature was the formative moment in my intellectual development and interest in twentieth-century European literature and history that eventually led to my study of the Holocaust. I was captivated by my professors' personal and political histories. Several of them Jewish, many had personal connections to European politics and conflicts, ranging from the Second World War and the Holocaust to escaping Communist countries, or fleeing other types of political oppression and persecution. Listening to their stories felt like touching history.

I never took a course on Holocaust Literature but focusing on Modern European Literature included Jewish writers and thinkers, such as Walter Benjamin, Joseph Brodsky, and Sarah Kofman. I was particularly drawn to writers and thinkers who were grappling with the Holocaust and its aftereffects in Europe in their writing, such as Thomas Mann, W. G. Sebald, and Wisława Szymborska. My favorite course, *Literature of the Self,* examined how individuals traumatized by war and exile wrote autobiographical texts about these experiences. Without realizing it, I was developing an interest in literary representations of twentieth-century historical traumas.

Graduate School: From Scotland to the Holocaust

After completing my BA, I decided to address the gender gap in my undergraduate education by attending the University of St. Andrews to obtain an MLitt in English Literature: Women, Writing and Gender. My dissertation would apply the feminist approaches of Hélène Cixous to Jeanette Winterson's novel about the Napoleonic wars, *The Passion*. During this time, but outside classes, I read Marguerite Duras' autobiographical account of the Second World War and the Holocaust *La douleur* (*The War*). The raw emotion of the diary section of this text—specifically her descriptions of her husband's wasted figure returning from Buchenwald and Dachau— struck me to the core. Also chilling was the description of her *Résistance* activities, including torturing a young German soldier for information. Whatever my ideas about war and Allied heroism were, this text disrupted them. Of her diary, Duras wrote, "it can't really be called 'writing' . . . I found myself confronted with a tremendous chaos of thought and feeling that I couldn't bring myself to tamper with, and beside which literature was something of which I felt ashamed."[1] What do we mean by "writing,"

I started to ask myself, what do we mean by literature? What can a diary representation of civilian war trauma offer that fictional representation cannot?

Even for Duras, whose fiction addresses traumatic experiences ranging from sexual violence to the atomic bombings of Hiroshima, her diary demonstrated a powerful counterpoint to straightforward and even experimental literary narration. Duras' diary recalls nursing her husband, Robert Antelme, back from near-death. She voices thoughts and feelings towards her husband, the French government, and Nazis that are at turns violent, rage-filled, and hysterical. The level of criticism she has received for her unfiltered anguish and rage (from literary critics and even Mitterrand himself) illustrates why most writers would remove such material from their narratives. To say she was disillusioned with France's response (we might call it complicity) to the Holocaust is an understatement. She writes:

> Seven million Jews have been exterminated – transported in cattle cars, then gassed in specially built gas chambers, then burned in specially built ovens. [. . .] One of the greatest civilized nations in the world [. . .] has just systematically murdered eleven million human beings with the utter efficiency of a state industry. [. . .] In order to bear it, to tolerate the idea of it, we must share the crime.[2]

Now this was an idea that I had not encountered before. The Holocaust was not a German problem, but a symptom of Western civilization. A civilization that, once primed for progress, had turned its cultural and technological achievements towards brutality. For Duras, it was a mistake to view the Holocaust as a German problem when so many other European nations had either been actively complicit or turned a blind eye. Reconciliation, for her, would involve collective responsibility, particularly on the part of France. Schooled in Christian Humanism, I was sobered by Duras' proclamation that we were not defined by such values as equality and freedom, but rather by the propensity for mass murder. After over a decade researching and teaching university students about the Holocaust—as well as Bosnian, Rwandan, Sudanese, and other genocides—I have come to appreciate her perspective even more with time. While I do not fully share Duras's dire vision of humanity, her warning against distancing oneself from the violent brutality of the Nazis remains prescient for me, particularly as white supremacist and neo-Nazi ideologies take root and flourish in the United States and abroad. I work with my students to displace their assumption that such events could never happen again, or that if they did, that they would never be the perpetrator or complicit bystanders.

At the same time I discovered Duras, I began to read Hélène Cixous' Holocaust writing. Born in 1937, Cixous grew up in Algeria with Jewish parents who fled Nazi rule in the 1930s. Both *Ex-Cities* (2006) and *Rootprints:*

Memory and Life Writing (1997) are her attempt to return to and reconstruct a family history that was permanently disrupted by the Holocaust. Before the Holocaust, there were fifty Jewish families in her mother's town of Osnabrück. After the war, there were none. "I was born a survivor," she writes, "I escaped by the skin of my teeth."[3,4] As I read Cixous, I gathered the names of writers whose "relations with war, racism, and the impulse to annihilate" were direct, and writers who would lead me straight into the Holocaust: Ingeborg Bachmann, Paul Celan, Nelly Sachs, and Etty Hillesum.[5]

Reading Duras and Cixous altered my thinking about war writing. I was struck by their sentiment that diaries are not "literature," but a dynamic form of writing that is more revelatory and closer to the true nature of one's personal experience than fiction. A genre that is, with its often inward focus and temporal proximity to events recalled, particularly suited to the conveyance of suffering. Second, that the Second World War and the Holocaust were, as Cixous put it, the "apex and nadir" of human suffering in modern times.[6] And, as Duras inveighed, that I had a responsibility to confront this suffering rather than distance myself from it. Finally, that women had expressed the significant personal and collective impact of the war and the Holocaust on women's lives. I wondered what could be learned about the Holocaust from reading autobiographical accounts like Cixous' and Duras' that were written in proximity to the Holocaust but were not based on personal experience?

Towards the end of my MLitt in 2006, when my supervisors Susan Sellers and Gill Plain invited me to stay on at St. Andrews for doctoral work, I asked to write my dissertation on European women's diaries of the Second World War and the Holocaust. Although I was then writing about contemporary British literature, they enthusiastically supported the project, another case of great trust and generosity from my women mentors. We agreed that I should return to the United States, where I could do the archival research the project would require.

I soon found myself back in Charlottesville, Virginia, because my husband had accepted a job at the University of Virginia. I read everything I could find about gender and the Holocaust, but locating the diaries proved more difficult. Scouring the collections and virtual databases, I found almost no published women's diaries of the Holocaust. Teenage and adolescent girl's diaries, a few; women's, almost none. "What's going on here?," I asked myself. Not having had any training in Holocaust Studies or archival work, I took the train to Washington, DC and showed up, unannounced, at USHMM research archives to look for women's diaries.

What is (not) in the archive

I quickly learned that archival work is as time consuming, frustrating, and expensive to conduct as it is rewarding. With the help of archivist Michlean

Amir, who patiently schooled me in archival practices and methodology, I fastidiously scoured the museum's collections for anything I could find resembling a diary, journal, or memoir in French or in English translation. Rarely were there full documents. Instead I pored over scraps and fragments hastily compiled in the face of destruction. In some more memorable instances: the charred pages of a diary found behind a radiator after the Warsaw Ghetto uprising (the pages Professor Jerzak's mother would translate for me);[7] a soft bound book permanently curved from being worn inside a kind neighbor's belt for three years after the Jewish writers were dragged from their apartment by the Gestapo;[8] and the annotated typescript of Renata Laqueur's diary of Bergen-Belsen, which has continued to compel me for over a decade.[9] These documents, comprising various and often hybrid genres, written by women and girls in a range of national contexts, raised far more questions for me than answers. As I pored over what I could find, I realized that I really needed to learn more about the Holocaust to understand what I was reading.

HEF Fellowship

Being accepted to take part in the Holocaust Educational Foundation's Summer Fellowship at Northwestern University in 2009 was a formative event in my education and research. In addition to creating a foundation for my future research and teaching, I met mentors and colleagues whose work and friendship have continued to enrich my scholarship and career. Sara Horowitz's course on women's Holocaust literature was particularly revelatory for me as she deepened my understanding of women's Holocaust experiences through her readings of such texts as Ida Fink's *A Scrap of Time* (1987) and Cynthia Ozick's *The Shawl* (1980), which I have since taught in my gender and genocide courses. John Roth, who led a class on ethics, inspired me with his ability to find scraps of hope and joy in the midst of overwhelming world events. Doris Bergen, Elizabeth Heineman, and Anna Hájková have continued to provide models of approaching history attuned to issues of gender and sexuality. I left Evanston that summer with a wealth of knowledge for approaching my archival research, as well as a new best friend, Hamutal Jakobson, who would cook me Israeli dinners and edit my doctoral dissertation a year later.

Motherhood and Mentorship

I do not think it is possible, as a feminist scholar, to discuss my career without examining the ways it has been affected by gendered forms of caregiving. In 2013, my husband and I moved to Cleveland, Ohio, a city where I knew no one. I had finished my PhD and then put it in a drawer as I nursed my grandmother, who was dying of ovarian cancer. Dr. Brooks, my Comparative Literature mentor, succumbed to cystic fibrosis the same week. The academic job market was still reeling from the reverberations of the 2008 financial crisis. I was, to put it mildly, unsure of my course. Fate would have it that I attended a Holocaust conference at the University of Portsmouth that summer. I gave a paper on representations of sexual barter in Renata Laqueur's Bergen-Belsen diary that produced some animated questions from a scholar whose work I knew and respected but had never met: Phyllis Lassner. Since that time, through the birth of my children and substantial maternity leave, and through my years of precarious employment, Phyllis has continued to mentor me and support my career. Phyllis also brought mentors like Alexis Pogorelskin and the late Rachel Brenner into my orbit. These women, who have been incalculably generous with their time, intellect, and encouragement, have kept me going through years of having no department, colleagues, or institutional support for my work. Because I am precariously employed as an adjunct professor, motherhood also constituted an eighteen-month hiatus from work and particularly from Holocaust scholarship. No maternity leave was available to me, and my twins occupied all of my emotional and physical energy. They were born on the eve of ISIS bombing the Bataclan in Paris and I remember my visceral response to this terrorist attack: Turn the news off; shut it out. It is, I understand, a great privilege to be able to shut out news of war violence and tragedy but it was my response as a new mother. This was also, not surprisingly, my response to gendered examinations of the Holocaust. I quite simply could not face anything to do with motherhood and childhood during the Holocaust for a substantial amount of time. The day arrived when I was ready to return to work, and I resumed my book research and teaching. In addition to my scholarly mentors, I have to express gratitude for my husband Stephen who has supported me practically, emotionally, and financially as I have worked contract to contract for little compensation, and for investing in the substantial costs of my archival research.

Between Literature and History

If precarious employment has given one gift to me as a scholar, it is time and freedom of movement. Spending time in the archives, holding the shreds and remnants of people's lives, and more often encountering the knowledge of their deaths, remains a poignant and fraught experience for me. The unlikely event that, amidst the wholesale destruction created by the Nazis, a diary—tactile evidence of an individual's inner life and humanity—could survive, remains incredible to me. While not a substitute for comprehensive historical approaches, personal narratives like diaries have a unique ability to connect their readers with what can be overwhelming large-scale historical traumas. I consider it a moral obligation of my work as a scholar and educator to bring these documents to light, particularly at a time when studies have shown that an estimated two-thirds of US young adults are unaware that six million Jews were killed during the Holocaust.[10] These efforts have taken different shapes: practical, pedagogical, and scholarly. For example, at the USHMM I often digitized the collections I was working with, collections that I continue to teach and publicly lecture on, as well as present to scholarly conferences and publications. In another example, I spoke on Renata Laqueur and Hanna Lévy-Hass' diaries of Bergen-Belsen at our local synagogue's Yom Hashoah commemoration. Having never before entered a synagogue, I was nervous to accept this invitation, but the congregation's response to Laqueur and Lévy-Hass's stories of trauma and resistance further cemented my belief in the power of personal narratives to engage individuals with the overwhelming tragedy and brutality of the Holocaust. In the face of what Duras called "the mass of death dealt by God's creatures to his fellows,"[11] these women's stories are a potent reminder that it was not a ubiquitous mass of Jews who were killed, but six million individuals with vibrant and complex lives and responses to what they were experiencing.

In some ways I continue to feel like a perennial outsider as a literary scholar working on women's diaries of both the Second World War and the Holocaust. Diaries, as Jochen Hellbeck notes, reside somewhere between literature and history and are equally vexing to both fields for the ways they challenge received notions of private testimony and factual representation.[12] This is a tension I feel acutely as a literary historian working on my generically hybrid book that addresses the questions Duras and Cixous raised in my early encounters: What do the urgency and immediacy of diary writing illuminate about women's traumatic wartime and Holocaust experiences? How did women, socialized to be the moral guardians of their communities, participate in, observe, and represent the moral and emotional landscapes of the Holocaust? How do women diarists portray themselves and other women engaging with the social ruptures created by war trauma—engagements that have often been intentionally omitted or excised from collective memories of the war precisely because they challenge ethical, political, and social norms that were restored postwar?

Uncomfortable Truths

Phyllis Lassner once asked me if perhaps I worked on the Holocaust because it was not my history. I have thought about that a lot over the years and, as time has passed, I have come to see how deeply and indeed uncomfortably those histories are connected—mine, and that of others. I learned only recently through reading Isabel Wilkerson's *Caste* (2020) that the Nazi regime looked to southern slave ownership and segregation laws as inspiration for the 1935 Nuremberg Laws that would serve as legal justification for the

Holocaust. So there is a relationship, then, between my family's centuries of slave ownership, participation in Southern Jim Crow segregation laws, and the Holocaust. These are connections that I have begun to explore with my teaching and research.

At Case Western, although I am an adjunct, I have been given the opportunity to design my own courses. I teach on women, war, and genocide in a general education department, and have also been able to give university talks and teach short courses on women's Holocaust diaries. Every semester I have found myself examining the conundrum of women's perpetration in more detail. This initially started with my teaching Wendy Lower's *Hitler's Furies: German Women in the Nazi Killing Fields* (2013). My students are always shocked to learn of the extent of German women's participation and complicity in brutal state-sponsored violence. Something I always tell my students is that two things are true: Women can perpetrate violence within systems that also subjugate them and open them up to gender-specific forms of violence. Being victimized, in other words, does not always result in empathy and compassion (often the opposite is true).

In 2019 I encountered Stephanie Jones-Rogers's groundbreaking study of Southern women's slave ownership, *They Were Her Property: White Women as Slave Owners in the American South* (2019), which I added to my syllabus. In a striking similarity to Nazi German women, Southern women played the gender card in abnegating responsibility for perpetrating violent white supremacy so successfully that they escaped historical scrutiny until recently. With few exceptions, feminist historians have exculpated both groups in similar ways by focusing on their subjugated roles in their respective societies. Yet as Drew Gilpin Faust notes of white Southern women's position in antebellum race and class hierarchies in *Mothers of Invention* (1996), "a lady's elite status had been founded in the oppressions of slavery, her notions of genteel womanhood intimately bound up with the prisms of class and race through which they were refracted."[13] I came to the difficult realization that, like the earlier generation of feminist historians, I had been engaged in revisionist history regarding the women in my family and the role they played in Southern slave-owning society. I had questions, and I turned to archives for the answers.

These are not questions that I would be capable of finding answers to had I not been trained in archival historical research and analysis of women's personal narratives through my work on women's Holocaust diaries. It's not just the necessary practical skills (and often, institutional access) required to engage in archival research that I believe have been necessary in my embarking on this project, but also the complex training in remaining objective while encountering devastating material that is often personal in nature. In this instance, I am facing the history of my family's enslavement, dehumanization, and exploitation of Black Americans across generations. I used my archival research skills to find evidence of my family's role in South Carolina's Native American massacres of 1715, substantial slave ownership spanning centuries, and investment in exploitative sharecropping practices continuing into the twentieth century. My family's copious record-keeping also revealed that some women in my family not only personally owned a substantial number of enslaved individuals, but also, as members of the United Daughters of the Confederacy, were active shapers of the Lost Cause ideology following the Civil War.[14]

The murder of George Floyd was a tipping point for me, at which time I felt a moral obligation to take accountability for my family's role in the United States' white supremacist history. To share the crime, as Duras insisted we should, by not distancing myself from my family's perpetration of historical traumas. I now share my family history with my students, and even assign diaries written by my slave-owning great-great-great aunt in the final months of the Civil War for my course.[15] These diaries detail the raiding of the Jervey and Ravenel plantations, their racist white supremacist ideology, and the story of a slave uprising led by enslaved women that was—to the women's great approval and relief—brutally suppressed by the murder of twenty-seven enslaved individuals.[16] While the history of American slavery is not comparable to the Holocaust, there are connections to be made between its xenophobic underpinnings and those of the Holocaust, not the least of which is women's roles as perpetrators and complicit bystanders whose support was critical in enabling both white supremacist agendas. The Unite the Right Rally, which occurred in my former hometown of Charlottesville, VA, and which resulted in the murder of activist Heather Heyer by James Field from my current state of Ohio, also provides a teachable connection between Confederate and Nazi ideologies. Ultimately violently protesting the removal of the statue of Confederate general Robert E. Lee, the rally began with torch carrying white supremacists and neo-Nazis surrounding Charlottesville's synagogue Congregation Beth Israel, chanting the Nazi chant "blood and soil." Carrying swastika flags, Confederate flags, and holding signs reading, "Jews will not replace us," they then marched to pay respect to the statue of slave owner and founding father of the United States, Thomas Jefferson. Teaching students of the historical context of such events and their ideological underpinnings, more recently including the insurrection of our nation's capital on January 6, 2021, is of paramount importance to me. You cannot properly resist what you do not understand, and it is my hope that this generation of students can resist the resurgence of white supremacist and antisemitic ideologies by meaningfully advocating for social justice on local, national, and international levels.

Conclusion

I have researched the Holocaust for more than a decade but remain daunted by how much remains to be learned. I am, by turns, frustrated by how much we don't know and fascinated by all of the new scholarship coming to light. I am a parent and an educator, fearful of the neo-Nazi and white supremacist ideologies rearing their heads in both the United States and other countries. In light of these threats, I am committed to researching and teaching about the Holocaust. This continues to feel like my most important work.

Notes

1 Marguerite Duras, *The War* (New York: Pantheon, 1986), 4.
2 Ibid., 49–50.
3 Hélène Cixous, "We who are free, are we free?" *Critical Inquiry* 19, no. 2 (1993): 204.
4 It would take Cixous another fourteen years after writing *Ex-Cities* to travel to Osnabrück and write the story of that haunted return to a city whose Jews had been handed over to death by their German neighbors. Cf. Hélène Cixous, *Osnabrück Station to Jerusalem: A Memoir*, trans. Peggy Kamuf (New York: Fordham University Press, 2020).
5 Cixous, 'We Who Are Free,' 206.
6 Ibid., 208.
7 Debora, 'Debora's Diary (1943),' Collection Acc.2002.74.1. USHMM, Washington, DC.
8 Frieda and Max Reinach Diary, 1939–1942, translated by Trude Koshland, Collection Acc.1999.A.0215, USHMM Archives, Washington D.C.
9 Diary of Bergen-Belsen (March 1944–April 1945), translated by Renata Laqueur, Renata Laqueur Collection, Collection Acc. 1995.A.1203, USHMM Archives, Washington, DC.
10 Harriet Sherwood, "Nearly two-thirds of US young adults unaware 6m Jews killed in the Holocaust,' *The Guardian*, Sep 16, 2020.
11 Duras, *The War*, 50.
12 Jochen Hellbeck, 'The Diary Between Literature and History: A Historian's Critical Response,' *The Russian Review* 63, no. 4, October (2004): 621–9.
13 Drew Gilpin Faust, *Mothers of Invention: Women of the Slaveholding South in the American Civil War* (Chapel Hill and London: University of North Carolina Press, 1996).
14 Karen Cox, *Dixie's Daughters: The United Daughters of the Confederacy and the Preservation of Confederate Culture* (Gainesville: University of Florida Press, 2003).
15 Susan R. Jervey and Charlotte St. J. Ravenel, TWO DIARIES FROM MIDDLE ST. JOHN'S, BERKELEY, SOUTH CAROLINA, FEBRUARY-MAY, 1865: Electronic Edition, Call number E529 .J57 1921 (Davis Library,

UNC-CH), University of North Carolina Documenting the American South, Beginnings to 1920, https://docsouth.unc.edu/fpn/jervey/jervey.html.

16 Details of this insurgency can be found in Thavolia Glymph's 'Rose's War and the Gendered Politics of Slave Insurgency in the Civil War,' *Journal of the Civil War Era* 13 no. 4 (December 2013): 501–32.

PART TWO

Great Britain

9

Before the Gate of Memory

Joshua Lander

In memory of David Lander

Jew-Boy

This chapter has two segments that loopingly entwine. The first section briefly examines how the Holocaust emerged in my formative years as a Jew growing up in Scotland, while the second looks at how my academic examinations of Jewish literature unearthed my own family's experience of the Holocaust. In truth, this chapter is as much about antisemitism as it is the Holocaust, though perhaps separating the two is impossible. Each section is yoked together by the faultiness of memory and a profound sense of loss; it is—in a roundabout way—my attempt to explain why I write on the Holocaust, antisemitism, and contemporary Jewish literature.

I grew up in Glasgow, Scotland, a city (and country) that has a dearth of Jews and Judaic culture. Still, I was educated in the only Jewish primary school in Scotland, a small and strangely charming little building located in Glasgow's southside (home to many of Scotland's Jewish community). This instilled in me a curious misunderstanding regarding my ethno-religious identity: Jewishness was ubiquitously Scottish to me and there was nothing strange or unfamiliar surrounding the entwinement of Judaism and Scottishness. Giffnock and Newton Mearns (two suburbs in Glasgow) had—and still have—an abundance of (mostly secular) Jews and my childhood was spent anxiously trying to prove I was as Jewish as them. My formative years perverted the logic of *Portnoy's Complaint*: Hashem, I often prayed, make me into a *Good* Jewish Boy; I wanted to assimilate into Jewishness and become as whole as the synagogue-attending, Hebrew-speaking boys in my class who outshone me physically and academically. So

I was rather taken aback when I was sent off to a secondary school in the west end of Glasgow, where not a single one of my classmates had ever encountered a Jew. I quickly gained two unflattering nicknames: Jew-boy and Halfknob. My classmates knew Jewishness through television shows like *South Park* and its characters Kyle and the antisemitic Cartman. Regrettably, the satirical bite of the show seemed lost on them, as many of my colleagues did indeed blame me for the killing of Christ.

My penis—a superfluous organ in my prepubescent years—aroused an astonishing degree of curiosity from my male peers, and many asked, with genuine interest, whether or not half my member was missing. The boys were likewise intrigued by my (tenuous) connection to the Holocaust. There was only one other Jewish boy in the entire school when I joined. I know this because a history teacher singled me out in front of the class before watching a Holocaust documentary to ask if I was able to handle the contents, and not cry like the other Jewish student. This content warning split the class in terms of what to watch: The spectacle of six million dead Jewish bodies piled up in impossible heaps, or me, now the archetypal token Jew, whom Mr. Smith promised would cry. I wanted to be stoic and brave, but not for myself; I wanted to impress Mr. Smith and show him I was better than that weak-willed other Jew. I didn't cry (in class).

In my fourth/fifth year of school, some classmates created a song for me which they called, "Grandpa was in the Hitler Youth." This dubiously titled tune begins pleasantly enough with a violin playing Klezmer music until Hitler's voice takes over, as a crowd bellows with adoration. All of this melts into silence, however, as the cacophony of sounds is replaced with the hiss of gas. In case anyone is tempted to consider this a sympathetic appraisal of the Holocaust, my sixteen-year-old classmate then counts to three in German, and launches into a rollicking machinegun fire chorus accompanied by screeching guitars and the following lyrics:

Shekel shekel money money
shekel shekel money money
shekel shekel money money,
Jew-ish bread!

I remember finding this hilarious. It was so ridiculously comical. This was antisemitism at its most banal, unthreatening, hollow, and absurd. However, in the second verse the two budding musicians up the ante. The singer puts on a strange accent that is supposed to mimic a shtetl Jew, and sings the following:

Gas chamber gas chamber
do we have to pay?
Gas chamber gas chamber

run away!
Gas chamber gas chamber
do we have to pay?
Gas chamber gas chamber
run away!

This recording—which I kept, perhaps knowing that someday it would prove useful in my literary endeavors—symbolizes the manner in which the Holocaust emerged in my secondary-school education. The Holocaust existed as a joke, an occasion ossified and obfuscated by the searing disconnect we felt from the event, one that was used to separate and distinguish me as the conceptual, impossible Jew. This was most apparent whenever we trundled along to the Greenie (the local newsagents) at the end of the school day to buy sweets and crisps. One particular student used to go around the boys asking for a pound or two, looking to "scaff" off someone, usually to no avail. Whenever he asked me and I said no, he'd reply by telling me to "stop being such a tight Jew"; if I relented and donated to his cause, he'd laugh and say, "See! Jews have all the money." I couldn't win! Assimilating into antisemitism effectively meant distinguishing Jewishness and its histories (including the Holocaust) as a negative, an identity to be shorn and shed; I was the quintessential self-hating Jew, a walking, talking Portnovian figure, anxiously gazing down at his member wondering what—if anything—was wrong with his *shmok*.

Discovering Philip Roth was an important turning point in coming to terms with my Jewish identity. That famous quote from *The Counterlife*'s Nathan Zuckerman perfectly encapsulates the emptying feeling antisemitism induces: "England's made a Jew of me in only eight weeks [...] A Jew without Jews, without Judaism, without Zionism, without Jewishness, [...] just the object itself, like a glass or an apple."[1] Roth gave me a voice to articulate the Jewish anxieties that emerged as a Jew dwelling in Scotland; he enabled me to identify the forces that had rendered my Jewishness into a grotesque vulgarity. These are strange sentences to reckon with; my (literary) relationship with Roth is strained, especially after reading the Blake Bailey biography, and yet Roth will forever remain an invaluable figure in helping me parse the antisemitism I experienced in Scotland. Such sentiments have been expressed by other British-Jewish writers. Anne Karpf, for example, echoes these same opinions in *The War After*, noting how the "lack of an identifiable British-Jewish literary canon reflected just how marginalized and unconfident British Jews were."[2] Thankfully, there is now a growing body of British-Jewish literature that has entered into the canonical mainstream. Spearheaded by writers such as Howard Jacobson and Linda Grant, these authors are blaringly examining and interrogating what it means to be a Jew in Britain and how the Holocaust has impacted British-Jewish lives. These writers' works simultaneously bring into question

Britishness itself, and how anglicization has affected British-Jewry's ability to commemorate and process the Holocaust. These questions were what brought me back to my family's archives and our own experience of assimilating into Britain during the Second World War.

Jew, Jew, Jew

Shortly after completing my thesis on Roth, I was invited to contribute to the recently published collection, *The Holocaust Across Borders: Trauma, Atrocity, and Representation in Literature and Culture*. My contribution focused on Judith Kerr and Eva Tucker, and the research I undertook brought me back to Britain, British antisemitism, and my own family's experience of the Holocaust. Recently, I uncovered a picture of my aunt and mother standing in front of what is now a chemicals factory in Vienna, Austria. My mother has her arm around her sister, a loving and protective gesture, as the two stand gazing at the property before them, sharing a poignant moment of reflection. My cousin—Sarah—took the photograph; she no doubt recognized the tenderness of the scene unfolding before her. The building they are facing was a residential block, and—for a while, at least—was where my grandfather and his family dwelt. According to my mother, Alexander Lander and his family fled the country in 1938 after Nazi Germany annexed Austria. He arrived in the United Kingdom in March 1939. The building photographed was—once upon a time—my grandfather's home, yet the object looming before the two women is almost entirely foreign, a place and space that signifies an unalterable vacuum. This gap remains prevalently searing in my mind's eye; it represents the chasmic liminality of being a Jew in Scotland today, living in what feels like a perpetual state between past and present, present and past. Yet this state of mind is one I overindulge in and foist upon myself. As my friends often jokingly say to me, "Jew, Jew, Jew! Everything's always about the Jews with you. That or the Holocaust. Jew, Jew, Jew!" As though I'm an invention of Howard Jacobson's.

Yet this is new to me; this immersion into my Jewishness took a very long time to emerge, in part because I had no language to articulate the dissonance I felt between my ethno-religious identity and the country I dwell in; this is what fiction and theory provided me: a voice, a very 'Jewy' voice. Returning to the picture, then, I think the awkward angle of the shot feels metaphoric; it encapsulates, in its stretched, distanced positioning, the insurmountable disconnect separating my family and me from our grandfather's past. When I first saw the photograph, I doubt I thought much of it, but when I looked again recently, I was struck by the multiplicities of meanings I could derive and invent. The building represents a place that was once home, yet the women pictured can only *imagine* what this space meant to their father. They remain—literally and symbolically—locked outside the building, unable to enter the past, signifying the violent chasm induced by the Holocaust and the Nazis' genocidal persecution of the Jewish people. Our family's disconnection neatly compliments Marianne Hirsch's point that "[i]n the face of expulsion and expropriation [. . .] home and identity are in themselves implausible and objects remain alienating and strange."[3] I have never faced exclusion or state sponsored dispossession, yet I am burdened by the sense that I feel "homeless" and that my identity as a Jew is fraught, in part because my claim to both Scottishness and Jewishness always feels tenuous (I was born in England and am incredibly divorced from Judaic culture). Yet I also know that these feelings likely have little to do with my grandfather's past. So many others in my family feel comfortable and happy and at home in Scotland as Scottish Jews. I'm always looking for neat, parable-style stories that encapsulate my own disconnect as a Jew. The picture of my mother and aunt, for example, is metaphorically ripe as I remembered a story of them attempting to enter the building but being thwarted by a disgruntled security guard who was disinterested in my mother's sentimental explanations. They were not welcome. However, this is wrong; this never happened. My mother and aunt never attempted to enter the building and were never pursued by anyone on their travels. I'm conflating family narratives: You see, it was my cousin who was chased out of a chemicals building in Budapest, Hungary. This was where my grandfather was born. The pictured building is a block of residential flats. I am trying to create meaning where there is none to suit my literary intentions.

Constructing Gates: In Memory of Memory

The tale of my mother and aunt's (fictitious) encounter with the guard reminds me of Franz Kafka's *The Trial*; or, to be more specific, it reminds me of Otto Dov Kulka's *Landscape of the Metropolis of Death*. Kulka's memoir details his infanthood growing up in the concentration camps; it is—as the title indicates—a haunting work that details the historian's struggle to articulate his violent and traumatic childhood in the death camps. Kulka turns to Kafka's parable from *The Trial* to explain his predicament. "Before the Law" describes an unnamed man's attempt to go through the gate of the law. He is repeatedly denied access by the guard standing before the gate. The man waits for years and bribes the guard with everything he possesses; the bribes are accepted, but still the man is not admitted. As death approaches, the man asks why no-one else has ever sought access to the law in all the years he has been there. The guard, sensing the man is close to the end of his life, reveals that the gate was built only for him, before finally closing it. Kulka leans on Kafka's parable to explain the mechanisms of the memoir he has written and how it has enabled him to metaphorically enter and exit his memories of the Holocaust:

this Auschwitz that was recorded here, which speaks here from my words, is the only entrance and exit—an exit, perhaps, or a closing—the only one that exists for me alone. I take this to mean that I cannot enter by any other way, by another gate to that place. Will others be able to enter through the gate that I opened here, that remains open for me?[4]

As a third-generation immigrant Jew and descendant of a Holocaust survivor, Kulka's gate metaphor resonates because it underscores the fricative nature of postmemory; my connection to the Holocaust feels strained and put on. I don't have any stories of suffering or tales of trauma that I can display or re-tell and there are no testimonies to lean on, either. I feel uncomfortable describing my grandfather as a "Survivor"; it feels like a term for someone else, someone more important whose story is more obviously entwined with the Holocaust as we associate it—the concentration camps. All I have—which seems measly in comparison—is faulty, half-remembered stories, myth, and fiction.

My grandfather never recorded his experience of escaping Nazi-occupied Austria; he never erected a gate for us to peep through. We know he and his family were forced to wear the star of David on their arms, were prohibited from entering public parks, and were barred from sitting on benches. The extent of their suffering and experience of prejudice is difficult to ascertain. Each of my aunts and uncles know fragments, but there is no monolithic narrative to eat from. All I have is scraps to sift through. This can be deflating because in order to retell our family's story I borrow half-remembered memories filled with (what I assume are unintended) fabrications; I feel as though I am writing over our history, transforming the lives of the Lander family into my own little fiction. I am desecrating in my attempt to describe.

The frustration of not knowing about my grandfather's experience is only furthered when I uncover a new story or detail. During a family get-together, my uncle produced an article he found that detailed my grandfather's journey to Britain.[5] Apparently, my grandfather—having made his way to Brussels—was in need of a hiding place after discovering the Nazis were planning on rounding up all known Jews in the area. He was offered a distinct sanctuary: a baker's oven.[6] But just as my grandfather was about to enter this caboose, which was filled with other Jews, he (pardon the pun) got cold feet and decided to chance his luck in the streets and alleys; he was lucky and remained undetected. Unfortunately, those Jews who had hidden in the oven were discovered and—we presume—sent to a concentration camp. The imagery of the tale is striking: In this post-Holocaust era, discussions of Nazi Germany and ovens inevitably conjure images of emaciated Jewish corpses, ash, and black smoke. We hear this story and imbue it with meanings and interpretations of our own; we alter the tale with our present-day knowledge, impregnating the narrative with an even more profound, disturbing meaning. What Alex knew in this moment is uncertain and unknowable, but *something* spooked him, *something* made him retreat from the oven and take refuge elsewhere. How cruelly ironic that the oven, of all places, was a refuge and hiding place for Jewish emigrants, and how bitter and terrible, too, that it turned out to be a site of treachery and death.

I was astonished by the story; I never knew the extent of my grandfather's suffering, the depth of persecution he endured. Nobody spoke of it, so nobody knew. "Persecuted," my uncle repeated the words back to me uncertainly, "you know, it's funny, I never thought of him as being persecuted." This blindness to his father's oppression surprised me initially, but upon reflection it is rather understandable. Indeed, in our extended conversation on the matter, he explained his position further. His father arrived in the United Kingdom with his college sketches (some of which my mother has framed) and his wooden skis, hardly items you'd expect a refugee to possess when hurrying from persecution. Furthermore, my uncle recalled a story wherein his father was boarding a train (potentially to Brussels but he isn't sure) when a Nazi officer stopped him to inspect his papers. As he did so, the guard jovially informed him that "we'll be seeing you again," to which my grandfather replied, "no, I can assure you, you won't." However, for whatever reason, the train was turned around and the same guard did indeed see my grandfather again. "I told you we'd see you again," he laughed. For my uncle, the story shows his father's experience wasn't cinematically violent; he was, all things considered, fortunate.

My grandfather did not—as far as we know—experience the torment of a concentration camp or any kind of Nazi-organized imprisonment. And to a degree, of course, my uncle is right. My grandfather *was* lucky; he escaped, yet I am wary of undermining the trauma he suffered. My aunt and mother both vividly remember watching my grandfather break down in tears at the memory of what he endured and witnessed. I think this is important to recognize: There are myriad memories and various constellatory ideas of my grandfather that cannot—nor should be—disentangled. Nor indeed should the trauma he endured be understated: His luck was not luck, it was displacement steeped in unfathomable violence and pain. Yet I think it is fair to observe that both my mother and uncle grew up wanting to grow *out* of their Jewishness; they wanted to escape from this religion of difference and become "normal people." Perhaps this is why they never set out to trace their genealogy and I now wonder how this impulse to become like everybody else has impacted the way we have—or have not—archived and remembered our history. My family's assimilatory turn has brought me back to questioning what anglicization has done to British-Jewry. Even in my own research, I began with *the* Jewish-American writer: Philip Roth. It did not even occur to me to look at or read any British-Jewish writers. My research is now animated by the desire to recognize and bring into focus *our* lives as Scottish and British Jews and our experiences of the Holocaust, even if we feel detached and separated from that facet of history.

My family are—for the most part—privileged, wealthy, and safe; we live comfortably and freely in Scotland. We seldom experience antisemitism; we don't know what it is to live under state-sponsored racial persecution. We cannot envisage what my grandfather saw, what he experienced, and what he knew.

We—my mother and I—did not know the route my grandfather took to arrive in the United Kingdom. Recently, however, my uncle revealed he had digitized my grandfather's passports, including the one issued to him by Nazi Germany. His journey suggests a deeper struggle than my uncle described. At one point, my grandfather had organized a visa to Cuba, but—for some reason unknown to us—this was cancelled. The tumultuousness of the process is absent, as is the emotional outpouring incurred by the displacement my grandfather endured. All we have is dates, numbers, and passport stamps. Yet the tangibility of the documents had a profound effect on me; indeed, this was the first time I had ever seen such visceral proof of my grandfather's persecution. I am astonished by the Nazi-issued passport; it affirms, in an almost violently disruptive way, my grandfather's traumatic dehumanization. The stamped, slightly faded J imprinted onto his passport makes real what we knew: Our family was persecuted for being Jewish. My uncle believes he had already shared this material with me, but this is simply impossible: I would never forget seeing such an arresting and powerful image. Would I?

My haphazard memory (and archival skills) are matched only by my eagerness to invest meaning where there might well be none. Alexander Lander established Lander Alarms in 1945. He did this because he studied engineering at college and this was his trade. Yet I cannot help but reinscribe his actions with a different meaning. My grandfather—the Jewish emigrant who was forced from his home, robbed of his citizenship, and transformed into a displaced "alien"—built a business oriented around the protection and preservation of the home; his company sought to prevent external forces violating private spaces. Ipso facto, I read (and thus transform) my grandfather's business into a signifier of resistance against fascism, a proud declaration of Jewishness. Ironically, though, his brand's logo is strikingly fascistic in terms of its aesthetic, as it has a dark red circle encased with solid black Ls. A few years ago, I wanted a tattoo and decided I'd like to get the Lander Alarms logo inked on my arm. I almost booked an appointment with an artist until a friend commented on the logo's unfortunate aesthetic: "It looks a bit fascist, don't you think?"

The bold, thick black lettered Ls combined with the red circle do—to a certain degree—remind me of the Third Reich's infamous swastika. The color schema suggests—as the Nazi swastika does—strength, stability, and power. The red circle, ensconced by the tilted Ls, is perfectly shielded, affirming the protective quality Lander Alarms offers. Doubtless, my grandfather would be horrified to hear such a comparison, but I cannot unsee the similarity; authorial intent is once again rendered useless when faced with the over-enthused reader. When I brought this resemblance to my family's attention, there was a mixture of responses. Some saw where I was coming from, whilst others were (politely) dismissive; these myriad interpretations continue to compel and excite me to delve deeper into the ever-emerging archives of our family, as the objects and documents left take on new meanings for the post-memory generation; they offer suggestive clues, hints at the impact and legacy the Holocaust has had on our family but are too fractured and fragmented to provide clarity. When I tell my uncle what I am writing, he listens attentively, intrigued by the literariness of the matter and its contents. When I discuss my interpretation of the above, he smiles and suggests I am overanalyzing, that I am imbuing my grandfather's actions with meanings that extend beyond their original purpose. It is a fair and true accusation, but what else can I do? The "truth" of my grandfather's intention is impossible to ascertain; and objective truth—that shibboleth of a concept—is entirely frivolous in terms of memory and postmemory. As Maria Stepanova writes in *In Memory of Memory*, "memory is concerned with justice, history with preciseness; memory moralizes, history tallies up and corrects; memory is personal, history dreams of objectivity."[7] This work is entirely animated by the impossible irreconcilability of the past and present; my academic and personal writing are yoked together by the same desire: "to connect what cannot be connected."[8]

Indeed, the idea for this chapter emerged from my inability to make sense of my grandfather's character. A few years ago my mother uncovered a video of him conducting what he claimed to be a scientific experiment. My grandfather was hanging cucumbers from the two glass pyramids he hand built in his garden and was using his wife's stolen stockings to investigate the effect light had on the vegetable. He had numbered every glass panel in his pyramids and the video showed him and his son taking meticulous notes regarding the "results" (the cucumbers in the stockings dried out, whilst the other ones he hung freely stayed moist). What fascinated me was the spectacle itself: I was witnessing my grandfather's eccentricity, vulnerability, and humanity. Here was a strange wee man conducting a strange wee experiment, without much in the way of purpose or rational; it was oddly touching watching this patriarchal figure being such an eccentric oddball. I felt very connected to him. I wept with laughter, whilst my mother wept with sadness and asked me—in a moment of protective cautiousness—not to discuss the contents of the video with anyone outside of our family (I guess this is my very own little *Maus* moment). I immediately wondered aloud if he had suffered PTSD from the Holocaust, an unfounded and spurious suggestion with little merit, yet one that emerged precisely because there is a vacuum in our family, a haunting, searing gap that will never be filled. My grandfather's eccentricity (I mean who the hell builds two giant glass pyramids in their garden anyway?) may or may not be as a result of his traumatic experiences; it is impossible to say because his past remains hidden, forever out of bounds and out of reach. All we can do is construct little gateways, fictions and stories to speculatively construct meanings, without any hope of creating certainty or objectivity that nevertheless parses and probes what it means to be a Jew living in the aftermath of the Holocaust; or in my case, what it means to live as a Jew without Judaism, without Zionism, without Jewishness.

Notes

1. Philip Roth, *The Counterlife* (London: Vintage, 2005), 328.
2. Anne Karpf, *The War After: Living with the Holocaust* (London: Minerva, 1996), 49.
3. Marianne Hirsch, *The Generation of Postmemory: Writing and Visual Culture After the Holocaust* (New York: Columbia University Press, 2012), 212.
4. Otto Dov Kulka, *Landscapes of the Metropolis of Death: Reflections on Memory and Imagination* (London: Penguin, 2014), 81.
5. Unfortunately, that article seems to have vanished.
6. It seems this story is not one well known in my family: none of my aunts knows this anecdote.
7. Maria Stepanova, *In Memory of Memory*, trans. Sasha Dugdale (London: Fitzcarraldo, 2021), 103.
8. Hal Foster, 'An Archival Impulse', *October* 110 (2004): 3–22, 21.

10

I Am Not Jewish

Joanne Pettitt

I am not Jewish. Why do I feel the need to declare that? It's not as if one *has* to be Jewish to study the Holocaust. But, then, I'm not of German descent either. Nor do I belong to any other group that was victimized by the Nazis: I am not gay. I am not disabled. I am not Roma. Etc. Etc. Etc. In other words: I don't have a personal connection to the Holocaust. Of any kind. True, my grandfather was a stoker in the Merchant Navy; he was stoking boilers off the coast of France on D-Day, apparently. And my grandmother was in the Land Army. So, I suppose like most British families, I have a (proud?) connection to the Second World War. But not really to the Holocaust. Not in any deep and obvious way, in any case.

I imagine that makes me somewhat of an outlier in the field. And, in case it isn't already obvious, by "outlier," I am pretty sure I mean "interloper." I say that because I have never quite managed to shake off the deep-rooted anxiety that, really, I am using the Holocaust. That, yes, it is my field of research and interest; and, yes, I am passionate about preserving its memory. But that at the same time, as my primary research area, the Holocaust has allowed me to pave a career for myself. The Holocaust pays my bills. What an appalling idea.

Would I feel less conflicted if I were Jewish? Or if I had some other connection to the atrocity? Perhaps. Who knows? A friend once told me that what I do is wonderful: "it's not your fight. And you do it anyway." That was nice to hear. I hope it is how others see me. I hope I am doing the right thing.

I wonder whether, subconsciously, this ambivalence is the reason I have always leaned towards the study of perpetrators. Somewhere deep down, I feel that I have no right to dwell on the pain and trauma of others. It seems somehow voyeuristic. No. Forget that. It is definitely voyeuristic. Reading book after book about human beings being tortured and murdered is not an easy task, but maybe there is also something in the idea that certain aspects of the atrocity should in any case remain outside the limits of representation. Maybe we don't have to be shown everything. Maybe we do. Maybe.

Studying Nazis is, in many ways, much more straightforward. It is also important. Without an understanding of what made the perpetrators tick we have no way of recognizing the warning signs that such an atrocity is likely to happen again: What motivated these people to commit genocide? How did they come to think of such atrocious deeds not just as morally justifiable but, terrifyingly, as morally *desirable*? What were the conditions that allowed these human beings to become monsters?

But I'm getting ahead of myself. Let's start at the beginning.

A Very British Upbringing

Academics have long-since acknowledged that the Second World War is one of the cornerstones of British national identity and, looking back at it now, I can see that it featured in my life—albeit peripherally—from a very young age. I didn't realize it at the time, but I was first introduced to the idea of the "bad Nazi" when I was very young, maybe only six or seven. My sister and I used to spend weekends at my grandparents' house, where we would insist on watching *The Sound of Music* over and over again (anyone remember video tapes?). To this day, I know the songs by heart. Certainly, the story of the naïve young governess and the stoic former naval captain captured my imagination in a way that few films have done since. I was transfixed by both the love story and the beautiful Austrian landscape; I am sure the film was the start of my love affair with the mountains. But how much did I really understand that final scene, when the von Trapp family finally made their escape across the mountains? And did I really comprehend the character of Rolfe, who so shamelessly betrayed his former love interest, Liesl? And did I "get" the bickering between the captain and "uncle" Max about whether one has a duty to be political in such times? In answer to all three questions: No, of course I didn't understand. In fact, the word "Anschluss" didn't enter my vocabulary until much, much later. But somewhere at the back of my mind, a seed had been planted: Nazis were bad guys.

If it wasn't *The Sound of Music* with my grandparents, it was *Dad's Army* with my dad. For those that don't know the show, *Dad's Army* is a comedy series following the Home Guard in the fictional coastal town of Walmington-on-Sea, supposedly the area of Southern England most vulnerable to Nazi invasion. The bumbling characters and their humorous attempts to protect British shores captivated the public, regularly pulling audiences of 18 million at its peak. Even today, reruns attract viewers in their millions. Safe to say, *Dad's Army* is something of a national treasure. The important thing here is what the series taught me about what it means to be British. The theme tune goes like this:

> Who do you think you are kidding, Mr Hitler?
> If you think we're on the run
> We are the boys who will stop your little game
> We are the boys who will make you think again
> 'Cos who do you think you are kidding, Mr Hitler?
> If you think old England's done

Ultimately, the series promoted an idea of Britishness that was steadfast and loyal, if not always entirely proficient. I was being raised, apparently, on the right side of the war, as part of a community that opposed fascism and the bullying tactics of foreign powers. I don't remember the Holocaust ever being mentioned—it is hardly appropriate content for a comedy series—but I do know that the series furthered my understanding of Germans (and especially Hitler) as the enemy and the Brits as the plucky and resilient underdog.

Adding to my growing list of cultural encounters with the war, I could also recite sections of Laurence Binyon's canonical poem "For the Fallen" off the top of my head before I was ten—it was on the wall of the working men's club my dad used to take us to on Sunday afternoons (I was obviously absorbing the words as I snuck sips of John Smith's ale off the table when my dad wasn't looking). Written in the immediate aftermath of the First World War, the poem has become an essential part of the British memorial tradition and, along with the poppy, forms the foundation of the UK's collective memory as it relates to both World Wars.

> They shall grow not old, as we that are left grow old:
> Age shall not weary them, nor the years condemn.
> At the going down of the sun and in the morning
> We will remember them.[1]

Each year, these lines are recited up and down the country at Memorial Day events, reminding us all of the sacrifices made by the war generation and the respect we owe to those that took up arms in defense of freedom and virtue. Even if the memory of the two conflicts tends to be blurred by these references, for many Brits, the truth is that it doesn't really matter too much: We were on the right side of the war in both cases and so our integrity/pride/virtue remains intact regardless.

The point is that I am a product of a very British working-class upbringing, and in my earliest memories, the groundwork for the "good British/bad German" paradigm was already being laid. I hadn't even left primary school yet.

My secondary school years passed in a bit of a blur. I remember there was alcohol (often a lot of it). And I remember there was plenty of youthful mischief with my friends. But I don't think I was the best pupil: I was certainly capable, but I was also boisterous, and my big mouth often got me into trouble with my teachers. I don't remember studying the Holocaust at school. *The Boy in the Striped Pyjamas* had not yet been written. But, nevertheless, I left at eighteen with some vague understanding that some bad stuff had happened to the Jews during the Second World War. Looking back, I don't really know where that knowledge came from: I didn't even see *Schindler's List* until much later. But somehow that information had filtered into my consciousness.

If I put my academic hat back on for a second, I suppose all of this says something about the proliferation of representations of the Second World War and Nazism, especially in Britain, where cultural identities are based in large part on (simplified) memories of the conflict. Of course, every country has its own "foundation myths" and stories, manners of being and remembering, and ways of understanding one's place in the wider world. In the case of Britain, the collective national identity is heavily steeped in memories of the Second World War, and much of our sense of self comes from knowing that we, the Brits, were on the right side of the war, that we fought Fascism alone and against all the odds. As skewed as this perception of history undoubtedly is, it continues to resonate in the cultural sphere, despite the work of many academics who have sought to set the historical record straight (or at least iron out the kinks). In many ways, this is something that I have spent my career working against: trying to de-anglicize my thinking around the war.

Anyway, at eighteen, I packed up and went traveling with one of my closest friends. By the time I came home, university was looming.

Student Years

Not long after I returned from my globetrotting adventures, I found myself as an undergraduate student at the University of Kent studying Comparative Literature and French. I can't honestly say that I had a good grasp of the discipline back then, but I was regularly achieving good grades and I very quickly realized that I wanted to be an academic when I "grew up." Despite this, I must admit that I look back on my undergraduate years with a degree of shame. I certainly threw myself into the course, but I did so with an air of arrogance that was deeply misplaced. How my lecturers put up with me and my cocksure attitude is anyone's guess.

It was, nevertheless, during these years that the Holocaust started to feature more prominently in my life. Primo Levi's *If This is a Man* was included on the reading list of a module about the relationship between fiction and power. Gudrun Pausewang's *The Final Journey* was on the syllabus for a course about travel literature (not a great book, by any means, but it gave me pause for thought). In my French literature and culture class,

I discovered Georges Perec's *W, ou le souvenir d'enfance*, a book which has remained with me as a powerful evocation of Holocaust memory. Outside of my studies, the publication of Markus Zusak's *The Book Thief* further expanded my interest in the period.

But still, these disparate parts had not yet developed into a concrete interest in my mind. And indeed, I was equally captivated by other pieces of literature: Mikhail Bulgakov's monumental *The Master and Margarita* was one such book, *The Adventures of Huckleberry Finn* and *Seven Years in Tibet* were two others. As different as these texts are in basically every way, I suppose I can say that I was beginning to lean into literature with a political focus; texts that addressed historical periods, and particularly moments of historical trauma, allowed me to get my teeth into something I considered both important and topical. But as I said, I don't think I really understood this yet.

In the meantime, I was having a great time embracing undergraduate life, and while I knew that I wanted to pursue my studies at postgraduate level, I did not yet have a clear conception of what this might look like. But as I came to the end of my degree and started pondering over what I would do for a master's. I tried to look back at the literature I had read over the previous four years. I realized that it was literature of the Holocaust that had had the most profound effect. Looking back on it now, I can't help but think about Adorno's reservations about the inappropriateness of gaining some kind of aesthetic pleasure from reading about the Holocaust: Was it precisely that pleasure that drove me into the field of Holocaust Studies? Was I guilty of the kind of voyeurism that I mentioned earlier?

In trying to deconstruct my "attraction" to Holocaust literature, all I can say is that there was a definite "punch in the gut" reaction: Reading about the genocide was like an emotional wrecking ball for someone who had come from a position of freedom and privilege, and who knew relatively little of world politics. I may have spent my youth surrounded by references to the Second World War, but the Holocaust hit me like a ton of bricks. I don't know whether this would have been acceptable to Adorno but, truthfully, this emotional and instinctive reaction is what led me into the field.

In the end, I drew up a proposal that brought together three of the authors I had discovered over the course of my undergraduate degree: Georges Perec, Gudrun Pausewang and Marcus Zusak. My project sought to analyze the representation of childhood in literature of the Holocaust. I was offered a place at the University of Warwick and so began my postgraduate career.

I didn't have an easy time at Warwick. If my arrogance had been allowed to fester at Kent, the professors at Warwick were very quick to knock me off that pedestal. What do you mean you haven't read Anne Frank's diary? "You need to go back to school," as one professor put it (slightly harsh, but also fair). In the following months, I looked at works as diverse as Janina

Bauman's *Winter in the Morning*, Art Spiegelman's *Maus*, Judith Kerr's *When Hitler Stole Pink Rabbit*, and Roberto Benigni's controversial film *Life is Beautiful*. I also revisited *The Book Thief* and I finally got round to reading *The Boy in the Striped Pyjamas*. It was a transformative time. Rather than cruising along with my previous "I already know best" attitude, I was suddenly aware of the huge gaps in my knowledge of both literature and history.

This new-found awareness set the tone for my future studies. What I learned at Warwick was not only about what books I needed to read, but also how to become a functioning academic: One who was cognizant of what she does not know and aware of how much there still was to learn. Any illusions of grandeur were quickly shattered. If I were to enter this field, as a non-Jew from a working-class background, and as someone who could quote *Dad's Army* but hadn't read Anne Frank, it was going to take some serious work. It was here, then, at one of the UK's top universities, that I was first aware of what would become a constant presence in my life: imposter syndrome.

To be clear, I have never spoken to another academic who does not have some fear, on some level, that they are not good enough, and that, sooner or later, everyone else will find out that they simply don't belong. I'm sure they exist, but my experience has been that most academics operate with a degree of insecurity. Personally, I tend to wander through conferences, meetings, seminars, lectures, grant applications, article submissions (etc. etc.) wondering when (and who) will notice that I am really not very clever, and that I really don't know much about anything.

Having said that, I'm not entirely sure that imposter syndrome is always a negative thing. To me, acknowledging the gaps in knowledge is an essential part of the academic experience; it pushes you forward and keeps you humble. Nevertheless, as you might have already noticed, as I moved out of my (painfully cocky) undergraduate years and into my postgraduate career, I was plagued with insecurity.

What on Earth am I doing here? What can I possibly contribute to anyone's knowledge of the Holocaust? Where do I fit in? Am I good enough?

In all likelihood, these insecurities were amplified because of the somewhat obscure way I had fallen into the field: I simply hadn't been brought up reading and learning about the Holocaust. Come to think about it, I hadn't really grown up reading much at all, I certainly hadn't been raised on a diet of Goethe and Schiller. I hadn't even encountered much Shakespeare. So I suppose I was also an outsider to the academy in that sense, too. Coupled with the fact that I have no tangible connection to the Holocaust and have thus always felt like a bit of an intruder on the grief and trauma of others, the conditions were ripe for my own version of imposter syndrome to develop and sustain itself. I don't think I'll ever overcome it, but I'm happy to accept it as part of my personal and professional journey.

PhD and Beyond

Back to my academic progress. Following my year at Warwick, I completed my MA and moved back to Kent for my PhD. Having spent the previous year reading and writing about children's literature, I opted, with the support of my supervisor, to change direction completely. I had found myself increasingly interested by the figure of the perpetrator and wanted to pursue my thinking in this area. Despite the impression given by Hollywood, Nazis did not do what they did simply because they were "evil." These people were human beings, subject to the same psychological, social, political, and ethical forces as the rest of us. So how did they end up doing what they did? And how does the body of literature that deals with these figures encapsulate the complexities of their characterization as simultaneously human and monster? These were my opening (and very broad) research questions. My proposal was straightforwardly entitled "Perpetrators in Representations of the Holocaust."

As with my MA dissertation, I was more or less starting from scratch, but I had four years to familiarize myself with what I soon discovered was a surprisingly vast and diverse set of works. In the following years, I did all the things you are supposed to do as an impoverished PhD student. I attended conferences, wrote articles for publication (another *very* steep learning curve), and took on professional development opportunities. As soon as I had passed my viva, I submitted a book proposal. Et voilà! A year after I graduated, my first monograph was published.

I'm skipping over this time, but really I was very lucky in the opportunities that came my way, and I have always been very grateful to those who have helped and supported me. Nevertheless, I think it is worth noting that studying the Holocaust comes with its own specific challenges. It incites emotional responses alongside intellectual ones, and often these drives pull in different directions. Entering into this arena as an outsider can be daunting, especially for junior academics. This might be another reason I have tended to focus on the representation of perpetrators, a topic for which the emotional baggage seems somehow rather less weighty.

Perpetrators

I said at the beginning of this chapter that I think I gravitate towards the study of perpetrators because it feels less voyeuristic. It is certainly the case that literary and filmic accounts that focus primarily on the role of those responsible tend to circumvent some of the issues surrounding more victim-centered narratives, at least in that they do not (generally speaking) wallow in the pain and suffering of others. Instead, the experiences of victims are—again, generally speaking—depicted in a more peripheral way. For some, this is in itself problematic: It shifts emphasis from those who ought to be remembered and honored and provides space for the consideration of those responsible for mass murder. As I argued, such narratives often incorporate well-known mitigations and justifications and, in so doing, they attempt to expose the complex web of circumstances that led to genocide. By consequence, such texts decenter the idea of individual culpability, instead making recourse to collective and societal responsibility. This can be a challenging proposition when our basic instincts tell us that Nazis are evil, and that's the end of it. At its core, my doctoral project sought to consider the role of the reader in this process and unearth the various oscillations that the texts produce that serve to complicate processes of empathy and identification. This research formed the basis of my first monograph, *Perpetrators in Holocaust Narratives: Encountering the Nazi Beast*.[2]

As I moved on from my doctoral studies, I started to focus on the ways in which the Holocaust is used as a paradigm to discuss other instances of atrocity and genocide. This is something that those working in the field of Comparative Genocide have long since been working against. What is interesting for me, though, is that Nazis have become archetypes of culpability that are used in much the same way as the Holocaust is used as an archetype of genocide. Their codified image is discernible across Hollywood and in numerous cultural productions. How this codified version of Nazism is used (and abused) in representations of the British far right is the focus of my current research. I suppose, really, this brings me full circle: I am the product of a British upbringing, raised in the knowledge that my countrymen righteously opposed Hitler during the war. But where is Oswald Mosley in that formulation? Or Colin Jordan? Or Nick Griffin? You see, while the British far right has never enjoyed the kind of political success seen elsewhere in the West, associated groups have existed on the peripheries since the 1930s (and even slightly before). This fact rarely features in public discussions of Britishness. Better understanding the links between national identity, Nazism, and British fascism is thus the main goal of my current research. Being more cognizant of the complexities surrounding Britain's history with fascism seems to be of particular importance today, when a combination of factors (including Brexit, the refugee crisis, the Black Lives Matter movement, and the coronavirus pandemic) has created an environment that is ripe for the recurrence of nationalist discourses and politics of exclusion, and in which the likes of (far-right/racist/Islamophobic) politicians) Nigel Farage and Tommy Robinson have been able to thrive.

Conclusion

For me, perpetrator studies is as important as it is topical. If we can't find a way to understand how people can become radicalized to the point of committing genocide, then we have no hope of preventing such atrocities from happening again. To do this, we have to face some difficult truths. Without entering into the now-infamous Goldhagen debate, we must acknowledge that the specific socio-cultural context of Nazi Germany enabled (and, indeed, promoted) certain ideological and ethical perspectives that gradually led many millions of Germans down the path of genocide.[3] Individual motivations varied, of course, and there was often some form of cognitive dissonance purported by the perpetrators post war, though it goes without saying that these claims should be taken with a pinch of salt. The point is that the conditions were ripe for Hitler to take power—to be *legally and democratically voted in*—and that these same conditions allowed the Nazis to implement their policies with the assistance of many millions of Germans. The kicker of all of this is that it places us—and particularly people like me, non-Jews—in a difficult position: Would we (I), in similar circumstances, under similar pressures, in a similar climate, have acted the same? Or would we (I) have had the strength to resist? As a very proud liberal, I would like to believe that I would have known better, but how can I possibly guarantee it? Indeed, many Nazi perpetrators are reported to have been loving family men and "good people", except for the obvious fact that they spent their days torturing and murdering other human beings.

In her monumental work, *Citizen: An American Lyric*, Claudia Rankine talks about issues of race in contemporary American society.[4] On an encounter between a black woman and a white woman, she elaborates on the difference between the "self-self" and what she calls the "historical self": As self-selves, these two women meet as equal individuals with freedoms to define their relationship in any way they so choose, but the historical selves are always there haunting the frame. Because one is black and one is white, and because, not so long back, one would have been powerless and, in all likelihood, the other would have willingly wielded the power. I am not sure how applicable this concept is to other walks of life, but I do know that history has shown us that the "never again" dictum is an empty and hollow call. Societies and individuals are, particularly in times of strife, all too happy to look for a scapegoat, and to draw lines down ethnic, religious, or cultural lines.

I am not Jewish.

Where would I have sat in history? What would I have done? What part would I have played? What side would I have been on?

Being aware of all of these issues, and especially confronting the fact that (to use Rankine's formulation), my "historical self" may not have straightforwardly aligned with my "self-self," I can only do my best to work within such a challenging field in a way that is respectful to the victims and their families. I stake no claim on the history of the Holocaust, and I have no desire to dwell on the suffering of others. I wish only to understand the history of the period, to contemplate what literature and film of the Holocaust tells us both about that history and about our contemporary contexts, and to consider what the atrocity says about what it means to be human. I can only hope that, in my small contribution to the field, I am able to walk this emotional and ethical tightrope.

Notes

1 Laurence Binyon, "For the Fallen" (1914). Full poem available here: https://www.poetryfoundation.org/poems/57322/for-the-fallen
2 Joanne Pettitt, *Perpetrators in Holocaust Narratives: Encountering the Nazi Beast* (London: Palgrave, 2017).
3 Daniel J. Goldhagen, *Hitler's Willing Executioners: Ordinary Germans and the Holocaust* (New York: Alfred A. Knopf, 1996).
4 Claudia Rankine, *Citizen: an American Lyric* (London: Penguin, 2014).

11

Representing the Holocaust in Britain

Sue Vice

I count myself very fortunate to have had the opportunity and autonomy at the University of Sheffield's School of English, where I have taught contemporary literature and film for the past three decades, to follow my enduring interest in Holocaust representation. But it was only on responding to the present volume's exploration of individuals' engagement with Holocaust Studies that I started to reflect on the fact that my experience is one which follows, and has indeed been shaped by, broader cultural trajectories: those of British Holocaust awareness and the development of the event's representation in the UK and beyond.

As a teenage reader of Holocaust literature, I did not contemplate my own historical position as someone born less than two decades after the end of the Second World War. Rather, it struck me as a necessary subject in its own right, demanding the highest degree of attention and reflection. In my mind at the time, it was proof that my skepticism was justified about the humanist tenor of the literature I was studying at school. I remember feeling particularly indignant at Wordsworth's reference to the "still, sad music of humanity," believing that he should have put it far more stringently, and was drawn rather to the bleak but, I thought, clear-sighted visions set out in Joseph Conrad's *Heart of Darkness* (1899) and William Golding's *Lord of the Flies* (1954), the latter famously inspired by its author's witnessing wartime horrors.

I'm still not quite sure if this conviction arose from, or contributed to, my engagement with Holocaust history. Even more difficult to articulate is how it relates to my interest in Jewishness itself, and I sometimes regret it is this period of suffering and death, rather than other aspects of culture and creativity, that I've spent so long thinking about. At the same time as my friend and I, who ran the Film Society, were insisting on screening Alain Resnais' *Night and Fog* (1955), in the face of the school's reluctance, I was also learning Hebrew and preparing for my bat mitzvah. Both these facets of a Holocaust backdrop and Jewish-identified consciousness are present in refugee writing, and I've been fascinated to try to trace how a British Jewish hybridity is negotiated in the work of writers like Karen Gershon and Judith Kerr, who became (to amend the title of Charles Hannam's Kindertransport memoir) "almost Englishwomen." The detail of this "almost" quality is present in work even by those with generations of British-born forebears, and I've been lucky to have the chance to explore the intersection of Jewish with British culture and history in other contexts such as Jack Rosenthal's "golden age" television dramas, as well as more recent examples including Robert Popper's widely loved television sitcom *Friday Night Dinner* (2011–21). The latter, in particular, seems to me to reveal just what is enthralling but also frustrating about the representation of Jewish life in Britain, since its details are accepted yet hardly noticed. As its title suggests, although the Jewish identity of the Goodman family in *Friday Night Dinner* is by no means hidden, I'm not sure that mainstream viewers are fully aware of what it signifies.

These examples of British-Jewish art might seem quite distant from Holocaust Studies. However, part of the horror of the wartime era and its lessons for the present is the doubt cast on the security of assimilation, and I've been drawn to reading the poet Michael Rosen's writing to this effect. As a member of a British family with Polish roots, Rosen has voiced his outrage at the Leave outcome of the UK's 2016 referendum on EU membership. Like many other writers with Jewish heritage, who until 2016 had seen Britain as a "promised land" and permanent home, Rosen has invoked the Holocaust as a warning—not so much to suggest that the Jews themselves will again be the targets of populist nationalism, but to imply that not enough has been learnt from that history. For me, Rosen's most resonant expression of this conviction is the title of his 2017 collection *Listening to a Pogrom on the Radio Today*, which jarringly makes the Brexit "program" synonymous with racialized violence through an apparent slip of the tongue.[1] So, looking back at my engagement with Holocaust Studies since my schooldays in the 1970s, I'd like to feel that it arises from a combination of its intrinsic and present-day importance, cogently conveyed in the literary and visual texts I feel most at home studying.

Returning to my formative schooldays, there were relatively few cultural sources available at that period of the mid-1970s nor a real sense of Holocaust discourse. I remember a friend referring to my interest in what she called "the massacre," for want of an overarching term. Through a habit of unsystematically scouring second-hand bookshops, some of the texts I managed to acquire—including Lord Russell of Liverpool's account of war crimes trials, *The Scourge of the Swastika* (1954), and Gerhard Schönberner's photograph anthology, *The Yellow Star* (1960)—centered on atrocities in what now seems a sensationalist manner. Whether focusing on the perpetrators as Lord Russell does, paying unfortunate *ad feminam* attention to Irma Grese, or on the victims' suffering, as do Schönberner's photographs, there appears to be an emphasis on individual acts represented from the outside. This seems to me now like a substitute for exploring either conceptions of the structure of a mass genocidal movement or the internal worlds of those affected.

By the same unsystematic means, I came upon examples of Holocaust literature, including Elie Wiesel's testimony *Night* (1958), and Piotr Rawicz's novel *Blood from the Sky* (1961), which felt more illuminating. In my personal mythology, I'm convinced that I first read *Night* when I was fifteen—the same age as Eliezer, the memoir's protagonist, when he was deported to Auschwitz (although recent editions claim sixteen).[2] Our worlds could not have been further apart, in a way that added to my sense of the importance of Eliezer's experience. At the time, I read it as a transparently accessible ego-document. It was only gradually that I came to reflect on its extremely eclectic aesthetic form, which I now see draws on styles and genres that range from kabbalah, Torah, and the New Testament to French existentialism and even the *nouveau roman*.

It was because its literary construction can seem invisible in the face of the terrible events described that *Night* was assigned as the first text undergraduate students encounter in the still-extant course "Representing the Holocaust" which my late colleague Bryan Burns and I established at the University of Sheffield in the early 1990s. The element of co-teaching seems vital for this course, and I have been lucky to share it at different times with Eleanor Kent, Jess Meacham and Jenni Adams, while currently I teach with another wonderful colleague, Carmen Levick. This shows that there is not one monolithic way to approach this subject and that tutors' engagement can include different preferences and motivations. Although many other testimonies have since appeared, the gradual emergence of *Night*'s textual history,[3] the early date of its publication and Wiesel's personal renown, mean that it continues to feel of contemporary relevance.

I started my PhD soon after the publication of Thomas Keneally's *Schindler's Ark* in 1982, but my wish to write a doctorate on Holocaust literature did not come to fruition. Surprisingly from a twenty-first-century perspective, someone I consulted said there was nothing left to say on the subject. However, I wrote a speculative chapter on *Schindler's Ark* and discussed with my then-supervisor the unexpected use of metaphorical discourse in what was taken to be a non-fiction rather than a literary work. I was able to continue reflecting on the form and genre of Holocaust novels nearly two decades later at Sheffield, leading to my book *Holocaust Fiction* (2000). Approaching Holocaust literature in this way allows me, and the English literature students who take our undergraduate course, to use the familiar practice of literary analysis to show the inextricability of formal elements from the emotive and ethical impact of the extraordinary events depicted. Although critics sometimes state their reluctance to comment on style when a Holocaust experience is at stake, I feel it is a way of honoring such work by responding to it as a complex artefact that generates specific effects. Some striking examples in my mind include the deceptively everyday tone used to narrate atrocity in Tadeusz Borowski's eyewitness short stories, and the rather different effect of impressionistic lapses into contemporary-sounding dialogue in Heather Morris's bestselling novels.

In the event, I wrote my PhD on Malcolm Lowry's *Under the Volcano* (1947). Despite its apparent distance from any Holocaust-related concerns, as a late-modernist novel about the final day in the life of an alcoholic consul in Mexico, its setting in the late 1930s and conclusion with imagery suggesting a coming apocalypse, nonetheless reveal the war's influence. My approach to the novel was influenced by the Russian critic Mikhail Bakhtin, to whose theories I was introduced during my BA by my inspiring tutor Steve Watts. Bakhtin's work came to prominence in the 1980s after the translation into English of his studies of the novel and carnivalesque imagery in the writings of Dostoevsky and Rabelais and it has continued to influence my thoughts ever since.[4] It seems to me that Bakhtin's theories enable, in a way other approaches do not, awareness of the fusion of form with content that is foundational to Holocaust literature.

The value of Bakhtin's approach in my view lies in his emphasis on a series of linguistic techniques rooted in a text's social context, some of which he claims are definitional to language-use itself, others specific to novelistic discourse. These include strategies that have been invaluable to my attempts at detailed readings of Holocaust literature and underlie the central questions about representing that event. Such an approach has helped me try to make sense of the ways in which aesthetic form is enlisted in the near-impossible task of representing this disaster. In such a way, detecting the inevitable presence of two voices even in first-person writing can reveal the crucial distinction between the pre- and post-Holocaust self. This is evident in memoirs such as Wiesel's, but also in fiction, particularly where the earlier self is a child. I've been struck by this for instance in Jona Oberski's short stories *Childhood* (1978), where the implied adult narrator's understanding is far greater than that of the focalizer, a very young boy imprisoned in Bergen-Belsen, thus generating an ethically oriented irony.

I've found that Bakhtin's notion of dialogized polyphony, through which different "voices of the day" interact to produce meaning, likewise has a distinct significance in Holocaust-related texts.[5] For instance, the deformation of language under Nazism, its murderous use of euphemism, re-naming, and erasure, can be exposed most aptly in literary form, in a way that demands the reader's active engagement. This approach has helped my efforts to understand experimental literary perspectives on the Holocaust era. We are given linguistic hints at the hidden past of the Nazi doctor protagonist in Martin Amis's *Time's Arrow*, where the supposedly innocent narrator in a post-war USA claims, in a telling echo of the Auschwitz slogan, that "Work liberates," while every phrase in Geoffrey Hill's poem "September Song," from its opening address to a deported ten-year old child, "Undesirable you may have been, untouchable/ you were not," is full of double-voiced meaning.[6]

The early 2000s in Britain witnessed the inauguration of the Imperial War Museum's Holocaust Exhibition, reopened in a new form in 2021, and the institution of a national Holocaust Memorial Day, occurrences which have augmented public and students' awareness of the wartime events. Once more, I realize that what seemed to be my own self-determined journey in considering Holocaust representation can be understood only against this backdrop. In 2004, my book *Children Writing the Holocaust* appeared, in an effort to unite the documentary with the aesthetic by analysing children's-eye-view texts written for an adult readership. The effect of such a perspective, which allows for a defamiliarized view of calamity, depends on the fact that, at the turn of the millennium, the events thus represented—or, perhaps more accurately, the ways in which they were represented—had become horribly familiar. It seems to me that this paradoxical situation has had equally conflicting results, including efforts at aesthetic experimentation to try to show the event anew.

In the present, my Representing the Holocaust course at Sheffield possesses a syllabus that has evolved over the three decades of its existence, the changes reflecting such developments as the greater attention now paid to questions of gender difference, non-Jewish representations of the camps, extra-concentrationary experience (in the phrasing of Griselda Pollock and Max Silverman) such as the "Holocaust by bullets,"[7] postmemory, intergenerational recall, multidirectional memory, and decoloniality. These new cultural perspectives have allowed me to ponder the remarkable insights on racism by the African American perspective of W. E. B. Du Bois on his visit to the post-war ruins of the Warsaw Ghetto, while my view of Resnais' *Night and Fog* has been fundamentally altered through Pollock and Silverman's convincing argument that the film does not wilfully skim over the fate of the Jews, as it had seemed to me, but addresses the rather different subject of the Nazis' over-arching system of punishment and control.

For over twenty years, the course concluded with a talk by Sue Pearson, who arrived in Sheffield on a Kindertransport from Prague in 1939 aged eleven. Sue sadly died in 2020, but her memory of the Nazi invasion of her home city and account of her work on behalf of refugees in the present always transfixed students, who often quoted her in their assessments. Since its appearance in English translation in 1995, the final text students encounter is something of a polar opposite, Binjamin Wilkomirski's *Fragments*. This work featured initially as a rare example of a child's-eye-view testimony, and subsequently, after its notorious exposure as a false account in 1998, as a literary case-study. The extreme alterations in this text's genre and standing make it a cautionary yet enlightening instance in the history of Holocaust representation, in which matters of translation into English are also important. I have learnt a great deal about my own motivations and expectations of such literature by having lived through the saga of *Fragments*' changing fortunes. This process began with my emotional investment in what I believed was a child's perspective on terrible individual suffering, followed by my initial resistance to early reports of the doubts cast on its veracity, and eventual acceptance of the fact that it is entirely invented, but of continuing interest as a fictional construct. I've had to admit that it was the ahistorical image of a suffering child that initially impressed me so much about *Fragments*. However, what is so frightening about contemplating the Holocaust is not only bodily or personal depictions, but also those of the bureaucratic segregation and gradual dehumanization of entire groups of people, as conveyed for instance in Chaim Kaplan's much less widely read Warsaw Ghetto diary *Scroll of Agony* (1965). It's perhaps because it balances these imperatives of the personal and the communal that I've found myself over the past decade so enthralled by Claude Lanzmann's documentary *Shoah* (1985) and its construction.

Such a watershed event as the exposé of *Fragments* influenced my decision to start work on *Children Writing the Holocaust*, because of its distinctive narrative viewpoint, but also my later study *Textual Deceptions: False Memoirs and Literary Hoaxes in the Contemporary Era* (2014), in which I considered the phenomenon of "survivor envy" in the context of other such inventions. Yet perhaps even more significant than the dubious truth-value of Wilkomirski's memoir, and other rare examples such as Misha Defonseca's *Surviving with Wolves* (1997) and Bernard Holstein's *Stolen Soul* (2004), is the wariness with which even self-declared Holocaust fiction itself is received. Despite being myself a champion of fictive forms, and the intertwining of form and content that the novel, poetry, and drama can offer, as studies of postmodernism, poetry, magic realism, perpetrator and counterfactual fiction have demonstrated,[8] even I have sometimes balked at fiction's turn not to the exploitative but rather to the sentimental or commonplace where the Holocaust is concerned. Rather than dwelling on the existential horror of an atrocity that was so widespread and involved so many collaborators in very disparate social settings, novels of this kind center instead on personal redemption or didactically impart a lesson. It seems to me that these effects are made to appear significant precisely because of the context of extreme suffering or depravity that they end up transcending. This is the case in John Boyne's novel *The Boy in the Striped Pyjamas* (2006) as well as more recent examples such as Kristin Harmel's *The Sweetness of Forgetting* (2012) or Catherine Hokin's *The Fortunate Ones* (2020).

I feel that this novelistic tendency arises from a reductive view of the Manichean distinction between innocence and evil that the Holocaust can seem to establish. At the same time, I've found works of this kind to be worthy of attention in revealing shifting cultural and literary trends. Although some of the best-known works of Holocaust literature, by such writers as Paul Celan and Charlotte Delbo, are also examples of European high art, the bestseller status of these other works can give us an insight into contemporary conceptions of the role of Holocaust memory. It seems to me that for instance Boyne's work is really a general plea on the part of an Irish-born writer to dismantle barriers between communities, while the lesson implied by Kirstin Harmel's book, which unexpectedly mingles Holocaust postmemory with a story about an American bakery, is that of the United States' status as a savior nation.

In this context, I have most recently been drawn to literary texts which challenge such myths to reverse entrenched assumptions about Britain and the war. In the aftermath of Britain's decision to leave the EU, novels such as Ali Smith's *Autumn* (2016) and Linda Grant's *A Stranger City* (2019) imply that the UK and Germany have exchanged roles as these are conceived in the British national imaginary.[9] The UK's very conviction of its own moral exceptionalism is shown to have brought about a decline into populist nationalism, a paradox embodied in these novels by the figure of a Jewish refugee whose safe haven now seems perilous.

As this suggests, in my own reckoning with Brexit, I've recently been drawn to reading not only fiction that responds to the aftermath of the UK's departure from the EU, but also non-fiction accounts of Britons retrieving the German or Austrian citizenship stripped by the Nazis from earlier generations. I feel this arises from a mixture of autoethnographic and political impulses on my part. I don't have any recent European forebears, nor do I have any known family connection to the events of the Holocaust. My father's ancestors came to Britain from Poland and Lithuania in the mid-nineteenth century. The inherited myth passed down about my father's paternal great-grandfather, Moses Vice, is that he was a Russian drummer-boy in the Tsar's army, but found conditions to be so much better when taken prisoner by the British that he became convinced it was the country for him. I don't know if any of these details fit with the historical record, and one day would love to look into it properly. I do know that Moses was not Russian but Polish, and that his original surname, Parzenczewski, which I discovered only when we located his naturalization certificate, was also misremembered in the mythicizing process. This document, revealing that acquiring British citizenship cost £50 (an eye-watering £4,000 today), also shows that Moses was the son of Jacob and Leah Parzenczewski, who presumably remained behind in his birthplace of Ozorków, a town just a tram-ride away from Łódź. This proximity has a grim significance in relation to the town's Holocaust-era history, since those Jews who weren't killed locally were deported to the Łódź Ghetto or directly to the death-camp of Chełmno. When I visited Ozorków in the 1990s, I noticed Parzęczew Street listed on the town plan, and thought for a deluded moment that it was so called in honor of Moses—then quickly realized it was the name of a nearby village, from which his own name no doubt derived.

The reasons Moses chose to change his name to Vice from Parzenczewski are shrouded in mystery. My father thinks he adopted an appropriate-sounding name (Weiss?) when travelling through Germany on his journey to the UK, which was then perhaps phonetically misspelled by a British border official. Moses arrived in the port city of Hull, where he spent the rest of his life. He ran a pawn shop and was, according to his obituary, also a philanthropist. He worked alongside his future son-in-law Samuel Leiberman, my father's Lithuanian-born maternal grandfather, as revealed by newspaper reports about thefts from the shop. All Moses' descendants remained in Hull until my father, the first to go to university, left in the 1950s. He married my Scottish-born mother in London, and she converted to Judaism a decade later out of her own convictions.

This story of my father's family, with its mixture of apocryphal and attested elements, follows the template for many such tales of nineteenth-century Jewish migration to the UK. It also has deeper resonances. No doubt this heritage has prompted my interest in the Holocaust, although it conflicts with my sense that the events are of universal and not just Jewish significance. I continue to feel that Moses should be congratulated for his foresight in leaving Ozorków, as well as touched by the fact of his family's settling so firmly in Hull (Samuel Leiberman, presumably a Yiddish-speaking man of markedly non-British origin, seems nonetheless to have been a stalwart in the local cricket team).

However, as shown by my (fruitless) researches into reclaiming Polish or Lithuanian citizenship, much of this myth of British welcome and tolerance has been thrown into question by the departure from the EU, an event at least partly expressive of xenophobic insularity. No wonder creative writers have turned to Jewish history as a model for the potentially malign future of the Brexit era. As well as the figure of a Jewish refugee from Nazism in the novels by Ali Smith and Linda Grant whose British safe haven now seems perilous, I've been struck that even works set entirely during the war, such as Tom Stoppard's play *Leopoldstadt* (2019) and Rachel Seiffert's novel *A Boy in Winter* (2017), have been described by their authors as responses to the contemporary era.

All this has motivated my recent interest in the topic of fictional efforts to envisage the notion of an exchange of roles between Britain and Germany. It might seem that examples of counterfactual fiction which imagine British wartime surrender and Nazi occupation, such as Len Deighton's *SS-GB* (1978), C. J. Sansom's *Dominion* (2012). and C. J. Carey's *Widowland* (2021), embody this trend. However, like much of the fiction about the real-life occupation of the Channel Islands, it seems to me that such writing has a reassuring rather than a cautionary function. The fate of the Jews in Britain is constructed as peripheral or unimaginable in these cases. It seems that the notion of genocide being prepared for or carried out on British soil exceeds these visions that address instead the social and cultural effects of occupation. In *SS-GB*, for instance, I've been struck that there are more references to German food and the un-British "ersatz tea" that has accompanied the Nazi occupation than to racial policies, while *Dominion* and *Widowland* each ends with an act of resistance that has equally little to do with the fate of the Jews. These fictional patterns unwittingly register the historical truth, about which I can only agree with Hannah Holtschneider's stark observation that the British war effort was directed at "the protection of the nation and the defeat of fascism on the continent" and not "the prevention of the genocide of Jews in Europe."[10] Yet these examples reveal writers' unwillingness to imagine a Britain in which racist anti-Jewish policies are instituted as well as their marginality to British myths of the war.

I've found the most striking literary attempt actually to envisage a British genocide in Howard Jacobson's 2014 *J: A Novel*, which definitely deserves a much wider readership. Jacobson's renown as a chronicler of British-Jewish life, in his earlier novels *Kalooki Nights* (2006) and *The Finkler Question* (2010), might make *J*'s genre of speculative fiction seem at variance with his usual wry realism. I've been startled and impressed to find that *J* depicts the aftermath of an atrocity enacted against a nameless group in an equally unnamed location, yet this effort at suppression simply highlights that the novel's setting is that of the UK after "a second holocaust" of the Jews.[11] The crime itself is referred to, with a mixture of euphemism and denial, as 'WHAT HAPPENED, IF IT HAPPENED', alongside such blunt hints as a character's musing that the absence of tourists in the nation's capital city was only to be expected, since "Who wanted a holiday in the environs of Babi Yar?"[12] I've been struck by the fact that Jacobson's work appeared two years before the referendum took place, yet gives a fictional version of the discourses of parochialism and inhospitability that generated its Leave outcome, giving it kinship to works by Franz Kafka or Albert Camus. Like these writers' novels, Jacobson's is rooted in the historical record, as shown by its allusions to antisemitic outrages in medieval England as well as Nazi Germany,[13] but transcends it through arranging such detail symbolically rather than chronologically.

It's been a revelation that the imagining of a genocidal or fascist society is unusual in a British context, and allies *J* with such earlier works about the specter of a home-grown Nazism as Storm Jameson's 1936 futuristic *The Second Year*, in which a prime minister uncannily named Hillier has taken dictatorial power in Britain at the head of the National State Party. Yet even Jameson's novel does not, despite its depiction of a murderous assault on a Jewish man, make central to this vision the fate of the Jews—or at least, as they are in *J*, an unnamed minority that their history resembles. I've found it revealing to read that Jacobson himself has declared *J* to be a British version of Philip Roth's *The Plot Against America* (2004) in showing the Jewish fate to be paradigmatic of a fascist takeover of democracy.[14] These sobering implications arise from the Brexit-related blow to British self-conceptions that I and many others struggle with.

I have long imagined the project of compiling a history of British Holocaust representation, which would highlight the unexpected variety and vibrancy of its expression as well as its necessary entwinement with local preoccupations. However, it is revealing that the present chapter has not been a template for that history. Rather, the kinds of significant cultural event in Holocaust representation from my British-located perspective are a forceful counter to any post-2016 narrowness in being extremely eclectic and transnational. The influence of, for instance, *Night*, *Schindler's Ark*, *Fragments,* and *The Tattooist of Auschwitz* relies on translation into English or publication in other anglophone contexts. While some of the milestones in this trajectory come from a British- or Irish-identified source, they often consist of works by refugee authors with hybrid backgrounds, or, in the case of such writers as Amis, Boyne, and Hill, have a global literary influence. I'd like to agree with Joseph Finlay's recent argument that the dual strands of Holocaust and anti-racist action in Britain arise from different contexts that it is nonetheless possible to bridge. Only Holocaust education can help avoid my fear that the wartime genocide was not, in the words of Jean Cayrol which conclude *Night and Fog* (1955), something that "happened only once, in a certain time and a certain place."

Notes

1 Michael Rosen, *Listening to a Pogrom on the Radio* (Ripon: Smokestack, 2017).

2 Elie Wiesel, *Night*, trans. Marion Wiesel (London: Penguin, 2006).

3 Naomi Seidman, "Elie Wiesel and the Scandal of Jewish Rage," *Jewish Social Studies* 3, no. 1 (1996): 1–19.

4 Mikhail Bakhtin, *The Dialogic Imagination*, trans. Caryl Emerson and Michael Holquist, (Austin: University of Texas Press, 1982).

5 Ibid., 276–7.

6 Martin Amis, *Time's Arrow* (Harmondsworth: Penguin 1991), 57.

7 Griselda Pollock and Max Silverman, eds, *Concentrationary Memories: Totalitarian Terror and Cultural Resistance* (London: Bloomsbury 2014).

8 Robert Eaglestone, *The Holocaust and the Postmodern* (Oxford: Oxford University Press, 2004), Jenni Adams, *Magic Realism in Holocaust Literature: Troping the Traumatic Real* (London: Palgrave, 2011), Joanne Pettitt,

Perpetrators in Holocaust Narratives: Encountering the Nazi Beast (London: Palgrave, 2017), Antony Rowland, *Holocaust Poetry: Awkward Poetics in the Work of Sylvia Plath, Geoffrey Hill, Tony Harrison and Ted Hughes* (Edinburgh: Edinburgh University Press, 2005), Glyn Morgan, *Imagining the Unimaginable: Speculative Fiction and the Holocaust* (London: Bloomsbury, 2020).

9 Johannes Wally, "The Return of Political Fiction?," *AAA: Arbeiten Aus Anglistik und Amerikanistik* 43 (1): 63–86, 81.

10 Hannah Holtschneider, "Holocaust Representation in the Imperial War Museum, 2000–2020," in Tom Lawson and Andy Pearce, eds., *The Palgrave Handbook of Britain and the Holocaust* (London: Palgrave, 2020), 389.

11 David Brauner, *Howard Jacobson* (Manchester: Manchester University Press, 2020), 178.

12 Howard Jacobson, *J: A Novel* (London: Jonathan Cape, 2014).

13 Brauner, *Howard Jacobson*, 179.

14 Quoted in ibid., 173.

PART THREE

Israel

12

Following in the Footsteps of Claude Vigée: From the Holocaust Trauma to a New Science of Judaism

Thierry Alcoloumbre

As a general rule, academics avoid including personal considerations in the presentation of their research. Speaking about oneself seems like a lack of modesty and akin to a subjective or "impressionistic" detour that fits in poorly with scientific objectivity. Nevertheless, autobiographical discourse remains a legitimate way of retracing an intellectual itinerary, to signal the experiences and the encounters that raised questions or suggested the means to answer them. This is particularly true for the Shoah not only because many of us, Jews, or non-Jews, were personally affected by the catastrophe but also because it shook the very notion of the human and with it the validity of the foundations of scientific activity. Personal examination here does not thwart science, but on the contrary strengthens it. In the following paragraphs, I will explore how the study of the poet Claude Vigée (1921–2021) led me to broaden my research on the Shoah and his influence on the intellectual movements that marked French Judaism after the Second World War.

My Encounter with Claude Vigée and the Question of the Shoah

More than twenty years ago, when I participated in a conference dedicated to the poet Claude Vigée, I did not imagine that my contribution would open up a new period in my career as a researcher and would lead me to the literature of the Shoah—a subject that I had always avoided hitherto, consciously or not.

My paper sought to answer a very precise question without any apparent connection to the European catastrophe. How is it possible for a Jewish poet, and for a French Jewish poet in particular, to write in his native language although he chose to live in Israel? From the time of Ovid to the present day, an exiled poet remains rooted in the land and people of his origins. Language is the living link that perpetuates his tie to them and renders possible the dream of return. But for the Jewish poet who has emigrated to Israel, origins and exile are paradoxically inverted. He grew up in a land of exile and it is a language of exile that shapes the depths of his identity. His arrival in Israel is a redemption, the return to the original identity of his people. But this redemption is *at the same time* an alienation because it separates him irretrievably from the geographical and cultural milieu from which he came. Writing for him is a paradoxical act, the expression of an insurmountable contradiction. How then is this act possible?

In reading Vigée, I discovered that he was not looking to eliminate this contradiction but that he was writing *within and despite it*. Writing is not really "possible," because it is not possible to be both an exiled Jewish poet and a Hebrew-Israeli poet. But at the same time, it is an inevitable attempt, because it corresponds to an existential choice that Vigée defined as the choice between life and death. One of Vigée's first books, *La lune d'hiver*[1] (*The Moon of Winter*), shows how this choice was first formulated during the Shoah: At a time when the Vichy regime was progressively placing Jews outside the law and forbidding Jews to publish poems, Vigée affirmed his desire to survive and to create in spite of everything. This desire led him to decide to emigrate to the United States in 1943 and then to Israel in 1960. Poetic writing is the affirmation against the Shoah, of Jewish existence as a metaphorical waterway crossing many lands and the Jewish poet as the ferryman. Research on Vigée and the Shoah thus helps to understand the stakes involved in his poetry, and his message for his contemporaries and for generations to come.

In *The Moon of Winter*, poetic expression, like Jewish life in general, is understood as an act of resistance. Vigée defines this act as the result of a choice, the choice of "life" over "death." The imperative of life has its source in the verse in Deuteronomy (30:19) where Moses says to Israel: "I have placed before you life and death, a blessing and a curse: choose life so that you are your descendants can live." During the Shoah this life was understood primarily as the physical and spiritual survival of the Jewish people, the affirmation of hope against the inevitability of death. It is in relation to this imperative that the young Claude Strauss decided henceforth to call himself "Claude Vigée," Vigée could be read as "Vie-j'ai" (which in French means "I have life"). Later the significance of the "choice of life" widened to encompass a much broader ethical and metaphysical perspective. Life is "our destiny as the living," and it is by realizing "our destiny as the living . . . that one obeys the will of God, not otherwise."[2] The love and respect of life for oneself and for others becomes a moral and aesthetic imperative that should direct one's personal life as well as one's artistic and literary creation. By contrast, Vigée tells us, "everything that deals with annihilation must be careful avoided and fled from. Most of all one must not worship it, be won over by nostalgia for death."[3] In this spirit, Vigée condemns the fascination for death that one encounters too often in Western literature.[4]

Thus through the experience of the Shoah and the Resistance, the poetic experience expresses itself as the adhesion to the universal life present at the heart of all human beings and of all of creation. The fight between Jacob and the Angel, recounted in the book of Genesis (ch. 22) is understood by Jewish tradition as a fight against the angel of death. For Vigée, this fight runs through all of human history. It opposes the Jews, the poet, and finally all men to all the forces opposed to their existence that try to destroy them. And it is for this reason that Vigée can write: "Jacob and poetry have the same destiny. Being a Jew or a poet, is one and the same thing."[5]

Vigée made me discover an intimate link between the experience of the Shoah and an ethical stand towards life in general and toward poetic creation in particular. This discovery inspired my own research and my reflection on the survival of the Jewish people. In my personal journey, I often encountered antisemitism; I witnessed the permanence of it in France, and of its resurgence under the cover of anti-Zionism. My student years in Paris were marked by the attacks perpetrated against the synagogue on Copernic Street in 1980, and against the Jewish restaurant on Rosier Street in 1982. I remember an article in the newspaper *Le Monde* comparing Rosier Street with a "street in Beirut," which suggested that the massacred Jews had been punished deservedly for the crimes that Israel (according to this same newspaper) was committing in Lebanon. *Le Monde* also held the opinion that "Jesus was a Palestinian": Thus, the hate against the Jewish state was placed in continuation with Christian antisemitism. More recently, Islamist terrorism hit my hometown of Toulouse (the shooting at the Otzar haThora High School), as well as Paris (the murders of Ilan Halimi in 2006 and Sarah Halimi in 2017).

Faced with these dangers, with the new menaces that weigh on the Jewish people and on the state of Israel, an oeuvre like that of Claude Vigée offered me two teachings inspired by Judaism and the Shoah. On the one hand there is the choice of "life" and hope, as noted above; and on the other, faith in the brother/sisterhood of man. Faithful to these teachings, I published a number of articles on Claude Vigée himself between 2013 and 2021. I showed the particular position occupied by Vigée in contemporary poetry in relation to the Shoah[6]; I also showed how his "choice of life" led him to criticize the fascination for death so often expressed in Western literature (Mallarmé, Kafka, T. S. Eliot . . .) and how Vigée feels a greater affinity for the writers of "immanence" like Paul Claudel or Albert Camus[7]; the memory of the Shoah and the anxiety before death remain ever present in his oeuvre, but he fights to arrive at the celebration of life.[8] Finally, I showed how Vigée conceives of Hebrew identity as a universal vocation as well as a fraternal dialogue with all of humanity.[9]

From Vigée to the "Paris School of Jewish Thought"

My research about Vigée led me to reconsider an entire facet of the postwar French-Jewish intellectual production as it was developed after the Second World War, culminating in the 1970s and 80s. After 1945, a number of French-Jewish intellectuals, who retrospectively have come to be known as the "Paris School of Jewish Thought,"[10] dedicated themselves to the reconstruction of Judaism in Europe. This group, which included, among others, Emmanuel Lévinas, André Neher, Léon Askenazi ("Manitou"), and Eliane Amado Lévy-Valensi, was united by a common purpose: To bring the core Jewish texts (Bible, Talmud, kabbalah) into dialogue with contemporary thought in the fields of philosophy, sociology, psychoanalysis, and history, with the aim of producing an original synthesis. Most of them (Levinas excepted) emigrated to Israel, participating in the great wave of the French Aliyah that occurred at the time of the Six-Day War. They wrote and taught from Israel and within Israel, in French and in Hebrew. All of them had a great influence on my intellectual and personal journey. They helped me to see my Jewish identity as belonging to the present time and gave me confidence in our future. As a student, I was particularly excited by the reading of Levinas' *Talmudic Readings* , of Neher's *Quality of Prophecy,* and by the teaching of Leon Askenazy at *Rashi Center*. When in Jerusalem in 1984, I met Eliane Amado Lévy-Valensi, who gave me her (then) recent book about Freud and Moses.

The Holocaust had a decisive impact on these four thinkers and on the way they found their calling. It shook their faith in the model of integration that had hitherto been offered to French Jews and pushed them to rediscover a Jewish identity that they reimagined as an aspect of human universality. To take them each in turn:

- In 1940, the shadow of the Vichy regime's antisemitic laws fell on a twenty-six-year-old André Neher, then a German teacher in Brive-la-Gaillarde in southwestern France. Dismissed from his position, he immersed himself in the Bible, writing and illustrating several Jewish texts, including a Passover Haggadah, with his father and his

- brother. When the war ended, he burned the dissertation he had begun on Heine and devoted himself to Biblical studies, in 1947 defending a thesis on the Book of Amos.
- During the same period, Emmanuel Levinas was a prisoner in Germany. Luckily his wife and children escaped the claws of the Nazis thanks to the help of friends, but most of the family members that remained in Lithuania were massacred. The experience of this barbarity contributed to his questioning of the model of classical rational philosophy and to the renewing of ethical reflections from Talmudic texts.[11]
- Eliane Amado Lévy-Valensi who lived in the southeastern region of France, also survived, but her mother was arrested by the French militia and deported to Auschwitz. After the war, Amado became a brilliant philosopher and psychoanalyst. All of her work is shaped by the murder of her mother.[12]
- And finally, for Léon Askenazi, the French-educated son of a family of rabbis and kabbalists, Vichy's antisemitic persecution revealed "a fissure in our relationship with French identity."[13]

It was Neher whose writings and teachings began the rediscovery of not only the Bible and Judaism, but of the Hebrew language and literature. In 1955, a chair of Hebrew at the University of Strasbourg was created for him. The university was known as a place of dialogue. One of Neher's colleagues there was the philosopher Paul Ricœur (1913–2005), and the two men would later collaborate. Neher's disciples, Benjamin Gross and Théo Dreyfus, for their part, became educators. In Strasbourg, with the encouragement of the High Rabbi Deutsch, Gross founded Aquiba, a Jewish lycée (high school), and ran it until 1967. Meanwhile, in Paris, in 1947, Dreyfus similarly became director of the Lycée Maïmonide (Maimonides).

In Orsay, near Paris, the educator and resister Robert Gamzon (1905–61) founded the Gilbert Bloch School with the goal of reconstituting the spiritual leadership of the Jewish people. When Gamzon asked Léon Askenazi to join him, the latter accepted. Nicknamed "Manitou" (a term of Native American derivation; it approximates to "Spirit") after the name of his totem[14] in the Jewish scout troop, Askenazi became the school's deputy director in 1947, then director in 1951. It may be said that French Judaism had three leading lights at this point: Neher in Strasbourg, Lévinas in Paris, and Askenazi in Orsay. Bonds of friendship linked the three men, and Manitou sometimes referred to Neher as "our teacher" ("*notre maître*")[15].

The journey of these four thinkers is analogous to that of Vigée. All of them made the choice of life against death, according to the meaning Vigée gave it,[16] and it is not by accident that André Neher, before even having known Vigée, consecrated a teaching to the theme of the struggle against the

Angel. It is precisely on the occasion of a lecture given by Neher on this theme that the philosopher and the poet met and that a friendship between them was formed. Benjamin Gross, the disciple of André Neher, gave his autobiography the title *To Choose Life*.[17] Levinas constructs his ethics on the fifth commandment (thou shall not kill). And Amado tries to go beyond the tragic dimension of Freudian psychoanalysis towards the optimistic idea of the transmission of identity between fathers and sons.

Beyond their respective differences, the most salient point of commonality between these four thinkers is their engagement in the service of Jewish culture and Jewish education. This engagement is characterized by a keen feeling of love for the Jewish people and their tradition, a concern for their continuation, and the passionate study of the great Jewish texts from both a scientific and existential perspective. This mindset does not contradict the "science of Judaism" *(Wissenschaft des Judentums)*, represented at the same time in France by the formidable scholar Georges Vajda (1908–81).[18] But it also led to some misunderstandings and tensions. Whereas the science of Judaism sought first and foremost facts and influences, the "Paris school" gave priority to philosophical reflections in search of meaning. The favorable eye with which these thinkers examined Jewish sources was often suspected, incorrectly, of having apologetic goals by representatives of the positivistic science. But in fact, for these thinkers it was less a matter of defending Judaism at any cost than of defending the idea of the contemporary meaning of Judaism for our generation. Their philosophical and scientific work is guided by an ethical consideration.

As in the case of Claude Vigée, my study of these four thinkers was not *a priori* linked to the question of the Shoah, but rather to my interest in Jewish thought. During my student years, André Neher was known for his research on Biblical prophecy, and Levinas for his philosophical reading of the Talmud. I had also followed the lectures of Léon Askénazi in Paris and had encountered Eliane Amado Lévy-Valensi in Jerusalem. But their teaching acquired a new significance for me in the last twenty years, during which we have seen coterminously a resurgence of antisemitism, as described above, and increasing scrutiny of the Jewish people in Western thought and culture.

This period was especially marked by the publication of two books which had a considerable impact in the Jewish and non-Jewish world. The first was the 2001 work by archeologists Israel Finkelstein and Neil Asher Silberman, *The Bible Unearthed: Archaeology's New Vision of Ancient Israel and the Origin of Its Sacred Texts*. In this book, the authors contest the reliability of the Biblical stories concerning the origins of Israel (the exodus from Egypt, the conquest of Canaan by Joshua, the Kingdoms of David and Solomon.) The second is the book by Shlomo Sand—written first in Hebrew and published in English in 2009—under the title *The Invention of the Jewish People*. Sand's principal thesis was that the Jews do not descend from the ancient Israelites, but are peoples who converted to Judaism, and that the idea of a Jewish "people" that is the heir to the "promised land," is a myth created by modern nationalism.

Finkelstein and Sand are respected academics: Whether accepted or not, their theses are legitimate to the extent that they obey the rules of scientific research and are open to debate. The problem is the ideological and dogmatic use that the antisemites and anti-Zionists have made of them. If the Jewish people and their belonging to the land of Israel are myths, what history can a Jew turn to? What legitimacy can the Jewish state have in the face of Palestinian claims? Is Jewish identity not called to dissolve itself in a multiplicity of arbitrary representations, none of which is authoritative? It should be noted that Shlomo Sand's thesis connects indirectly with the thesis of Nazi theoreticians, taken up later by the Palestinians, according to which the Jews are not Semites and that the Jews who colonized Palestine are not the descendants of Judah. Taken to the extreme, one could conclude that the Jews have no other choice but assimilation to the Christian world or massacre by the Palestinians.

It is in this context that the oeuvre of the Jewish thinkers I have cited took on such importance for me. Their ethical positioning, taken up by Claude Vigée, was reinforced by the Shoah: It consists in affirming a love for the Jewish people, faithfulness to its tradition, and a love of science. Philosophy and science can be used to critically examine Judaism but they must also be submitted to critical examination. In this spirit I have published studies on Beno Gross and on Eliane Amado Lévy-Valensi[19] and in 2017 I tried to define what might be the goal we could give to comparative literature in universities.[20] My recent research, although not dedicated to the Shoah, remains inspired by its teachings; following André Neher, I became interested in the thought of the Maharal[21] in particular. André Neher found in this thinker existential and moral principles that can help us to live as Jews after the Shoah and to face the challenges and dangers of modernity.[22]

Conclusion

Thus, the study of the Shoah and the Resistance has played a revelatory role for me. It has allowed me to clarify, starting with Claude Vigée, the itinerary of postwar Jewish thinkers. It has also allowed me to think about our own itinerary, as contemporaries of these thinkers or twenty-first-century successors. The famous question asked by Theodor Adorno about the possibility of poetry after the Shoah could also have been asked about the possibility of the humanities after the Shoah. In both cases, the answer is positive. But also in both cases, this affirmation passes through a renewal. Neither poetry nor science can be practiced after the Shoah as they had been before. Certainly, scientific objectivity remains the rule, but this objectivity cannot be cut off from the educational and existential goals from which it draws its justification and meaning. In this perspective I find an echo of the teaching of the French humanist François Rabelais, who wrote "Science without a conscience is but the ruin of the soul."[23]

Notes

1 Claude Vigée, *La lune d'hiver* (Paris, Flammarion, 1970, Honoré Champion, 2002).
2 Claude Vigée, *Le fin murmure de la lumière* (Sion : Parole et Silence, 2009), 188.
3 Claude Vigée, *L'Extase et l'Errance* (Paris : Grasset, 1982), 108.
4 See namely *Les Artistes de la Faim* (Paris : Calmann-Lévy, 1960).
5 "Dans le Défilé", in *Délivrance du Souffle* (Paris : Flammarion, 1977), 38.
6 "Situation de Claude Vigée" ["The Situation of Claude Vigée"], *Pardès*, n.56/2 (2015), 51–69 ; "Holocaust, Exile, and Redemption: Variations of Style in Claude Vigée's *Winter Moon*", *Ma'aseh Sippur (No. 4) Studies in Jewish Narrative*, Bar-Ilan University Press (2018), 397–415.
7 "Un Hébreu de passage : note sur l'hébraïsme de Claude Vigée" ["A Hebrew passer by. Some remarks about Hebraism in Claude Vigee"] *Perspectives de Jérusalem* 22 (2015): 39–68.
8 "Kafka dans l'œuvre de Claude Vigée" ["Kafka according to Claude Vigee"], *Judaica: Beitraege zum Verstehen des Judentums* 3 (2015), 113–30.
9 "La condition humaine dans La Lune d'hiver" ["The Human Condition in Claude Vigée's *La Lune d'hiver*"], *Peut-être. Revue poétique et philosophique* (Association des Amis de Claude Vigée) 7 (2015) : 79–87. "Paris et Jérusalem dans la pensée de Claude Vigée" ["Paris and Jerusalem. According to French Israeli Poet Claude Vigée"], *Perspectives de Jérusalem*, 23 (2016) : 163–80.
10 See Shmuel Trigano, "Qu'est-ce que l'École juive de Paris ?", *Pardès* 23 (1997) : 27–41.
11 See namely E. Levinas, "The Name of the Dog, or Natural Rights" in *Difficult Freedom: Essays on Judaism*, trans. Sean Hand (London: Athlone Pres 1990), 151-3: Bobby the dog was "the last kantian in Nazi Germany" (153).
12 See Sandrine Szwarc, *Eliane Amado Lévy-Valensi. Itinéraires* (Paris : Hermann, 2019), chapter 2, 61–83.
13 Koginsky, Michel (ed.), *Un hébreu d'origine juive: hommage au Rav Yehouda Léon Askénazi Manitou*, (Jérusalem : Ormaya, 5758-1998), 26.
14 In the French Scout movement, the "totem" is the name of an animal or a symbol attributed to members according to their physical or moral characteristics.
15 Askénazi, Léon, *La Parole et l'écrit. II. Penser la vie juive aujourd'hui*, ed. Marcel Goldmann (Paris : Albin Michel, collection *Présences du judaïsme*, 2005), 46.

16 See A. Neher, *They Made Their Souls Anew*, trans. David Maisel (Albany, NY: State University of New York Press, 1990).

17 Benjamin Gross, *Choisir la vie. Le judaïsme à l'épreuve du monde* (Paris: Editions de l'éclat, 2015).

18 Neher and Askenazi had Jacob Gordon as their teacher, who was trained in the science of Judaism. See Jacob Gordin, *Écrits : Le renouveau de la pensée juive en France*, ed. Marcel Goldmann (Paris, Albin Michel, collection *Présences du Judaïsme*, 1995).

19 "Benjamin Gross et les études maharaliennes" ["Benjamin Gross and Maharal Studies"], *Perspectives de Jérusalem* 23 (2016) : 143–61. "From the secrets of the Soul to the secrets of Kabbalah: The Contribution of Eliane Amado Levy-Valensi to psychoanalysic theory" (Hebrew; *Da'at*, Bar-Ilan university, in progress).

20 "La pensée juive française: chance de renouveau pour l'université israélienne ? L'exemple de la littérature comparée" ["how French Jewish Thought may contribute to the renewal of Academy in Israel. Comparative Literature as an example"], *Pardès* 59 (2017): 139–51.

21 The Maharal of Prague (Rabbi Yehuda ben Betzalel Loewe, 1512–1609) was one the most important Jewish thinkers of the Renaissance.

22 "Ethique et laïcité d'après le Maharal de Prague" ["Ethics and Secularism according to the Maharal of Prague"], *Pardès* 62 (2019): 107–26.

23 *Pantagruel*, ch. 8.

13

Where Did Those People Go?

Karen Alkalay-Gut

Introduction

It was the portrait in my in-laws' dining room that began my journey back—a somewhat comical rotund man smoking a cigar, that seemed to be placed there as a warning of the dangers of overindulgence. He was known in the family as Gromek, from a grotesque character in a Danny Kaye comedy called *Knock on Wood*, and placed opposite the dining-room table in order to remind us not to eat too much. But this complacent man seemed to command a deeper presence and demanded more than a comic response. My mother-in-law, who had completed her doctorate in Berlin just before the war and was known to have extensively experienced night-life, must have known much more about this character, but dismissed the subject and went on to talk about other issues, other paintings. I would have to ask elsewhere.

There were books about the painter, Shalom Sebba,[1] and there Kurt Gerron's name was mentioned as belonging to this figure. Not only was Gerron a well-known German-Jewish actor, the singer who opened Berthold Brecht's *Threepenny Opera* with "Mack the Knife" and co-star of Marlene Dietrich and Emil Jannings in *The Blue Angel*, but he was also a prolific actor and director who appeared in ninety-seven films, although most of these were now unavailable including his last, *Hitler Builds A City For the Jews*.

How had he met his demise in Auschwitz after filming a propaganda "documentary" on Theresienstadt for the Nazis? So much was known and yet so much obliterated, even scenes cut from popular film. Obsessively I researched his past, and each missing detail struck me slowly as something familiar, something vaguely to do with my own history. But I could not find the connection.

Why was I so interested in a single person when the emphasis has always been in the popular discussion on the enormity of the numbers? Yet in 2019 when I was awarded the Rubinlicht Award for a publication in Yiddish, I didn't give the speech that had been expected of me, about the necessity of revival of that language. Instead I translated a poem of the unknown initiator of the Leyb Rubinlicht prize:

SNOW IN AUSCHWITZ

That night a downy snow fell
And covered the site with a veil of white
Through the barred barrack windows.
We stare at its whiteness by the glare of the fire.

The Auschwitz chimneys spew out their flames
To faraway heavens in the quiet of night
The red and snow-white colors mingle together
And shimmer in the pastoral symphonic cover.

See how the symphony from that wintery night,
When flames from the crematoria united
With heaven-sent white snowy glory—
Distracted the king of demons from augmenting the agony.[2]

It was the first and only poem the distinguished audience had ever heard by Leyb Rubinlicht, whose works are in public domain, and for some the only poem encountered about the individual experience of watching a crematorium in operation.

I know it is necessary to discover much more about Leyb Rubinlicht, a man who left a fund for Yiddish poetry because he had no heirs and apparently hoped that someone, somewhere, would try to make some kind of contact with the heritage in his poetry. His was a voice that cried out to be heard sometime in the future.

At that point, it began to occur to me that my research into the history of Kurt Gerron's portrait and that translation of Leyb Rubinlicht's poem was far more than curiosity or whim. There was something of myself buried there—the history of my own relatives in the Holocaust, a history of my own that had been erased.

The jovial face masked a terrifying past. I watched Gerron's films that had not been destroyed and most of them featured a Jewish "type"; either wicked, or greedy, or a fool. Gerron was the obese magician and pimp of *The Blue Angel*, the crooked banker, the swindling lawyer. Why were films like these available when the equally classic films of his had cut him out? Why had his name been besmirched in the only film publicly available at festivals?

Prisoner of Paradise (2002), a film about Gerron's alleged pact with the devil, suggested that the movie he made for the Nazis in 1944 was to him a trade, a piece of propaganda to which he contributed in exchange for his own life. I watched it again and again, and each time he seemed a more and more pathetic character—I was almost tempted to follow the film's argument and blame Gerron for agreeing to be forced into making it, even though he did not escape a shameful destruction in Auschwitz. That was when I recognized the feeling—the guilt my parents must have felt for attempting to survive. The blame that was attributed to Gerron may have been shared by them, too.

Although my father kept silent, my mother would occasionally refer to fragments of terrible events as if I knew the entire story of her life, and all her family. Sometimes my father's sisters, who spent the war years in Stutthof concentration camp, would supply miniature anecdotes, often with no chronological context. Much of what they told me had been forgotten but details began to emerge in my memory—details that would be fleshed out in unexpected moments.

I began to search libraries and archives for verification of these details. Sometimes the stories led to dead ends but sometimes they could be traced more fully, in all their complexity and horror. In one case, my Aunt Chasia mentioned one officer at Stutthof who would choose one woman from the lineup he'd order in the middle of the night, and implied that she would be beaten and raped. Chasia referred to him as Max. Years after her death, I discovered he was Max Pauly, and was in charge of the 5,150 prisoners at that camp.[3] He had been executed for war crimes, but not for the rapes and murders he committed at Stuthoff. The English translation of the trials notes: "None of the commandants of the Stutthof camp stood before a Polish court. SS-Sturmbannführer Max Pauły, from September 1942 commandant of KL Neuengamme, was tried together with other members of the staff of this camp in Hamburg ... Pauly, sentenced to death for the crimes committed in KL Neuengamme, was executed on October 6, 1946."[4] I quote this sentence in Chasia's memory, in the hope that this information that made her shudder at the recollection of his name never reached her.

The conflation of the fate of my family with facts and erasures in Gerron's life and death drew me ever deeper into the question of facts—what was not available to survivors? What has since been discovered and written down? What has been distorted by memory or witnesses or censors or even a computer glitch? What can be recovered? I found myself writing poems about the images from my family's past as they emerged. Some of them came in Yiddish, a language in which I had first heard the stories of my mother and her family, a language in which I had experienced encounters with refugees my parents were obsessed with rescuing, a language in which I could imagine my lost relatives speaking. I translated them into Hebrew and then later into English:

> There are no photos
> not of grandma, nor of grandpa
> I've never even seen
> a word they wrote.
> I never met
> my mother's brothers and sisters,
> I've never even heard their voices.
> But sometimes
> a few words
> a few sentences,
> return to me,
> reminders
> from my past
> that they are still here.
> And they are seeking a way
> to tell their stories
> to show their faces
> to have their voices heard.[5]

It was not something over which I felt I had control.

> When they tell you to remember
> they mean there is a possibility
> you might forget. But in me
> there are brothers and sisters
> who were never born
> it has nothing to do
> with memory.[6]

The Association of Yiddish Writers, Beit Leyvik, together with the Foundation for Yiddish Culture, encouraged me in my writings in that language, and Rivka Bassman, the wonderful Yiddish poet, helped me polish them. Even though she had been in Bergen-Belsen, and had suffered terribly herself, her assistance was focused on helping me make poems from memories, no matter how sentimental and grisly. These poems appeared in Hebrew and Yiddish (*Yerusha*, 2019) and have now been published in Yiddish and English (*Inheritance*, 2021)

I had known Rivka Bassman for at least forty years when my parents asked me to drive to Kibbutz Hamaapil, where I met Rivka's husband, Mula Ben-Haim. "I babysat for him!" my mother exclaimed. Since my father's family had lived next door to my mother's family, and Mula had lived across the marketplace from them, it was a real reunion. It was probably the first time they had reconnected since their youth, when my father found his siblings after they were released from the camps. But while my parents were musing over the past with Mula, I wasn't listening—I was only the driver and much more interested in the kibbutz than their reminiscences. I didn't even know about Mula's heroism in a movement called the *Bricha*, "The Escape," which saved countless refugees, perhaps even some of my relatives. Only as I write this do I begin to understand that they had all been involved in some kind of united effort, and that my parents' escape had also been engineered by some sort of organization.

At the request of the publisher, I translated *Yerusha* from Yiddish into Hebrew, but after it was published I felt I had just begun, that with each sentence I understood just a bit more about what had been going on around me. I found myself writing more poems, this time in English. I had written many before, but they were never conscious attempts to recreate the past. Sabine Huynh, friend and writer in French, translated the poems, connecting with them through her own exile from Vietnam, and she began to urge me to write more of my experiences. Without this encouragement, I could never have imagined the poetic value of digging into my own past. Only when *Survivre a Son Histoire/ Surviving Her Story* was published did a flood of memories begin to emerge; the dialogue between them and the stark lists and articles published on the internet brought forth further facts, further stories of individuals that suddenly stood out from the vast history of numbers.

This is what became my goal: Reconstructing the lives of individuals, from the forgotten star of stage and screen (Kurt Gerron), to the benefactor who created my prize (Leyb Rubinlicht), to my parents' escape on the night of Hitler's invasion, to my partisan aunt (Malcah Kravitz).

Silence

I grew up with the gesture of silencing. Someone begins to speak about their experience in the Holocaust; someone else whispers their name, and all become quiet. I grew up surrounded by people who shushed one another. Even as they built new lives and new families, many of them had pasts that needed to remain hidden, not just forgotten.

As soon as we were ensconced in a home of our own, a year after our immigration to the United States in 1948, we began to house refugees. Sometimes an entire family would move in for a few months—gaunt parents and a confused child, always with no luggage. My brother and I would be in charge of helping the child acclimatize to America and teaching them some English. Sometimes it would be a man who would hold secretive conversations with my parents after we'd been sent to our rooms. Or sisters from somewhere so foreign their very odor was suspect, because they used strange ingredients like garlic. Or a boy with teeth that rotted as they emerged from the gums. Or a couple whose children had disappeared and we were meant to help substitute for them. Or a friend's seamstress mother who spoke of her past as we sat by the machine pedal and threaded needles. But always there would be sudden breaks in the conversations, sometimes a sudden awareness that children should not be exposed to such tales, that it was difficult to thread needles while being told about children wrenched from their mothers' breasts and thrown again a wall.

But it was not only a question of inappropriate subjects for children. There were also dangers in the McCarthy era—real or imagined. When my brother brought home a new journal entitled "U.S.S.R.," my father exploded. "They watch the newsstands!" he shouted, and we had no idea who was watching or what they were looking for. Only after my father's death did I learn of his imprisonment as a teenager in Lithuania for socialist activities. Only as an adult did I learn of his later persecution and imprisonment in Danzig and the escape engineered by my mother and her sister from Danzig to England days before Hitler's invasion on September 1, 1939. My own reaction was to release the information as soon as I could in this poem:

Night Travel

On that night in Danzig the trains did not run.
You sat in the bus station till almost dawn
knowing that if you could not get out,
the invaders would find you, grind you among the first
under their heels.

Toward morning an announcement came of a bus,
and without knowing where it would go
you raced to the stop.
But the Nazis were there first, and you watched
as they finished their search –
checking each traveller for papers,
jewellery, a Jewish nose.

Among the passengers you recognized
a familiar face—a German woman—sitting
with someone else you'd seen
in the neighborhood.
They winked a greeting,
waited for the soldiers to leave,
and jumped out—
pushing you up in their place.

Thus you escaped to Berlin, remaining alive
by keeping silent through the long train ride

from Berlin to Cologne in a car filled with
staring German soldiers—

And arrived the next day in Holland,
black with fear and transportation.[7]

But the true history of that trip, the physical feeling of the voyage of escape, did not reach me until the existence of the internet. I had traced Gerron's journey from Berlin to Paris to Holland, to Westerbrook and then Theresienstadt, in my attempt to understand the experience of repeated escapes. It had helped me understand why Gerron let himself be easily discovered—wandering the streets in confusion when the Nazis invaded. Now with the help of Google Maps, I could gain an appreciation of that dangerous journey my parents took through Germany during the invasion of Poland, could see how many stops, how many busses, the duration. I could begin to understand why my mother described my father's face then as "black."

Having traveled day and night, my parents arrived in Vlissengen in the Netherlands and from there took a ferry to Harwich, England, where they were granted leave to land on the condition that they leave the country when their "training" was finished. They were "safe" this time. Their journey to Palestine several weeks before had failed, and they were returned to Danzig. But the trauma of that journey through Germany to safety must have dwarfed all the others, despite many future travels.

One example: When they left England for the United States on the Queen Elizabeth II, I was just recovering from whooping cough, and there was a terrible fear I would not make it through Ellis Island—I was kept in our tiny cabin for most of the journey and warned many times not to cough. Apparently the warning succeeded, because I remember that after long consultations with the doctor at Ellis Island, my father and I were allowed to join my brother and mother on the mainland. And my father was trembling.

My mother mentioned a key detail of the trip from Danzig—that they couldn't speak during the trip, or even buy food, lest their Yiddish accents give them away. Their constant feeling of safety being only transient may also have contributed to their later unwillingness to speak.

But there was also a real and constant danger in speaking. Not all secrets were safe to voice. Some were shameful and some dangerous. My father's youthful political involvement got him into trouble in Poland/Lithuania, and had to be kept from his chatterbox daughter, especially when she began writing stories and publishing them in the Yiddish newspaper, The Forward. Knowledge of his socialist past during the McCarthy era would have been sufficient to deny him citizenship and have us all deported.

I now realize that one of the women we helped must have been a kapo (a prisoner who acted as a guard). I am not sure, but her twin sister hinted that to me when I asked her why she didn't speak with her closest sibling. She wept that her sister had betrayed her people. I was not old enough to enquire further, and now cannot even remember her name, but because both women were childless and showered me with attention, their faces remain clear to me.

Another close cousin used to shush his wife whenever she would begin to speak of their partisan past, because (I later learned online) he had led a revenge battalion and knew the time of retribution would come some day. Many of the internet sites that reveal he was a sergeant major in the partisans are now missing post-war details that had been published in the 1970s and 80s. The information I first saw online has been erased too—I assume to protect future generations, and even today I respect his silence. He was long gone when the Belorussian government announced a list of traitors and asked for information of their whereabouts, but his silence had come at the cost of his son's disdain for his father's supposed cowardice. His wife, on the other hand, was always praised for her partisan background and her escape from the Warsaw sewers. Sometimes what we *don't* know skews relationships for the next generation.

My mother's anecdotes usually focused on pre-war days and her many brothers and sisters. Although she wept at their loss, she did not explain where they and their families had disappeared to. Perhaps she never knew.

She found testimony in Yad Vashem—the World Holocaust Remembrance Center—that one of her sisters, Basya Berenzyk, born 1910, had perished in Auschwitz, but there is no mention of her in the Arolsen Archive of the camp's prisoners. But given that the wrong birthday has been attributed to her in Yad Vashem suggests that the sister-in-law who wrote the testimony may not have been an accurate source. And Batya's husband and three or four children seem to have vanished—whether in the crematoriums or into orphanages, I do not know.

Although I myself drove my parents to Yad Vashem in Jerusalem that day, my mother never mentioned that she herself had recorded an entry for Batya, or one for her elder brother, Moshe Sharon, as having been shot in Lida together with his wife and the children, and for her second brother, Motel, who died in Majdanek. Their wives and children were also not recorded. Further queries yielded no additional information.

But she could not keep silent when it came to her youngest sister, Malcah. The poem I wrote about her a few years ago has been reproduced many times, in the hope that someone might be able to help me to add to the story, but to date no more information has been found.

Her Story

I have never been able to tell her story
Sometimes it escapes me, sometimes I am not sure
it could really have happened, sometimes I read

different accounts of her demise, or a paragraph
from some testimony jogs my memory and the terrible days
when I first heard what happened to her return.

This much is in my blood:
I was conceived on the day she died.
This much is in my blood.
She blew up trains.
The courage came from her uplifted chin
and the two infants she watched
dashed against the wall of their home.
Avram twelve months old and Masha two years.
my first cousins.
They too—in my blood—all that is left.

If I can write of these babies,
I can manage the rest—
following her path as she escaped
the prison camp with her husband
And joined the Otrianski Otriade
Lenin Brigade, Lipinskana Forest.

I can feel her mouth, her narrow lips clamped
as she bends over the delicate mines,
solemn as in the photo when as a child
she sat with the rest of the choir
unsmiling amid the festive singers
unwilling perhaps to feel poetic joy
perhaps destined for so much more.

There are at least three accounts of her death:
the partisan Abba Kovner told me she was caught
in a mission and hung. He looked away when he spoke,
not piercing me as always with his tragic eyes,
and I knew there was more he would not say.

Another book states she lagged behind the platoon
escaping an attack, perhaps pregnant,
and was imprisoned in Zhetl.
The jail was ignited, perhaps by accident,
and she was just one of the victims.

When Mother first told me the story
she had just heard at the hairdresser's,

I was only a child, and outraged
that she was weeping, tears
rolling down her face. She knew
all I cared for was my own life,
and her latest discovery
of the fate of her youngest sister
a disruption.
But who else could she tell?

The loft in the barn, she said,
Partisans were hiding there—three women,
her husband and her. They came
and set the barn afire. He helped
the women first, and his wife came last.
But she didn't come, was burnt alive.

Malcah Malcah who saved all our lives
Malcah who was waiting for them
when the ship brought them back to Danzig
after they were barred from the Holy Land,
who found them the agricultural visas to England
and saw them off the night that Hitler invaded.

But there is no real story.
All that remains is a faded snapshot
a few sentences in unread memorial tomes,
and me, who cannot tell any story for sure.[8]

How can I know anything about Malcah for sure? Even her appearance is a mystery. Perhaps she can be identified in the photograph of a group of partisans frequently reprinted, but not mentioned even in the Zhetel book.

Could the woman pointed to here be the same sister? All I have to identify her are baby pictures, in which she, the youngest of eleven children, was not central to the family. Even in an illustrated diagram of the early resistance in Zhetel, hers is one of the names that appears, but her photographs are absent. Since I accessed the site itself, in 2021, the site itself has been blocked as well.

In addition to what I wrote in the poem, there are other confusing elements. In testimonies from the Zhetel Memorial Book Years ago, when I first looked for her on the web, I found three entries. The book has now been translated into English and the spelling is different for two of them She is listed as a partisan hero under the name Malka Kravetz,[9] but the entries are vague. One witness writes:

At four o'clock in the morning we crossed the Podyavark small river and approached the old, former camp near Karshuk. 25 partisans died that day including the girls from Zhetel: Henie Gertzovsky, Miriam Levenbuk and Maliye Kravetz.[10]

Another witness testifies:

The third platoon leaves on an assignment. Maliye Kravietz, Mirke Levenbuk and Lyuba Inderstheyn decide to join them. It is not a good time to separate from the platoon...They walked into a German ambush. The men managed to escape. The women fell into the hands of the murderers.[11]

But what happened after that? My mother wrote in Yad Vashem first in 1967, and then again in 1978 after the details had been given to her by a witness she met at a beauty parlor. When I first found it, I was so excited I couldn't work out how to download the actual document. But even on my small screen I could see my mother's pain. Circumstances of death, the form said in Hebrew. "Burnt alive," she wrote in Hebrew, in the Otrianski Otriad, Lenin Brigade, Puscha Lipinitsianska, she added in Polish, the Lipinskana Forest. Her own name was in Yiddish, and her handwriting was unusual in its irregularity. From my experience with her I recognized it as emotional. The first time I found this document, in the 1970s, it was under Malcah's married name, Kravetz, but when I looked for it again in the 80s, the name was not there. Looking at the document more closely, I realized that parts had been removed and overwritten. The date given is January 1978, marked over what looks like 1965. 1965 was the year of my mother's first visit to Israel, before she knew the details of the passive role of Malcah's husband, Wolf, in her death. In 1978, Malcah's married name disappeared. His name was tippexed out, and although the last name was mentioned further down between the lines, his first name was omitted. Between 1965 and 1978, Wolf Kravetz was erased by my mother because she discovered he had helped other women to safety but left Malcah for last, too late to be rescued.

There remained some evidence clear to me, but unreadable to a translator who could not decipher the handwriting. Malcah's place of death was originally translated as the Loire Valley. It would transpire that more errors had been inserted into the evidence. The English version of this was lacking in all but basic detail, and it was my fault. It followed a complaint I had made about the wrong transcription. When, sometime in the 1990s, I discovered the mistranslation, I wrote to Yad Vashem to correct Malcah's name and place of death, and to include the details my mother added in Hebrew to explain that Malcah had been burnt alive. A warm letter soon came, agreeing with my corrections and promising to correct the errors. It was more than a decade later than I checked those corrections, only to find that they had been replaced by lacunae. I have since attempted to correct the elision, but was told there is a long waiting list for record amendments ahead of me. Perhaps by the time this chapter appears in print, the basic facts will be have been corrected, but in any case, I am certain that connections that might have been made in 1965 from a more accurate document are no longer possible.

These mistakes alone in my aunt's history would have been enough to confuse scholars, but there are more. Her name, Malcah, is sometimes given as Maria, Maliyeh, or even Male. Most of the information sites about partisans that listed her when I first began to look for her, such as http://www.thepartizans.org/member_eng_frame.asp?id=2127&cat=com and http://www.partisans.org.il/, no longer exist. When I downloaded information from them over two decades ago, it never crossed my mind that both would disappear. The first site claimed she was killed in Zhetel, the second that she was hanged in Koprizi. My mother's claim in the Yad Vashem pages was that Malcah was burnt alive in Zhetel and she repeated this often, with great fervency. I have found no other evidence of this, but every other account she gave me has proven true.

Some of the other sites about Malcah and other relatives disappeared soon after I found them, and I have not been able to trace their sources. I had not realized how ephemeral the information would be. It had not occurred to me that the silence some survivors maintained was to avoid some future persecution for murder in Belarus. And who can imagine what a mother who had witnessed the murder of her babies might be capable of? The further away in time, the farther away Malcah—the human being— becomes. All the information I can find now melts her into a mass of victims.

If the data on Malcah proves nothing else, it shows something of the slippery, ever-changing stories of the individuals whose history has yet to be told, and the urgency of pinning down and recording each item of information before it disappears.

Notes

1. Karlheintz Gabler, *Siegfried Shalom Sebba, Maler und Werkmann: Mit Œuvre-Verzeichnis der Druckgrafik* (Berlin: Thiele & Schwarz, 1981).
2. Leyb Rubinlikht, *A shmues mitn harts: ider* (Tel Aviv: Nay-lebn, 1975), 22.
3. Grabowska, Janina, " Prisoners", *Monography Of Kl Stutthof,* https://web.archive.org/web/20090122183745/http://kki.net.pl/~museum/rozdz6.htm (accessed September 29, 2021)
4. Grabowska, Janina, "Responsibility For Crimes In Stutthof. Processes" *Monography Of Kl Stutthof,* https://web.archive.org/web/20090122183745/http://kki.net.pl/~museum/rozdz13.htm (accessed September 29, 2021)
5. Karen Alkalay-Gut, *Inheritance/Yerusha* (Tel Aviv: Leyvik House Press, 2021).

6 Karen Alkalay-Gut, *Inheritance/Yerusha*.
7 Karen Alkalay-Gut, *Ignorant Armies* (New York: Cross-Cultural Press, 1994), 9.
8 Karen Alkalay-Gut, *Survivre a son histoire/Surviving her story* (Paris: Corlevour, with the aid of the *Fondation pour la Mémoire de la Shoah*, 2020), 26–30.
9 Kaplinski, Baruch (ed.), trans. Janie Respitz, *Pinkus Zhetel*, "Partisan Heroes From Zhetel, 440.
10 Kaplinski, Baruch (ed.), trans. Janie Respitz, *Pinkus Zhetel* "The Participation of People from Zhetel in the Liptchanska Partisans," 379.
11 Kaplinski, Baruch (ed.), trans. Janie Respitz, *Pinkus Zhetel* "The Last Ambush," 379.

14

Untold Story, Indirect Course: My Path into the Field of Holocaust Literature and Representation

Michal Ben-Horin

An early memory. I am about four years old, perhaps less. I stand in a room, probably not bigger than a few square meters. A long, black, display case faces me. The shelves are very high, almost reaching the ceiling, and are covered by heavy glass doors. Behind the glass I see dozens of puppets dressed in colorful clothes. I peer closely. The sight of them fascinates me. But it is not just the sight that is captivating. The sound is, too, as I would learn many years later. The woman who owned the puppets spoke German and even taught German. One of her students was my father, who was born to parents who emigrated in the 1930s from Poland to Eretz-Israel. The only "foreign" language he knew when he graduated high school was English. Yiddish was the language my grandparents spoke to each other, but never to their own children. Hebrew was the language they had to speak when they arrived in the new land as pioneers (*Halutzim*) and settled in the Beit She'an Valley, leaving their families behind them in Kraków and Rzeszów.

A later memory. A painting hanging on the wall in the bedroom of my grandparents on my father's side. The painting is that of an old man wearing a long black cloak that covers his whole body. He has a long beard and a huge black Hassidic hat on his head. This was my great-grandfather, whom my grandfather hardly mentioned. My great-grandparents had twelve children. Only my grandfather survived the Holocaust.

A much later memory. I spent a few months in Berlin completing my MA thesis on the historical novel written in German by the Jewish Czech writer

Max Brod. On returning to Israel, I visited my grandparents on their kibbutz. One of the first questions my grandfather asked me was: "Nu ..., how are our German friends doing?" The question shocked me, not so much the sarcastic tone but rather the pain I could feel behind the words. At that moment, all I could do was nod back to him with a pale apologetic smile. The guilt was already there. I felt that I had disappointed him. As if I had crossed a border I should not have crossed, in getting an education in Germany which was not only a geographic place, but also the origin of evil that devastated his world. As for my grandfather, who lost his family in the Holocaust but never really talked about them, he never went back to Poland, let alone Germany.

Looking back at these moments, I realize how they embody the beginnings of my journey into the field of Holocaust literature and representation, namely my own need to find an explanation for my father's fascination with the German language, for my great-grandfather's absence, and for my grandfather's Yiddish gesture which reverberated within the Hebrew. However, as much as this journey continued, I didn't share it with my family. It was as if we were on two different roads that never actually met. What did I know about their lives in Europe before they arrived in Israel? Very little. I didn't ask and they didn't tell; or was it the other way round? When I was taking my first steps as a young researcher at Tel Aviv University's Department of Comparative Literature, and could tell my grandparents about my interest in European culture in general, and German literature in particular, they were no longer alive. My grandfather died as I was starting to write my doctoral dissertation, and he never really knew what I was working on. It was too late to ask him to tell me about his childhood in Europe, on the one hand, and to share with him my insights about Europe, on the other, both of which made the questions I was examining as part of my personal and professional journey even more acute. Presumably, sharing my work with my grandfather while listening to his own stories would have given me direct access to my family's past. I could have dealt with the loss of my grandfather's parents and siblings in the Holocaust consciously instead of sensing the burden of an unspoken horrific past which is passed over and continues to haunt subsequent generations. At the time, this was impossible. Only by looking at the devastation generated in the Holocaust by exploring its representations in literature written by others (including Germans and Austrians) was I able to process and reflect on this trauma. This opened an indirect route for me into my own family stories, which I slowly began to discover.

From Emek Yizre'el to Tel Aviv

Not only was the path that led me to the stories of my family somewhat circuitous, but so too was my way into academia in general and the discipline of Holocaust literature and representation in particular. My first active steps into the world of German culture were in the field of music. I grew up with stories about my mother, a talented violin player who preferred not to make music her career. As a young girl, I wanted to become a pianist. My piano lessons began when I was ten years old. I had the honor of taking piano classes with Galila Ruebner, a gifted pianist who lived on the kibbutz. Years later, I would combine my childhood piano practice and my professional interest in the aesthetic representation of the Holocaust, which was not part of my own biography, at least to the extent that no one from my close family ever talked about it. Moreover, I felt strongly that the realm of music offered an effective tool for the study of trauma. Painful experience cannot be articulated or formulated with words. As a non-verbal art, music reverberates with such experience. Playing musical instruments may thus suggest a therapeutic potential. Following this idea, I was interested in how music was incorporated by writers who searched for non-verbal means of dealing with the trauma of the Holocaust.

As for my own music practice, what began with my piano playing on the kibbutz in Emek Yizre'el brought me to the city of Tel Aviv. I was accepted into the Academy of Music at Tel Aviv University. However, by the end of my first semester in the Academy, I realized that I was missing the verbal aspect that was absent from the instrumental music. At that point I decided to apply to the Department of Comparative Literature in addition to my music studies. I was fascinated by the German novel—which was strongly related to music—as well as by Israeli writers, whose work expressed dialectic relationships of longing for and denial of European, among them musical, traditions that were written anew in Hebrew. In retrospect, I understand that this fascination was a part of my growing interest in the ways of representing the Holocaust.

Even as a teenager reading works of literature, I developed an interest in fictional spaces that lay beyond the familiar and the local, and that provided me with ways of dealing with reality. Immersed in the lyrical voices of Israeli poets, such as Dahlia Ravikovitch, I would be transported to distant oceans and exotic continents that opened for me perspectives on loss and desire. The German novel too gave me an emotional glimpse of this imaginative power by traveling in remote worlds that were created in a foreign language. For example, I recall the strong impression that Fontane's *Effi Briest* had on me, in which the obstacles the protagonist experienced testified poetically to the social and cultural boundaries of the bourgeoisie, or how fascinated I was by Goethe's critical depiction of German idealism in *The Sorrows of Young Werther*. In *Wilhelm Meister*, Goethe introduces the broad possibilities conveyed with an extreme creativity, but also points to the dangers that lie in the aesthetic realm, such as locking oneself into a fantasy world that cannot entertain any alternatives offered by reality. Distancing myself from the local, namely to search for the other as a return to the self, played a role in my developing research and shaped my path into the field of Holocaust Studies. I became interested in how literature, especially prose works that were related to music, shed light on a historical event and the emergence of collective memories, while accounting for the personal mechanism of repression. This became the point of departure for my doctoral dissertation on how German writers represent the Nazi past.

Another writer who influenced my academic choices without ever becoming an explicit case study was Yehuda Amichai. My parents had poetry collections in their library, and as a child I would open them from time to time in an attempt to read a few poems. I still recall Amichai's disturbing depiction of destroyed cities intertwined with poetic images of loss and belonging. I didn't understand what the words meant at the time; the resonance of their sound, however, while reading them aloud, left an indelible impression that kept haunting me. What I didn't know as a young reader was that Amichai, who was lauded as a national poet, as well as being part of the *Palmach* and a soldier in the War of Independence, also wrote, but was never published, in German. I was unaware that his birth name was Ludwig Pfeuffer and that he was a son of an Orthodox rabbi; born in Würzburg, Germany, he emigrated with his family to Israel in 1935. Amichai's repression of the German language demonstrated the dialectical relationship to German culture in the emerging Jewish Land of Israel. Discovering this as an academic, combined with a reading of the growing scholarship in the field, played a role in my decision to focus on the relationships between Hebrew and German. At this point I also became aware of the short correspondence Amichai had with the Jewish Romanian poet Paul Celan, who lost his parents in the Holocaust, after the latter's visit to Israel in 1969. This encouraged me to look at ways of interweaving the stories that were a part of the national narrative and those that were repressed or excluded by it. Looking at the negation of exilic life stories, which were barely present in the national narrative I was raised with on the kibbutz, I was confronted not only with the collective dilemma that characterized Israeli society since its foundation, but also with my family's personal dilemma.

In tracing the memory of the Holocaust in works of literature in German and in Hebrew, my research enabled me to explore these quandaries. This, however, happened much later; back then, I decided to pursue my interest in literary studies, and applied for an MA degree in comparative literature. Meanwhile, I completed a two-year teaching diploma and began to teach literature in a high school. However, after a year of teaching I experienced tremendous frustration. I was clearly at a crossroads. At that point, I started to work on my MA thesis. I decided not to pursue the issue of German-Hebrew dialogue in Israeli poets and writers, but rather to focus on the historical novels of Max Brod, which gave my interest in German culture new imputes. In order to deepen my research and language skills I applied for a scholarship that enabled me to spend a few months in Berlin.

Berlin and Jerusalem

In Berlin I took courses at the Freie Universität and worked in libraries, including the collections in The Center for Research on Antisemitism (Zentrum für Antisemitismusforschung, or ZfA) and the Staatsbibliothek. I was particularly interested in the emergence of Jewish nationalism in Europe and the role the genre of the historical novel played in the formation of a Jewish national identity. I looked at how works of literature contributed to the shaping of national characteristics, such as the model of "Muscular Judaism," and how the novels disseminated and revealed these ideas throughout communities of readers in German or German-language readers. As a part of this project, I examined the relationships between history and literature and how a historical event is represented, shaped, and depicted in the realm of the poetic text. For example, one of the case studies focused on Brod's depiction of David Reubeni, a sixteenth-century Jewish political activist, and how this depiction demonstrated Brod's critical conception of modern Jewish nationalism.

Life in Berlin did not revolve around my thesis alone. From a young age, I was disturbed—and at the same time deeply moved—by the texts we read in class and by the ceremonies on Holocaust Memorial Day in which we participated every year. During the months I spent in Berlin, I met German students and got to know a few grandchildren of veteran Wehrmacht soldiers, which opened a whole new perspective for me. As a native Israeli, who had been educated in the Israeli education system, I knew nothing about the perpetrators, nor the lives of their children and grandchildren. There were the Jewish victims—I could hardly consider dealing with the German perpetrators: It was far easier to think about them as inhuman. When meeting their grandchildren, however, I could no longer maintain this position. This realization led me to the understanding that flesh-and-blood humans, not demons, were responsible for the horrific crimes. It was also in Berlin that I first experienced the public debate regarding the memory of the Holocaust. I recall watching the speech Martin Walser gave on television after being awarded the German Book Trade's Peace Prize in Frankfurt's *Paulskirche*. I also remember the response of Ignatz Bubis, who served at the time as head of the Jewish community in Munich. He expressed his pain and anger toward Walser's irresponsible attitude regarding the German past. The public discourse that followed the debate in the German media stunned me. I could not understand the demand made by some of the debaters, including Walser himself, for a *Schlussstrich*, namely the drawing of a line under what he regarded as an obsessive preoccupation with the Holocaust. This "celebrated" event had a powerful effect on me, and would contribute to a turning point in my academic interest. I decided to conclude my research on the German Jewish historical novel as a formative tool of a Jewish national identity, and focus instead on the German novel in the second half of the twentieth century.

On my return to Tel Aviv, I submitted my MA thesis and applied for a doctorate. My dissertation dealt with post-1945 German literature and how German and Austrian authors responded to, reflected on, and wrote about the events connected to the Second World War and the Holocaust. I was curious about how people who related to the perpetrators explained the Third Reich and its crimes to their children and grandchildren. I wanted to learn how they depicted these years in their novels; what roles their literary characters played, and how writing their novels helped them to work through the traumatic experience. While working on the literary material, I noted the prominent role of music in the poetic descriptions. One way of explaining this was to trace the alliance between music and literature in German Romanticism since the late eighteenth century. Music is a non-verbal art and—in contrast to the visual arts—a temporal one, which interferes with accepted meanings. Accordingly, music became a profound tool for expressing what cannot be represented by words or concrete images, such as events connected to the theological (for example, an experience of revelation or transcendent insight) or the psychological realm (for instance, a psychic mechanism generated by traumatic experience).

I therefore wished to examine how music provided these authors with such powerful tools and enabled them to expand the boundaries of verbal representation in dealing with the disaster. I focused on novels by Thomas Mann, Günter Grass, Ingeborg Bachmann, and Thomas Bernhard. Each writer used musical intertexts in addition to sound and rhythmic components which were tied to more than the semantic level. Their work told of Germany and Austria in the twentieth century by confronting their literary characters and readers with the Nazis' crimes. Reading their work enabled me to view the Holocaust through a foreign lens. In exploring how they dealt with ethical responsibility and worked through trauma, I was able to discern new possibilities as well as barriers.

Working on my dissertation was an important stage in shaping the theoretical framework that I would use in my subsequent research projects. I was trying to integrate various disciplines—including music theory and poetics, memory studies, and cultural history—that would enable me to obtain a critical perspective on questions that had apparently interested me long before I reached academia. On my return to Israel, I submitted my dissertation. I obtained a post-doctoral position at the Rosenzweig Center in Jerusalem and a year later started to teach at the Hebrew University of Jerusalem. Some time later I applied for another post-doctoral position, this time at the University of Haifa. Here I explored the characteristics of European romanticist and modernist aesthetics, and how they have been dialectically embedded in prose by Israeli writers such as Yehoshua Kenaz, Nathan Shaham, Ruth Almog, and Yoel Hoffmann, whose novels have traced the memory and representation of the Holocaust.

Throughout my work on the project, I was struck by the relationships between private and collective memories. I examined the notion of diaspora negation (*shlilat hagalut*) as it emerged in the final decades of the nineteenth century and its implications for the Jewish national discourse during the twentieth century. At the core of this conception was a binary model: The New Jew, a forerunner of secular Jewish nationalism, an independent warrior, a worker of the land and a sovereign of a territory, as opposed to the Old Jew, the weak and helpless victim of violence and pogroms in the diaspora. I tried to follow the impact of these trends as well as how they reflected my own experience as a third generation of pioneers who founded the kibbutz. I was particularly interested in my own grandparents, who left Poland in the 1920s and the 1930s, and I could not help wondering what European—and even more, what *Jewish*—traditions they had passed down to me. I recalled my decision to study German, a European language that was connected to the discourse of the diaspora. Yiddish, however, was also such a language, but although my grandparents spoke it, they did not pass on their knowledge to their children. If I wanted to learn about the history of my family that was not told at our house, why then did I not choose Yiddish? Gradually I became aware of psychological processes and strategies of collective and private censorship, and how each of us develops our own immune system or rejection in order to survive. Meanwhile, I began to publish my first articles based on my dissertation and the new comparative project that followed. A year later, I received a Minerva Scholarship and moved with my family to Germany. In 2007, we moved to the United States. The academic discipline of *Germanistik*, as I knew it from Jerusalem or Berlin, turned into German Studies.

Gainesville and Philadelphia

At the University of Florida, I started teaching courses in German literature, and also in Hebrew literature and culture. The latter gave me an opportunity to not only to explore with the students the repertoire of modern Hebrew literature, but also to focus on the relationship between literature and history, culture and memory, and the arts and music in Israel. Through the encounter with the students, Jews and non-Jews alike, I became aware of the relevance and the power of the aesthetic realm in exploring issues of human rights, oppression, and violation of marginal populations. The Holocaust was a part of the discussions we had in class alongside the study of other twentieth- and twenty-first-century atrocities. We read texts by German and Austrian authors, as well as Israeli and (to some extent) American writers. We looked at the literary generations in the context of the formation of collective memory. The students shared their own stories and family histories, some of which were connected to the Holocaust.

In 2009, I received a fellowship from the Center for Advanced Judaic Studies in Philadelphia. My proposed project focused on the Jewish Austrian composer Arnold Schoenberg. I was back in the realm of music, this time not as a pianist or as a reader of literature, which connects to characters or repertoire from the musical world, but as a listener of a musical piece. I looked at Schoenberg's opera *Moses und Aron*, which included texts based on the Hebrew Bible, and which conveyed, among others, Schoenberg's anxiety in facing antisemitic violence. Schoenberg began to work on the libretto during the 1920s and composed only two acts of the opera before he fled from Germany, through France, to the United States. The project examined the question of representation through exploring the relationship between the sacred and the secular, and between the musical avant-garde and the Jewish tradition. In his letters, Schoenberg connects the opera's creation to his return to the Jewish faith after escaping from Germany. Through this project I found myself once again questioning the modes of expression of the non-representable. At the core of Jewish faith (Second Commandment) is the prohibition of creating an image of God. In his opera, Schoenberg elaborated this prohibition by developing image–word dialectics by means of a new musical technique (twelve-tone composition) to express traumatic experience. This technique was also used in his 1947 oratorio *A Survivor from Warsaw*, a testimony to the catastrophe. Following other scholars, I could not avoid comparing the two musical pieces and how the first, even though it was composed before the Holocaust, already embodied the problem of representing the non-representable and expressing the magnitude of the disaster. Music was not the only pertinent factor here. The figure of the stuttering prophet also drew my attention. In the biblical story, Moses, who stutters, needs his brother Aron to speak for him to the people. Schoenberg demonstrated Moses's "broken" language by the Spoken Song (*Sprechgesang*), a vocal style that interferes with the melodic style of the Beautiful Song (*bel canto*).

Through the figuration of the broken language, I found my way back to the poetic work. This time, however, the core of my research was not the musical composition with regard to verbal text (Moses' Spoken Song), but rather the verbal text with regard to musical components. This was also encompassed in my understanding of translation and the way I listened to the sound relationships between source and target languages. At the same time, a colleague told me about Tuvia Ruebner's autobiography, written originally in German and later in Hebrew. In addition, I learned about his translation into German of his own poetry, written initially in Hebrew, which he published from the 1990s onward. I argued that the way Ruebner moved between the languages, German and Hebrew, enabled him to work through his life experience—first the loss of his family in the Holocaust and later other losses in the family he built in Israel. But I needed more time to delve into this story that also connected me with my own biography—living on the kibbutz, dipping into the arts as a way of working though painful experience, learning about my family's stories, and reading and listening to the stories of others. We returned to Tel Aviv at the end of that year because of academic jobs. However, for me, settling down was still out of the question.

Back to Tel Aviv

I returned to Tel Aviv University, where I taught a course on German literature. I also joined the European Forum at the Hebrew University in Jerusalem, where I taught a few courses on German culture. I also started teaching literature in high school, too. This time, however, it was a completely different experience. I developed an independent program that was approved by the Ministry of Education. I came to appreciate the hours I spent with these young students who attended my literature classes. I loved listening to their original ideas and unusual way of thinking. They demanded from me a revision of my pedagogical approach, as I had to explain sophisticated ideas in a way that would be relevant for them. I learned a lot from this challenging experience, which also made me a better lecturer, and perhaps a better scholar. To my surprise, sharing with my students a varied German repertoire of novels, plays, visual art, and cinematic texts to explore Holocaust representations was more challenging than I could have envisaged. For the students, the Holocaust was conveyed by Jewish writers, thinkers, and artists. I learned that an expanded introduction was needed to explain the rationale of the course and that the Holocaust could be viewed from different angles and perspectives.

Despite the new opportunities and varied experience, I did not have enough time to make progress on my research. For this reason, I was happy when I finally received a tenure-track position at Bar-Ilan University. My first book, on German and Austrian post-1945 authors, was already in print with De Gruyter and I also completed a co-edited volume on the literature of the German author W. G. Sebald. In both cases, prose by non-Jewish writers demonstrated an aesthetic lens through which the issues of the Holocaust were explored. Sebald's prose, however, was already a part of German post-reunification. His stories of the Jewish victims (Max Farber, Jacques Austerlitz, among others) enabled me to look at issues Germany was facing after 1990 and how the crimes of the Nazis, the history of the Third Reich, and the responsibility or negation of responsibility for that history played a role in post-reunification collective memory.

The representation of the Holocaust was at the core of a translation project that at this point seemed to me the right time to pursue. I used translation theory in the context of comparative literature and the twenty-first-century debate around world literature to explore the phenomenon of autotranslation (Hebrew and German) in Tuvia Ruebner. I realized that for the poet, the initial move into Hebrew and the subsequent return to German was his way of maintaining the dialogue with the living and the dead. German was the language Ruebner spoke to the close family in Bratislava, among them the parents and sister that he lost in the Holocaust. Writing in German was both a way of preserving their memory but also locked him into the world of the dead; writing in Hebrew was a way out of this world and its price of oblivion. The transition between the languages facilitated the memory of the dead without giving up the communication with the living. I found these conclusions to be of particular relevance for the prose work of Aharon Appelfeld, who had been born in Chernowitz. His mother, who also spoke German, was murdered by the Nazis; he escaped to the forests and survived the Holocaust. I focused on his Hebrew prose, written in Israel, throughout my inquiry into the relationship between trauma and language, literature and testimony. I argued that the German repertoire, including its musical components, was embedded in Appelfeld's Hebrew poetics which sought modes of Holocaust representation. The role of a poetic language that can testify to the catastrophe, as opposed to the language of historical documentation, was the core of my work on another poet from Chernowitz, Paul Celan. I first studied Celan's prose in its Hebrew translation, while trying to ascertain the relationship between German, Hebrew, and Yiddish in light of Celan's notion of Jewification (*Verjudung*). As I read Celan's poetry, I discovered another string from my old musical passion by listening to its sound components and how they facilitate unique modes of testifying to the disaster.

Looking back at my engagement with the memory of the Holocaust, it is hard to detect a direct route. However, when trying to tell the story of how I arrived at this place, as I am now doing, the seemingly non-connected pieces do cohere after all. But this is what autobiography is all about; the ability to make a story out of the inconsistent moments of our lives—a storytelling that imbues such moments with meaning. Tracing my path into the field of Holocaust literature and representation, this autobiographical essay opened with my early interest in German culture and the Romanticist movement both in music and literature. The story continued with my MA thesis on the German-Jewish historical novel that revealed for me the dialectics of the Zionist movement—the binary models of the old and new Jew as were also embedded in the education system I grew up in, including the silence about the personal family stories of my relatives who were murdered in the Holocaust. This silence led me, in my doctoral dissertation, to look at the stories of others, which gave me a different perspective on the Holocaust in light of the debates following the German reunification in the 1990s. From literary theory, I moved to musicology in my research on the biblical opera by the Austrian-Jewish composer who testified to the Holocaust by new musical means. And, finally, translation research brought me back to Jewish poets and writers who moved between languages (translingualism) and media (transmodality), to bear witness to that which challenges verbal and historical representation.

I returned to explore issues of Holocaust representation in my projects, even though they are not part of my biography as I am neither a second- nor a third-generation Holocaust survivor. I have chosen to deal not necessarily with archival documents and historiographic methodologies, but rather to explore the aesthetic realm of literature and the arts in searching for answers. The foreign sounds I heard as a child of the German my father wished to acquire, the violin playing my mother would not turn into a profession, or the family stories about life in Galicia and Poland that my grandparents from Lviv, Kraków, or Rzeszów did not tell me in Yiddish, nor in Hebrew, and certainly not in Polish, all paved my way into the academic field of Holocaust literature and representation.

15

Too Much, Too Little: A Personal Journey through Holocaust Narratives

Keren Goldfrad

Introduction

She was waiting in line to receive her verdict—left or right. It was not hard to figure out. Those on the right were healthy young women, whereas those on the left were unfit for labor. Finally, her turn came, and she was extremely surprised when the officer's finger pointed to the left. After all, she was only in her twenties. Bella refused to accept her fate, and she decided to somehow sneak back into the line. When the guards were not looking directly at her, she managed to slip back, and waited anxiously for her turn again. She faced her judge and looked him in the eye awaiting her verdict once again. Her eyes widened in shock when the finger pointed left. Her feet did not budge, but she was pushed abruptly to the left. It took her a few seconds to come to her senses and decide not to give up. Driven by her relentless passion to live, she snuck back in line and blended in with the crowd. "What if the officer recognizes me?," she thought to herself. The frightful thought accompanied her as she approached the angel of death for the third time. She was afraid to look him in the eye and so she just watched his finger anxiously. It swayed to the right.

    I did not have the privilege of hearing this story directly from my paternal grandmother Bella, who was killed in a car accident when I was ten years old. But it has haunted me since my uncle recounted it in front of a few family members. Shoah stories, such as this one, experienced by all four of my grandparents are part of my personal identity. They are part of my essence. They are at the base of my nightmares and my daily thoughts.

Sarah could scarcely breathe. The bunker was so small, she could hardly understand how twelve grownups managed to be there without moving the whole day. During the night, they crept out of the bunker and stretched their weary muscles and aching bones. They also looked for food and water. The bunker was situated in a forested area owned by Sarah's family in Czechoslovakia. She was there with her newly wedded husband, who her parents would never have approved of, had they still been around. They managed to survive in this manner for six months, until the Day of Atonement, when the men felt they needed to go out of the bunker in order to stand upright and pray. That is when they were spotted.

Savta Sarah, my maternal grandmother, was my confidant. She would always ask me about my friendships, dreams and aspirations. I remember going to her apartment, close to the beach, where she would sit patiently peeling an apple and ask me to recount my experiences and thoughts. This act of peeling a piece of fruit is etched in my mind, for it felt as if she was gently peeling my reserve and my outer defenses. We were so close and yet looking back retrospectively at those blissful and cherished moments, I realize that she did not recount her Holocaust experiences to me during those long conversations. This changed when I had to do a history project in eleventh grade on the Holocaust. Most students found material for their paper in the library, but I decided to take this opportunity to interview my two remaining grandparents, Savta Sarah and Saba Yechezkel, my paternal grandfather.

Yechezkel, unlike most of his fellow Auschwitz inmates, was used to physical labor. He had worked cutting leather in Będzin, Poland, since the age of fourteen in order to help his elderly parents and six siblings financially. It pained him to watch his two close friends get a beating each time they did not do the work quickly enough. Yechezkel did not think they would survive much longer. Shoving two blocks of cement into the mixer every fifteen minutes was arduous work, especially for these famished, weak inmates. "Come closer to me," Yechezkel whispered to his two friends, "stand on each side of me and the guards will not notice the pace of your work." His solemn belief in the Almighty pushed his strength to the brink, until one day, walking back to the barracks in a daze, he slipped on the ice and broke his arm. Going to the infirmary could be a death sentence, but the pain was unbearable. There was no other choice! The doctor tied two metal rods on both sides of his arm. The bombing was already underway and eight days later the German guards hastily rounded up all the remaining inmates and started marching out of the gates. The sick people in the infirmary were left behind. That wretched fall had saved him from the Death March.

Exposure to such stories gripped my attention and led me to research and investigate testimonies to better evaluate their power, diversity and possible meanings. The more I delved into these personal accounts, the more evident it became that each act of witnessing bears its own unique quality; each testimony adds a fragment to our understanding of the Holocaust; each story serves to expose yet another angle, another experience and another viewpoint. My earlier work attempted to analyze how literary artists managed to represent their unique traumas, as well as the literary genres which were chosen to best convey these experiences. However, in this chapter, I would like to focus on a number of pedagogical projects that strive to entice and engage students when learning about the Holocaust. Looking back retrospectively at these projects, I have come to realize that they all touch upon a dilemma or an issue that troubled me personally over the years. A Talmudic Tractate relates a quote by Rabbi Hanina:

I have learnt much from my teachers, from my friends—even more, **and from my students—most of all.**[1]

This well-known tractate embodies a humbling message, especially for experienced teachers. Personally, after teaching a subject year after year, I find students' reactions to their first encounter with the material both refreshing and insightful. Moreover, the process of intense questioning and reasoning between me and my students in an attempt to achieve an in-depth and clear grasp of the content becomes part of my own learning experience.

Teaching and Studying Holocaust Narratives

Learning historical facts and figures is at the core of Holocaust education but approaching this sensitive topic from a factual perspective may distance many of our learners. My introspective journey sharpened my realization that my thirst for knowledge in this field stemmed from the emotional impression left by my grandparents' stories. These short, simple and direct accounts about individuals, who have a name and a familiar face, facilitated my understanding of the incomprehensible numbers and the vast devastation of the Shoah. Based on the significant impact that my grandparents' testimonies and other Holocaust narratives imprinted on me, I believe that these tools should be used when introducing the Holocaust to students in order to better engage and motivate them. My fortunate meeting with Karen Shawn in 2005 reenforced this belief and we began working on a pedagogical project entitled "The Call of Memory."

The project consists of two volumes, an anthology of short stories about the Holocaust, and a teacher's guide.[2] The twenty-seven short stories chosen for the anthology were selected carefully in order to personalize the statistics and factual data without traumatizing the learners. Each of these stories is accompanied by two chapters in the teacher's guide, a literary analysis chapter and a pedagogical chapter. The two chapters complement one another so as to give instructors a holistic approach to teaching the Holocaust.

Both the anthology and the teachers' guide are organized chronologically and thematically into ten sections offering a variety of perspectives, responses and reflections on the Shoah. This unique approach to teaching the Holocaust does not begin with numbers, facts, and other historical data, but rather gently lures the reader into a singular scene which conveys a more personal encounter with the protagonist's specific predicament, struggle or difficulty. Such an approach enables learners from different grades to relate to and engage with age-appropriate material and pedagogy.

After the anthologies were published in 2008, we learned that the United States Holocaust Memorial Museum distributed both volumes to a number of groups of American educators who visited the museum. This was especially meaningful to me since this same museum framed a picture, taken by Roman Vishniac, of my great grandfather, Chaim Simcha Mechlowitz. The famous picture, known as "The Farmer,"[3] which to the best of my knowledge is still hanging on the fifth floor of the Museum, has a direct relation to two distributed anthologies co-edited by "The Farmer's" great-granddaughter. The untold story of Chaim Simcha, as well as of countless others murdered in Auschwitz, continues to be learned and recounted decades later.

Prof. Shawn and I continued to collaborate on an additional pedagogical project. "The Sunflower Project" invites American and Israeli university students to discuss the moral questions that arise when learning about the Holocaust and other genocidal acts of the twentieth and twenty-first centuries. Based on the second edition of Simon Wiesenthal's thought-provoking book, this international online project requires participating students to read *The Sunflower*,[4] delve into other related Internet sources and hard-copy texts, and develop a dialogue concerning the complex questions raised in these sources. Some of the dilemmas proposed in these forum discussions included the possibility and limits of forgiveness and reconciliation after the Holocaust and other genocides, and the rights and responsibilities of the second and third generations of victims and perpetrators of genocide.

These forum questions, focusing on forgiveness and reconciliation, are not hypothetical in nature. In fact, I recounted to my students a personal incident that occurred when I was in a hotel in Tiberius with my extended family for the Passover holiday. While we were having breakfast in the dining room, a German tourist approached my grandmother and asked if she was a Holocaust survivor. Following her positive response, the man kneeled by her chair and asked her to forgive the German people for the atrocities committed during the Holocaust. I remember being shocked by her definitive "no." Only after reading and discussing with my students some of the essays responding to Simon Wiesenthal's profound questions, such as the responses of Moshe Bejski and Eva Fleischner, did I comprehend my grandmother's response. My personal experience may illuminate the importance of exposing students to a variety of perspectives and giving them a chance to explore ideas with others who come from different countries, cultures and beliefs. In the last few years "The Sunflower Project" has also expanded to include students from the Czech Republic and continues to offer students from diverse cultures and backgrounds a unique learning opportunity while creating closer inter-cultural connections.

Another pedagogical project aimed at university and college students focuses on children's Holocaust testimonies. "Voices of Child Survivors" is a multidisciplinary pedagogical project providing students with a methodological model for analyzing Holocaust testimonies in general, and specifically children's Holocaust testimonies.[5] The project consists of three modules that focus on different Holocaust contexts: The first concentrates on Hungarian children whose testimony was collected in the Aschau DP youth center in 1946;[6] the second module centers around children from East Galicia who were witness to "Aktzyas" between 1941 and 1943;[7] the third module contains testimonies of children who were "on the run."[8] Many testimonies collected from children seem laconic, brief, and devoid of feeling. A multifaceted approach, which combines analyses from the fields of history, linguistics, and literature, reveals layers of meaning and exposes hidden expressions and emotions that may have gone undetected otherwise. In addition to the integration of the analysis from these three fields, the modules created in the framework of this project consist of pedagogical suggestions and ideas so as to provide instructors with a variety of teaching tools that encourage active learning and learner engagement strategies. Working on this project with Joel Walters, Boaz Cohen, and Rita Horvath was an enriching experience. Surprisingly, while working on these children's testimonies, Boaz stumbled across the testimony of my husband's uncle, written in Aschau. My family's history was the starting point in my journey of researching the Holocaust; little did I know that my research would lead me back to it.

"Worlds Meet: The Sciences in the Jewish World" is an elective course given at Bar-Ilan University to students from different faculties and departments.[9] Within the framework of this course, professors from a variety of scientific fields are invited to give students a lecture explaining and illustrating how their research coincides with Jewish faith. For the last nine years, I have chosen to give my lecture just before the "Shavuot" holiday (Pentecost) and entitled it "What is the connection between Shoah and Mount Sinai?" The title builds upon a well-known idiom in Hebrew "What is the connection between Shmita[10] and Mount Sinai?" In modern Hebrew, this idiom is used to express a rhetorical question when comparing seemingly unrelated items, analogously to the English idiom—how can you compare apples and oranges? Nevertheless, a closer look at both the Hebrew and English parallel idioms reveals a strong thematic connection.[11] During this session, students are exposed to a variety of literary responses concerning the complex issue of faith and the Holocaust. As a religious person, this topic has continuously captivated, troubled, and distressed me, but I always remember my paternal grandfather, Saba Yechezkel, telling me how his faith gave him strength and courage. Indeed, some of the literary responses portray this attitude while others reveal a rupture of faith or a reinforcement of disbelief. It is quite difficult to ignore or stay apathetic to the issue of faith in the face of the Holocaust. The session encourages students to read and discuss an array of responses and narratives that are less widely known.

Five years ago, I began another lecture-based project designed for American students who come for a summer science research program at Bar-Ilan University.[12] The title of the lecture is "Ethics and Aesthetics in Holocaust Literature and Film," and during this session we discuss the issue of ethical boundaries of aesthetic representations of the Holocaust. It begins with the assumption that literature and film, or art in general, present the viewer and reader with a point of view, a spectrum of emotions and thoughts. Art represents the individual perception of reality of the person who creates it, and eventually art helps create a new reality in which the perception of the artist is infused into the collective perception of history. We, through art, get a glimpse of reality as it appeared to the artists, and their perception is imparted to us, enabling a broader understanding of the human experience. Based on this assumption, students are presented with examples of books, plays, and movies that pertain to one of three categories of Holocaust representations: Art that includes historical inaccuracies;[13] art that is represented in seemingly inappropriate genres for the Holocaust;[14] and unrepresentative fables.[15] A discussion then ensues regarding the ethical concerns and implications for each of these categories and whether students think they should be introduced and taught to teenagers for educational purposes.

Omission and Excess in Narrative

In the first part of this chapter, I introduced a few personal narratives recounted by my grandparents that are embedded deeply in my life. Reflecting back on the pedagogical projects presented in the second section, it seems that in addition to the educational goals set out in each of these projects, they may have been my way of processing and confronting my family's personal accounts through the teaching of testimonies and literary narratives. These projects enabled me to deal with Holocaust narratives from a variety of perspectives in order to address my own burning questions pertaining to issues such as ethics and religion. Alongside them, I continue to delve into literary analyses of Holocaust narratives in order to expand my theoretical understanding of the various undercurrents and motives that present themselves within these texts. Doing so helps me reexamine my relation to both my family's personal narratives as well as the pedagogical projects. Recently, while working on a new literary project focusing on two of Ida Fink's short stories, I was intrigued by a recurring aura of obscurity surrounding her works.[16] Later I came to realize that this obscurity characterizes many personal and literary Holocaust narratives. I would like to focus on two possible ways in which narratives could be obscured: The first one being the omission of details while the narrative is created, and the second being the excess of added meaning and significance to presented details while the narrative is received.

There may be numerous reasons and causes for details to be omitted out of personal narratives. They could be conscious or subconscious, out of shame or trauma. After my great-aunt passed away, her daughter revealed a secret to me. I found out that my maternal grandmother omitted the fact that she had had a baby during the Holocaust and the baby was taken away from her. I was not with my mother when I heard this information, and I remember how shocked my mother was regarding this unknown fact that my grandmother omitted from her testimonies and accounts. We did not want to confront my grandmother regarding this omission, but shortly after her eighty-seventh birthday, she revealed this detail to my mother. "Maybe I have a half-brother somewhere in this world," my mother would say to me, and on her trips to Europe, she found herself absently looking for strangers that bore some kind of resemblance to our family. Since this important piece of information has surfaced, I cannot help but wonder what other details have been left out, never to be known.

Omissions were also identified in a few of the pedagogical projects mentioned in the previous section. For example, while working on children's testimonies, as part of the "Voices of Child Survivors" project, it was not surprising that most academic students felt the testimonies seemed laconic and devoid of feeling after the first reading. However, a closer guided analysis using the multifaceted approach that integrates the linguistic, literary and historical research techniques revealed details that children omitted—consciously or otherwise—as a way of dealing with difficult moments that their psyche could not handle. Certain handwriting features, for example, can indicate intense emotional hotspots that may include detail omissions, such as neatly written versus messier parts; places where the pen or pencil has been pressed hard on the paper; places where the writing continues even when the pen has run out of ink; changes in letter-formation; spaces left between words; and places that contain inkblots. Indeed, in some cases, recognizing patterns of silence within a testimony is as important as paying attention to the direct statements that were made concerning a specific event within the testimony.[17] This phenomenon could be the result of the testifier's own efforts to prevent the testimony from becoming a re-traumatizing force.[18] The same feeling I had learning about the missing details in my grandmother's story motivated me to take part in the efforts to recover omitted information from these children's testimonies.

The multidisciplinary approach used while working on the children's testimony project, drew from methods used in other fields of research, the most central of which was historical inquiry. Dan Diner, in his book *Cataclysm: A History of the Twentieth Century from Europe's Edge*, explains that omissions unavoidably exist in every historiographical narrative and "no historical presentation located beyond mere chronological recollection can avoid the hazards of selection."[19] This approach guides the theoretical aspect of Diner's usage of memory in historiographical writing; acknowledging the omissive nature of narrative, both historical and that of collective memory, allows Diner to use memory in his interpretation of major twentieth-century events in order to create a multifaceted historical image. History, being the objective component, invites inquiry about facts and evidence, whereas memory, being the subjective component, guides the narrative through the many perspectives surrounding historical events. Diner does not only tell us what happened; he devotes a significant part of the book in contemplation of how to approach what we know had happened. Diner explains his choice to focus on the catastrophes of the first half of the twentieth century by pointing to the centrality of those events to a variety of collective memories: "the century's dominant historical narration has been determined by its catastrophic first half for both contemporaries of the period and the generations that followed."[20] Looking back, the burden of the few details recounted by my grandparents over the years shaped the entire course of my family's lives, as well as my own. These details felt like crumbs, specks, morsels of information, but their weight drew us further into the gaps between them, of everything unsaid.

Obscurity can be caused by the lack of detail in narratives, but also when the presented details invite a multitude of interpretations. In his book, *The Genesis of Secrecy: On the Interpretation of Narrative*, Frank Kermode writes about the exegetical process surrounding parables from the Holy scriptures. According to Kermode, "all narratives possess "hermeneutic potential," which is another way of saying that they must be obscure."[21] That hermeneutic potential is the result of the relationship between a highly valued narrative and its receivers, during which excessive meaning is attributed to each and every detail. An example of this relationship can be found in the hermeneutical traditions of the Bible: The divine source of the narrative accounts for the significance of all the pieces of information presented within it. Unlike the gaps created by omission, the obscurity in the Holy scriptures is caused by details which seem out of place and therefore call for interpretation. In the case of Holocaust narratives, the added historical, collective, and sentimental value that those stories carry within them causes the need for interpretation of seemingly odd details.

My current study of a few of Ida Fink's works revealed to me the inevitable exegetical process engulfing the reader when hermeneutically analyzing and piecing together obscure and odd details in order to create a coherent flow of ideas. In her story "Traces,"[22] for example, Fink portrays a twenty-two-year-old woman, who barely survived the Holocaust, as she tries to find her lost sister two years after the end of the war. Being the only survivor in her family to escape the concentration camps, she knows it is up to her to find the lone family member who may still be alive. Remembering that her parents somehow smuggled her little sister out of the Ghetto with false identification papers to be hidden in a Polish peasant's house, she tries to collect as much information as she possibly can from the townspeople in order to locate her lost sister. She learns that the Kempinski couple who supposedly hid her sister died a couple of years earlier, and so she latches on to every piece of information provided by surrounding witnesses. Since the story is seemingly set out as a play, the reader does not gain access to the sister's thoughts and unexpressed feelings and can mainly create a flow of events based on the dialogues between the characters. One odd detail that stands out from the "Elder's" account highlights Kempinski's extraordinary gardening talent:

> He had a temper worse than the devil himself! But what a gardener! If you saw his cabbage. Heads like the domes of an Orthodox church. And his snapdragons—they were this big! He talked to his flowers. Why not? People talk to animals, why not to flowers?[23]

Since the story has an obscure ending, which does not disclose the whereabouts of the younger sister, the reader assigns a great deal of significance to every revealed detail, in order to decipher possible underlying hints planted by the narrator. This description, delivered to the reader by the town Elder, presents an example of an odd detail that seems out of place within the context of this narrative. Such a dissonance creates an excess of information that in turn calls for explanation and generates a variety of interpretations: Could it be that Kempinski was hiding the girl in an underground cellar, and talking to his flowers was his way of masking his communication with her? Or, maybe his cabbage heads were as big as the domes of an Orthodox church because the ground was fertilized by dead people's bodies, one of whose was the little sister's? Complicating this hermeneutical process even further, the reader cannot ignore the writer's own wartime experience when finding out that Fink and her sister were smuggled out of the Ghetto and hid until the end of the war using false identification papers.

Journeying back to my grandparents, I remember asking my father and uncles, why my grandmother Bella, who was incarcerated in Auschwitz, did not have a number tattooed on her arm. Since my grandmother was killed in a car accident when I was ten years old, I could not ask her myself, and when probed, this detail generated differing interpretations. I remember as a child hearing that she did not have a number because she was very resourceful and managed to hide under the table, thereby escaping the tattoo procedure. Over the years, this odd detail which never fell into place generated other interpretations as well.

Conclusion

The obscurity around Holocaust narratives, which accompanied me throughout my life, fueled my motivation to shed some light on the opaque parts of my family's history. Understanding two possible causes of such obscurity in narrative—omission and excess—helped me understand and reflect on my own process of interpretation when analyzing the details left by my grandparents. That said, my access to Holocaust narratives through my family's personal accounts cannot be taken for granted. The further we get from the historical point in which those events took place, Holocaust narratives become more and more distanced from the current generation's personal experience. Moreover, the traumatic contents of Holocaust history and literature makes it difficult for students to engage with the material as well as for teachers to teach it. The pedagogical projects that I conducted and took part in showed time and time again that methods such as encouraging independent inquiry and utilizing active learning tools spark curiosity and increase motivation to continue and explore this thought-provoking subject matter. The hermeneutic potential contained in literary Holocaust narratives poses a challenge as well as an opportunity for future researchers and activists, who will need to further analyze and explore the vast amount of material that has yet to be researched.

Notes

1 Rabbi Hanina, *The Babylonian Talmud*, Tractate Ta'anit, 7a.
2 Karen Shawn and Keren Goldfrad, eds., *The Call of Memory: Learning about the Holocaust through Narrative: An Anthology* (Teaneck, NJ: Ben Yehuda Press, 2008). Karen Shawn and Keren Goldfrad, eds., *The Call of Memory: Learning about the Holocaust through Narrative: A Teacher's Guide* (Teaneck, NJ: Ben Yehuda Press, 2008).
3 "The Farmer," The United States Holocaust Museum, https://www.ushmm.org/collections/the-museums-collections/collections-highlights/vishniac-collection/photo-gallery/the-farmer (accessed September 30, 2021).
4 Simon Wiesenthal, *The Sunflower* (New York: Schocken Books, 1998).
5 "Voices of Child Survivors: Children's Holocaust Testimonies." Modules prepared with the support of the Conference on Jewish Material Claims Against Germany, Inc. and the Rabbi Israel Miller Fund for Shoah Education, Research and Documentation. Joel Walters, Rita Horvath, Boaz Cohen, Keren Goldfrad.
6 "From Hungary to Auschwitz and Back," Western Galilee College, https://cwg1945.org/wp-content/uploads/2019/07/Module-1.pdf (accessed September 30, 2021).

7 "Children in the Midst of Mass Killing Actions (Aktzyas)—Eastern Galicia," Western Galilee College, https://cwg1945.org/wp-content/uploads/2019/07/Module-2-.pdf (accessed September 30, 2021).

8 "Children on the Run in a Land of Genocide," Western Galilee College, https://cwg1945.org/wp-content/uploads/2019/07/Module-3-.pdf (accessed September 30, 2021).

9 Keren Goldfrad, "Mount Sinai and Holocaust Literature," in *Worlds Meet: The Sciences in the Jewish World*, ed. Avraham Gottlieb (Ramat Gan: Bar Ilan University Press, 2018), 296–309 (in Hebrew).

10 Shmita, in Jewish Law, means that during the seventh year of a seven-year cycle, the land of Israel should lie fallow and cannot be cultivated.

11 In the English idiom, both apples and oranges are fruits, so there is room for comparison. In the Hebrew version, Rashi who coined the term, responds to his own question by answering that mentioning Shmita in the context of Mount Sinai shows that all the commandments and all the details of those commandments were given on Mount Sinai. The answer explains the connection between Mount Sinai and Shmita.

12 "Summer Science Research Program," https://www.biu.ac.il/en/faculties-programs/programs/summer-science-research (accessed September 30, 2021).

13 Some film adaptations of historical novels change certain facts in order to create more drama. One such historical novel is Nechama Tec's *Defiance: The Bielski Partisans*, which was later produced as a film directed by Edward Zwick. Some of the battles that occur in the film never actually took place, but were added to make the movie version more thrilling.

14 Examples of seemingly inappropriate genres may include Art Spiegleman's graphic novel *Maus*, or the Hebrew Opera "And the Rat Laughed" which is based on Nava Semel's book and composed by Ella Milch-Sheriff.

15 Examples of unrepresentative fables may include Bernhard Schlink's *The Reader* or John Boyne's *The Boy with the Striped Pyjamas*.

16 Ida Fink, *Traces: Stories*, trans. Philip Boehm and Francine Prose (New York: Metropolitan Books, 1997). Ida Fink, *A Scrap of Time and Other Stories*, trans. Madeline Levine and Francine Prose (Illinois: Northwestern University Press, 1995).

17 Keren Goldfrad, "Voices of Child Survivors: A Multidisciplinary Approach to Children's Holocaust Testimonies," in *From Testimony to Story: Video Interview about Nazi Crimes, Perspectives and Experiences in Four Countries, Education with Testimonies*, eds. Dagi Knellessen and Ralf Possekel (Berlin: Stiftung Erinnerung, Verantwortung und Zukunft (EVZ) 2015), 2.

18 Boaz Cohen and Rita Horva´th, "Young Witnesses in the DP Camps: Children's Holocaust testimony in context," *Journal of Modern Jewish Studies* 11 (2012):103–25.

19 Dan Diner (2008), *Cataclysms: A History of the Twentieth Century from Europe's Edge*, trans. William Templer with Joel Golb (Madison: University of Wisconsin Press, 2008), 3.

20 Diner, *Cataclysms*, 9.
21 Frank Kermode (1979), *The Genesis of Secrecy: On the Interpretation of Narrative*, (Massachusetts: Harvard University Press), 45.
22 Fink, "Traces," *Traces*, 155–81.
23 Fink, "Traces", *Traces*, 168.

16

"Why Don't You Move On?": A Sort of Play in Three Acts and Three Standing Ovations

Roy Horovitz

Prologue

Time: March 2013.

The TimeKeepers, a theater production I am acting in, is touring South Africa.

It is the first time that we're performing in a country where the majority of the audience has little connection to the Second World War or the Holocaust. Every show that we do is followed by a Q&A, with sessions often lasting longer than the show itself. The audience is very heterogenic: young, older, whites, blacks, Jews, Gentiles. For some members of the audience, our show is the first time that they hear about the concentration camps and the Jewish yellow star.

One night, a white woman stands up and says: "Your show is very moving. It was a good theatrical experience, but why don't you move on? Seriously?! I really don't see the point in you coming here, all the way from Israel, with another play about the Holocaust. It's been what, seventy years already ... Move on! What's wrong with you, trying to make the whole world feel guilty and sympathize with you? Come on, guys, give us a break."

She was very articulate and charismatic. Within seconds, she transformed the whole vibe and managed to turn it against us. Furthermore, I immediately realized that she certainly had a point: Israeli theater *does* have a serious, central preoccupation with the Holocaust. It *does* seem like we are not "moving on" ... What could I say? All eyes turned to me with great anticipation; I took a deep breath.

"Look," I opened. "In my opinion, the customer is always right. If you find our play to be an anachronistic piece, what can I do but feel sorry? However, may I please ask you something?"

"Sure."

"You aren't Jewish, are you?"

"No, I'm Christian."

"No offence please, but to the best of my knowledge, some 2,000 years ago, there was a man named Jesus. He ended his life on the cross and ever since then the Christian world hasn't stopped blaming the Jews for his unfortunate fate. One body, a long time ago, whereas the Holocaust involves the loss of over 6,000,000 bodies of our people, just seventy years ago. Do you really think that something is wrong with our proportions? Let me assure you: Once you move on from your single case, we'll reconsider."

I don't know how where I got this answer from. All I do remember is that woman turning pale while I enjoyed the loudest applause I'd ever received in my entire career, and an unforgettable standing ovation (the first one, two more to come later on in this chapter ...). It certainly brought an end to the discussion that night, but the questions still stay with me: Should I / we move on from the Holocaust? Is it possible? And—above all—*do I want to?*

Act 1: Child and Adolescent

It is seven years later. I have a PhD in literature and theatre, and I receive an invitation to write a short academic autobiography about my work in the field of the Holocaust, both as an artist and a scholar. This invitation is a great honor, yet raises a reflexive question (why me? What could I contribute?) and how to even approach the matter. I study the genre and find that the goal of an academic autobiography is "to shed light on your history, as you do for the history of someone else ... To analyze as a historian, the link between the history that you make and the history that made you."[1] Something deep inside me is drawn to this mesmerizing retrospective adventure. A quick overview revealed that over the years I have indeed accumulated quite some mileage in exploring the Holocaust: writing essays, teaching relevant courses, and no fewer than ten productions that I either directed or participated in (which I usually also initiated). The opportunity to tie what seemed like sporadic episodes to a holistic narrative appeals to me, so I sit and write.

I was born in 1970, the youngest child in the family, born much later than my siblings. My mother, Miriam (may she rest in peace), was born in Israel to a large family of rich merchants, who came to Israel from Aleppo, Syria.

My father, Yitzhak (may he also rest in peace), was born in Berlin in 1927, his parents' only child. In January 1933, when he was six years old, Hitler came to power. A few weeks later, a few children beat up my father in the school yard. My grandfather understood it was time to leave Germany. The family made Aliyah to Israel (then Palestine) and settled in the city of Haifa. Thirty-six years later, I was born in that very same city.

My father and his family escaped Europe and the horrors of the Holocaust before it was too late. They fled, but their spirit remained behind. They kept the language and mentality of their homeland, and yearned for European culture all their lives. This yearning was never spoken of, but through some miraculous alchemy their memories also trickled down to me. The Holocaust haunts me. My friends always joke that if I do not read a Holocaust book at bedtime, I won't be able to fall asleep and whenever I go on vacation, I always make sure to pack *Sophie's Choice* or *Every Man Dies Alone* . . . The Holocaust remained unspoken in our house. To satisfy my immense curiosity, I obsessively consumed books, films, and TV shows on the subject.

One of my earliest memories is watching the documentary series *Pillar of Fire* on Israeli television. I first learned of the existence of the innocent-looking showers, that were in fact gas chambers, in the death camps while watching one of its episodes. I can still remember the dreadful sound of the heavy doors shutting on the miserable victims. For years, I would shower with the shower curtain open, and got into the habit of smelling the water, before taking a shower, just to check. This continued throughout my adolescence. The showers at the basic training camp in Israel where I was based after being drafted into the army at the age of eighteen, had no curtains. There, the question of "to close or not to close" became irrelevant.

I was a sensitive and introverted child. I discovered theater in fifth grade. A friend from school enrolled into a drama class and convinced me as well. It was love at first sight. Playing characters, standing on stage and improvising, I felt that I found my place. I quickly combined my interest in the art that I discovered with subjects that fascinated me. When we were asked to present characters and monologues, I instantaneously chose to perform Weiskopf's monologue from Joshua Sobol's play *Ghetto* (which later became my permanent dramatic monologue, which I performed in every audition, including the one for acting school):

> Oy oy oy, ay ay ay! Why the crying, why the weeping? Times are hard? So what's new? When did our people have it easy? Hardship makes us strong. Take me, for example. Before the war I had a little tailor's shop. The Germans came, pushed us into the ghetto. The shop's gone. Finished. So did I cry? Of course not. Will tears bring it back? Hell no! Instead of crying I held my wise Jewish Kopf in my hands, and I said to myself: Why do they call you Weiskopf? You've lost your shop, it's true; now if you lose your Kopf— you're kaput . . .[2]

I savored the immense gift that acting offered. For the first time in my life, I could not only read about things, but also act them out physically. I discovered the power of theater, the art of both the fleeting moment and the present which makes it possible to return to the scene of the crime, to resurrect the dead, and sometimes even find happiness and beauty amid the horror.

The coupling of the Holocaust with theater raises complex aesthetical and ethical questions, or to use Joshua Sobol's quotation of Hermann Kruk: "no theater in a graveyard." Yet at the same time, linking the two concepts is widespread. After Weiskopf, I moved on to Yossaleh, the protagonist of Ben-Zion Tomer's *Children of the Shadow*, and the *Poisonous Mushroom*—a musical revue of Bertolt Brecht, which I directed with my classmates at school. As a theatergoer, I also found myself drawn to "Holocaust plays" such as Hanoch Levin's *The Child Dreams*.

The Holocaust features centrally in Israeli theater. No other historical event or theme has such intensive treatment in Israeli art. The South African woman was right: Israeli theater is not letting go of the subject! One hundred original Israeli plays can be classified as "Holocaust plays." This number is not surprising: Drama has always found extreme situations deeply alluring; and the horrors of the Second World War offer fertile ground for inspiration.

A salient feature of Israeli theater's treatment of the Holocaust is the manner in which it focuses only on Jewish suffering and ignores the historical common fate shared with other victims of the Nazi regime and the dreadful war. As Yuval Noah Harari states: "history isn't a single narrative, but thousands of alternative narratives. Whenever we choose to tell one, we are also choosing to silence others."[3] In my own works, I wish to enter in this exact space, to tell the untold story and make place, alongside the Jewish story, for the suffering of others: homosexuals, Japanese, second- and third-generation survivors and even the Germans themselves. I try to draw that veil of Israeli dramaturgy around these and other issues that Israeli playwrights tend to ignore. For instance, I commissioned two prominent playwrights (Hanoch Reim and Roi Rashkes) to each write a play (*Stills*, a semi-documentary play, written by Reim and directed by me, was staged at Habima National Theater in 2001; *Sadako–The Crain Princess*, written by Rashkes, tells the story of the Japanese girl Sadako Sasaki, "Japan's Anne Frank," who was a victim of the atomic bomb dropped on Hiroshima. The play was staged in Tzavta in 2015 under my direction). I also brought and staged foreign plays written by playwrights from Germany, South Africa, the United Sates, and Australia. To fulfil this dream, I had to first finish my military service. Once released from the IDF, I auditioned for the top three acting schools in Israel (with Weiskopf's monologue, of course) and was accepted to all three. I chose Nissan Nativ Acting Studio. My father agreed to pay for my studies if I promised him that, after finishing them, I would study a "real" profession that would provide me a safety net. I made the promise (but in my heart, I didn't promise to keep it).

Acting classes are an intensive and visceral experience. Those were challenging years for me, but they shaped me as a professional and a human being, for better or worst. I would just say that I now try to be a better, more sensitive teacher to my students, than some of my own teachers were.

Act 2: Actor

I left acting school without a sense of security. Unlike my classmates, I had no job offers waiting for me. I experienced doubts as to whether I could make it. I traveled to England to rest and to find focus. Benny Barbash's book *My First Sony* had just come out and I took it with me to London and read it with bated breath. The novel follows the unraveling of an Israeli family from the point of view of the son—eleven-year-old Yotam. The boy is obsessed with documenting and tape-recording everything. In *My First Sony*, I found my first dream role. I convinced Barbash to adapt his book into a one-man show, which premiered at the Theatroneto Festival in 1996. The show was received enthusiastically by critics and audiences alike and has been running ever since, for over twenty-five years. The book was translated into many languages and became an international best seller. It is taught in prestigious universities like Harvard and Yale, to which I was also invited to perform. I also toured with the play in Canada, South Africa, Germany, the Netherlands, Slovakia, Australia, and Egypt. The play's successes gave me back my confidence and established the long line of "Holocaust-plays" in my career:

> And so, Dad became a ghost writer, which is someone who writes other people's stories for them and signs their names. Each of these survivors had his own way of telling their story. There was Sonya Kravitz of Grodna, who lived for two years in a pit, in a pigsty, with good Gentiles, and before important things she would say to Dad: "pay attention!" Or: "write it in my words!" Or: "let me emphasize!" For example, she said "Inside it, inside our pit, in the pigsty on the banks of the river Niemen, childhood passes by. The clothes we brought with us are too small, the shoes don't fit. Henya, who was a year old when we came, learnt to speak. I got my period. Emphasize!"[4]

While I was working on the play, I also fulfilled my promise to my father and enrolled at Tel Aviv University. I studied psychology, but soon switched to BA studies in the Theater Department, continuing to reassure my parents that this course could provide me with the "security net" they had wished for. I finished my studies (with distinction) and immediately continued on to my master's degree; I also began to teach in the department, taking on courses for students of acting and directing. In one of them, I focused on monologues and dialogues from Holocaust plays. At the same time, I was invited to teach Israeli theater at the University of Texas at Austin and in the Hebrew Program at Middlebury College, Vermont. Witnessing students from Saudi Arabia and Egypt encounter Israeli plays was an unforgettable experience for me. At the same time, I also started working as an actor, first in Haifa theater and later in cinema (including a very silly film alongside Antonio Banderas and Sir Derek Jacobi).

However, my highlight as an actor came with my next Holocaust show, *The Timekeepers*, by American playwright Dan Clancy, winner of the Obie Award. If, in *My First Sony*, the Holocaust was in the background, in *The Timekeepers* it is front and center. The plot of the play takes place in Sachsenhausen concentration camp and depicts an encounter between three prisoners: Jewish watchmaker Benjamin (yellow star); Hans, a flamboyant homosexual (pink triangle); and a German criminal (green triangle), who acts as a kapo, watching over the other two. Hans and Benjamin fix watches that the Nazis plunder from their victims.[5] At the beginning of the play, they are suspicious of each other, but quickly form a strong friendship. The uniqueness of the play lies in the way it combines brutal scenes (like the one in which the kapo makes Hans perform oral sex on him) with moments of humor (Hans and Benjamin as the "odd couple"):

Benjamin: I am married to Sarah for twelve years now. I knew her all my life. Our families were friends—even as little children our families would say: "Sarah and Benjamin," "Benjamin and Sarah" . . .
Hans: If my father had to say: "Hans and Kurt," "Kurt and Hans," he would probably throw up.[6]

One of the salient features of new and controversial writing about the Holocaust, dating from early 2000, is the fact that it incorporates humor into Holocaust stories. For example, the heated debate surrounding the release of Roberto Benigni's film *La vita è bella* (1997) is well remembered. This mix of horrors and comic devices was seen by some as an amoral reduction of the historical truth.[7] Yet, those in favor of the genre have claimed that humor is an inseparable part of the human experience and can be used as an effective psychological survival mechanism in times of stress, pointing towards the plethora of testimonials regarding the existence of wild humor in the ghettos and the camps.[8] This ethical and aesthetical debate was also present in our rehearsal room, and we kept asking ourselves how the audience would react to this play. We were worried not only about the humor but also about whether the Jewish-Israeli audience would be able to accept an a Jewish prisoner being depicted *alongside other victims*. This panoramic representation, as stated above, can find no equivalent in any original Israeli Holocaust play.

The Timekeepers first premiered in 2002, at Tmuna Theatre, a small fringe venue, and quickly became a huge success. The critics raved about the play. It ran to hundreds of performances and represented Israel in prestigious festivals around the world, including twenty-five shows at Edinburgh Festival, and won the "Audience Choice" Award in the International Fringe Theater Festival in Edmonton. *The Timekeepers* became the most internationally toured Israeli play (alongside Hanoch Levin's *Requiem*). Many of the tours were funded by the Israeli Ministry of Foreign Affairs. Thus, for instance, in 2010, the play was sent on tour to San Francisco as the representative of "Gay Israeli Culture" (some viewed it as a cynical attempt to "pink wash" international opinion of Israel and present it in a liberal, flattering light, given the rising criticism of the incumbent government's policies). I remember vividly one particular trip to Germany in 2008. I invited my father to join us, thinking that returning to Germany would offer him some kind of closure. I could not have anticipated what was to come: At the end of the celebratory show, we sat as—we usually did, we three actors from Israel—for a Q&A with the audience. The discussion was in English with the German theater director hosting. At a certain point, a man from the audience got up and spoke: "thank you for a wonderful evening. I especially liked that Hans and Benjamin, the protagonists of your play, are not nice. When Hans, for instance, blackmails Benjamin and doesn't give him news about his son until he receives some payback from him, it sends an important message that the victims were also racist and homophobes, not just the Nazis, and that we're all human. That each one of us is also a Nazi." A murmur passed through the crowd, I saw the host beside me move in discomfort.

Suddenly, my father stood up from his seat in the middle of the fifth row and gave a long monologue in fluent German. I could see that he was very upset, but since I do not speak the language, I could not understand a word he said. Naturally I looked to the host who was supposed to translate for us, but he was transfixed by my father. Once the speech was over and my father sat down, something incredible happened: The crowd stood up as one and clapped (the second standing ovation. Remember? To be continued . . .). I could not understand what had just taken place, but one thing was clear: My father was the star of the evening and had stolen our thunder! They later explained to us that he, who could not stay silent, said something along these lines:

> I was born here in 1927. When the Nazis came to power, my schoolmates beat me because I was Jewish. I return here, seventy-five years later, with my son, not to hear one of you clearing his conscience and comparing victim to victimizer. If the play showed us a lack of solidarity between the different prisoners, it is because someone put them in an impossible situation in which they had to survive at all costs. There are people who are responsible for the horrible situation they found themselves in. We did not come all the way here from Israel so that someone here will use

us to cleanse the Germans' guilt. And we will not leave here until everyone is clear about the humane and historical lesson that is to be learned from this event.

Five years later, when I myself stood before the member of the audience in South Africa and answered her in a similar fashion, my cast members joked that "the apple did not fall far from the tree."

In *The Timekeepers*, which is still running, I found the ultimate recipe, one that would define my later works, as an actor and mainly as a director: Focusing on a private case (that the viewers can connect with more easily than with abstract masses), expanding the narrative beyond the Jewish context, and injecting the humor that I find necessary. Comic relief is as vital as oxygen if we are to grapple with this subject.

Act 3: Director and Scholar

After receiving my master's degree, I directed dozens of plays in most theatres in Israel. Many of them were "Holocaust plays." I was also fortunate to work with two of the best actresses in Israel, Lea Koenig and Miriam Zohar, both Holocaust survivors, and now in their nineties.

In *The Haunted Stage*,[9] Marvin Carlson presents a holistic conceptualization of theater as a "memory machine." In using this metaphor, he shows that each component of any production carries with it its own significant cultural history. He argues that a salient characteristic of every theater show is its "ghosting": Each participant brings to the stage his or her own "ghosts" of personal and professional biography, and these ghosts act as a crucial part in interpreting the work. The encounter between actors and audience, the pillar of every theatrical event, does not take place in an empty mental space:

> The "private" lives, real or imagined, of famous actors and actresses have been a source of great interest to the theatre going public and have unquestionably affected that public's reception of the artists' work.[10]

In this context, it would be difficult to find two other actresses whose physical presence and public personas are so identified with the memory of the Holocaust and Jewish culture in Eastern Europe as Koenig and Zohar. Between 2011 and 2021, I directed Koenig in no fewer than eight different productions, and Zohar in four. I will briefly discuss a few highlights:

Koenig is the daughter of two great Yiddish actors. She considers it a sacred duty to preserve the Yiddish language and its glorious culture. I bore witness to her dedication when we traveled to New York in June 2019. The city was hosting an international festival to celebrate 100 years since the foundation of the first Yiddish theater in town. Koenig performed a show that I directed at The Museum of Jewish Heritage. It included monologues and songs in Yiddish and won the hearts of the audience. When the clapping subsided, someone shouted: "what about something in English?" The actress took the microphone and said something along these lines:

> Excuse me, ladies and gentlemen. Tonight, I came to you to speak in the name of the great Yiddish authors and poets. There are performances in English in many other places in this city, every night. But Yiddish was sentenced to death. This great culture was pushed away and not allowed to thrive. I, myself, perform in Israel, every night, in Hebrew. Not in the language my parents spoke. So forgive me, but tonight I will speak in no other language.

And again (a third time, halleluiah!) the audience gave her a standing ovation.

I directed Zohar in 2017 in *Certificate of Life*, a play written by Jewish-Austrian playwright Ron Elisha. The protagonist, Clara Reich, is a Holocaust survivor who is required to come, on a yearly basis, to the German consulate to renew her certificate, which allows her to continue receiving her pension. Reich takes advantage of this annual appointment to make the young German clerk there miserable, and degrades her continually: "Her welfare is not my primary concern," she explains.[11] In a typical monologue, she confronts the young clerk with the absurdity of their bureaucracy:

> For twelve long years, the German people expended every fiber of their being in annihilating us. They tried everything in their power, from bullets to piano wire to starvation to torture to gas. And then the war ended. And the dust settled. And, to their utter disbelief, there we were. The Jews. Still alive . . . And so, every year since the fall of the Reich, the very same Germans who were consumed with orchestrating our deaths insist that we prove to them that we are still alive . . . So I ask you: Is that or is that not an irony of the most delicious order?[12]

Certificate of Life is also a comedy drama. Watching Reich confront the German clerk gave the Israeli audience a deep sense of satisfaction. In the survivor's caustic words, they saw a proper "Zionist" response to the murderers and their heirs.

My next collaboration with Zohar carried a similar quality. We worked on Victor Gordon's *You Will Not Play Wagner*. Here, she plays Esther Greenbaum, a rich American Jew and a patron of an international conducting competition that takes place every year in Tel Aviv. One of the competitors, a young Israeli, wishes to conduct a piece of Wagner's music and causes a scandal. The play revolves around his confrontation with Greenbaum, who refuses to lift the ban on playing Wagner in Israel. At the apex of the play, the heroine gives a poignant monologue:

> My past's irrelevant; just one of thousands who survived, many of whom live here, who experienced worse, much worse—thousands—straight from the camps with nothing—less than nothing, to a new country that all too often, to its shame, failed to even bid them welcome—did not know what to do with them; shunned them, looked away, saw them as weak, pathetic—a danger, yes, to the spirit of the new Jew who'd resolved not to give one inch to *anyone* ever again. *Never again.* No submission, no surrender, no gas . . . and let me say it so you clearly hear—*No Wagner! You, Yaakov, will not play Wagner* . . . No doubt the time will come when they *will* forget or just no longer care . . . where people like me will become an obstacle to what they see as progress.[13]

The production premiered during Miri Regev's turbulent time as Minister of Culture, when the subject of cultural boycott and artists' self-censorship was at the heart of public debate. Zohar, who was not afraid to voice her opinion against Regev's policy, was happy to take part in a play that encourages critical thinking.[14]

I completed my PhD in 2019, and immediately joined the Department of Comparative Literature in Bar-Ilan University as a senior lecturer. My practical work in the theater nourishes my academic research and vice versa: Back in high school, after watching *Ghetto*, I wrote an extensive paper on cultural life in the Vilna Ghetto, for which I received a national award from the President of Israel at the time, Chaim Herzog. My writing is practice based and I aspire that it may always have a practical application in the field of theater. In recent years, I published articles about the (lack of) representation of the "pink Holocaust" in Israeli theater and my work with the Koenig-Zohar duo, which I view as a calling. I truly regard it as a generational "passing of the torch."

Epilogue

Theater is the art of the present—as the great acting guru Stella Adler taught us: "On stage, it is always present." And yet, good theater strives towards timelessness. Returning to the question from the South African woman with which we opened—"Why don't you move on?"—my answer is: Because I do not wish to! The Holocaust continues to drive me forward with deep intensity. I keep extracting valuable lessons from this event: If the Nazis attempted to reduce the personal identification spaces of their victims by labeling them as "Jews," "communists," "homosexuals," "Gypsies," and so forth, then I seek to avoid definitions and expand my horizons. I constantly strive to widen the perspective: To act, direct, research, and teach both in Hebrew and in English, in Israel and abroad.

In the next year, I am planning to direct two more plays that reflect on the Holocaust. Just like in the shower room of my childhood, I have no intention of closing the curtain.

Notes

1. Pierre Nora, *Essa is d'ego-histoire* (Paris: Gallimard, 1987), 7.
2. Joshua Sobol, *Ghetto*, trans. Jeremy Sams. Scene 9. Never published.
3. Yuval Noah Harari, *Homo Deus: A Brief History of Tomorrow* (London: Vintage Publishing, 2017), 205.
4. Benny Barbash, *My First Sony*, trans. Dalia Bilu (London: Headline Review, 1999), 141–6.
5. The Oscar-winning film, *The Counterfeiters* (Best Foreign Film Category, 2017), which presents the story of the Nazis use of prisoners with artistic skills to counterfeit British bills and coins during the war, also takes place in Sachsenhausen.
6. Dan Clancy, *The TimeKeepers*, scene 3. Never published.
7. See, for instance, Kobi Niv, *Life Is Beautiful, But Not for Jews: Another View of the Film by Benigni*, trans. Jonathan Beyrak Lev. Filmmaker Series, No. 107 (Lanham, MD, and Oxford: The Scarecrow Press, 2003).
8. See, for instance, Itamar Levin (ed.), *"Meebe'ad ladma'ot"* ("Beyond the Tears: Jewish Humor Under the Nazi Regime") (Jerusalem and Tel Aviv: Yad Vashem, Yedioth Ahronoth, 2004).
9. Marvin Carlson, *The Haunted Stage: The Theatre as Memory Machine* (Ann Arbor: University of Michigan Press, 2003).
10. Ibid., 85.
11. Elisha, Ron. *Certificate of Life*. Scene 11. Never published.
12. Ibid, Scene 2.
13. Gordon, Victor. *You Will Not Play Wagner*. Scene 2. Never published.
14. For instance, this is how the play presents the young conductor's arguments: "Banning music does nothing—nothing to stop antisemitism; how can it? *Parsifal* should contribute no more pain to a Jew than a Mercedes driving through the streets of Tel Aviv—and shit, look around—there're enough of them! It makes no sense—none at all—I refuse to be part of such thinking ... Look around you. We don't ban **them**, their technology—even their money—no—so we ban their culture. Why? Because that way we protest while we sacrifice nothing. We repeat their stupidity! ... like **them**, like Chairman Mao Zedong, we ban culture! To our shame, we choose the same path" (Ibid, Scene 3).

17

Intersecting Narratives: When East Meets West

Yvonne Kozlovsky Golan

Forward: A Mizrahi Child Approaches the Holocaust

The first person I looked up to, who was not a family member, was the Israeli envoy to the United Nations from 1968 to 1975, Yosef Tekoah. His fiery speeches and display of self-confidence towards the Arab states and their verbal assault on our country aroused great pride in me. Israeli television, then in its infancy, frequently aired news broadcasts consisting mainly of "us versus them." I was unfamiliar with the Holocaust or with the existential anxiety that characterized Israeli society, and therefore did not understand Ambassador Tekoa's passion. When I began asking questions about the war and his approach to it, my parents replied that this was because of what had been done to the Jews in the Holocaust and because we were Israelis. Then I understood that being a Jew was a big deal and apparently also aroused jealousy, as my father said. When I asked, "What's the Holocaust?" my parents said that it has to do with Ashkenazim and emphasized that it was none of my business. I was born into a family of *Olim* from Iran; a conservative, traditional family that jealously guarded its privacy. In hindsight, I understand that they felt that it was not theirs to deal with the experiences of others, especially such horrific ones.

I never thought I would become involved in the subject of film in law, much less the Holocaust. My family is not one of survivors and did not experience antisemitism in its most profound and painful form. When the war was raging in Europe, my parents were just coming into the world. My family had a dual approach to Israeli society: On one hand my parents were

Zionists, but on the other they viewed Israelis with disdain, scorning them for their lack of respect to their fellowmen and their blunt directness in conversation. In fact, outside of school hours, only two avenues to the outside world were open to us: television and the mobile library, which visited us twice a week.

The movies I watched in my childhood were very limited and broadcast in an unchanging loop for decades. Once a year, like clockwork, Israeli television (which had only one station at the time) aired the play *The Diary of Anne Frank* on Holocaust Remembrance Day. It was interesting, but the end-without-an-end always frustrated me. I wanted to know what happened to her, finally. As a native Israeli who was uninvolved in the Holocaust narrative, I did not really connect to her character: To me, she seemed like a regular child with problems that were just like mine. I did not respond well to the obligation to read her diary. In hindsight, I know that this obligation should have been accompanied by better preparation: No one took into account that there were children unfamiliar with contemporary history and why one should be afraid of others or hide from them.

That same year (1973–4), when the BBC serial *The World at War* was aired, I was fascinated by the narration and the historical events; the opening titles with flames conjuring up the faces of leaders and personalities from the world wars opened a window to a world that was beyond the small circle in which I lived. Since then, my historical consciousness has been shaped by the screen: Through it, I connected to the world and understood the media's power to generate change, to enhance and reduce knowledge, to shape national and historical identities. In time, watching and analyzing the media corpus became a significant part of my life. As a professional situated at multi-disciplinary research intersections, I have implemented these insights to strengthen and shape the consciousness and knowledge of the students in the MA Interdisciplinary Research Program for Culture and Film Studies I established at the University of Haifa.

But let's not get ahead of ourselves. In my first years of school, the Holocaust was, in the deepest sense of the word, *obscure* for me; like viewing a coin submerged in deep water. I was exposed to the Holocaust on several occasions, which in time became a central part of my personal and professional life as a Holocaust researcher, to the extent that every event became a subject of study and investigation. I could not rest until I got to the bottom of things.

The first occasion was during a visit to my grandmother's house. The neighborhood she lived in was a mix of *olim*, among whom lived the Hungarian Madam Sarah, her husband, and their dog. They were a somewhat odd, childless couple. Once, Madam Sarah confronted a group of children she thought wanted to harm her dog. She erupted into a bout of hysterical screaming, and cried and wandered around, as if it was not her anxiety for her dog that was troubling her but something else entirely, something that was not there. The people sitting on their balconies watched her, laughed, and mocked her. My grandmother leaped to her defense, shooed away the children, and said to the other neighbors, "Leave her alone, she escaped Hitler's clutches." I did not understand who Hitler was and what kind of clutches he had, but my grandmother hushed me and said no more. I was told that Madam Sarah was a poor soul who must be treated with compassion. Only thirty years later, after lengthy research on disturbed and abused women in the Holocaust, did I understand the causes of her post-traumatic behavior.

The second occasion was at a school assembly. We were summoned to the yard to listen to a young woman who sat at one edge of the yard. Our principal, Ella Handler, wore black; in fact, she always wore black to ceremonies; only many years later did I understand that she had lost her entire family in the Holocaust. The speaker was named Rachel. She sat on a wooden chair and possessed a transparent beauty. To me she seemed like a nymph that had emerged from a place I knew nothing about, and then she began telling her story from a distance, as if it had nothing to do with her. I don't remember much of the story, but what I do remember is etched so deeply in me that to this day I know and comprehend the power and importance of testimony, and especially of filmic testimony, which became one of the central means of incriminating the Nazis in the Nuremberg trails. Over time, photographic testimonies became a very significant part of my research.

I was fascinated by Rachel. Her heroic story, her beauty, and halting voice with a foreign accent touched my heart. I wanted to know more and why. I felt I was part of her story even before I heard it. When I came home, I asked if we had Holocaust survivors among us and was answered in the negative. "But surely there is someone with a tattoo on their arm?" I queried. During the next few weeks, when we had guests, I closely observed their bare arms, but to no avail. My parents explained to me: "It happened in Europe, to the Ashkenazim; we had other troubles." My parents seemed to understand the boundaries of Holocaust memory and their place in Israeli society: At the time, these boundaries were very clearly defined, as were those who were included within them and those who were not.

We lived in the Givat Shaul neighborhood of Jerusalem. To the right of our street stood "the nuthouse," which was not to be mentioned and looked more like a prison, housing "special" and very strange patients. The few figures we managed to see—people in pale blue pajamas and shaved heads wandering around the yard—frightened us. For some reason, I recall pink shiny heads among the shadows cast by the pine trees. Today, I know that what I had seen was perhaps my first encounter with Holocaust survivors and with the image of the *Muselmann*, whose meaning I understood only decades later. The expression of such images formed the basis of my research of Holocaust consciousness among viewers. The face of one of the patients, who looked straight at me, is engraved in my memory to this day. It held neither light nor darkness, just emptiness and astonishment. I encountered this look once again in movies about the liberation of the Nazi concentration camps, which were the subject of my research at Yad Vashem.

I had no choice but to return to my haven in my beloved world of literature. At school the teachers had several books in a well-locked closet that was seldom opened, and there was no municipal library in our neighborhood. However, we had a mobile library that came by twice a week, so my reading pace was determined by its arrivals. I would leave the library with a stack of books on the Holocaust. The stories were so vivid that at night I was afraid the Germans would knock on our door and take us away. My anxiety increased further when I realized that we would not know how to speak in "Nazi" with the Germans, and that would really be the end of us. Things began to make sense to me: Jews—jealousy—hatred—persecution—annihilation. From that time on, I was able to fit the figure of Yosef Tekoah very well in the puzzle.

Forbidden Love

The dramatic event that shaped my historic and national consciousness occurred to me on the personal level in the tenth grade, when I was fifteen years old. I was chosen to be a member of a municipal youth delegation to the United States. Before we left, we were asked to host a delegation of athletes from Austria, or to be exact, from Tyrol. I gathered two of them to my house: Peter and Johan. As a gift, I received a picture book describing the grand views of Tyrol and its beautiful sites. A strong chemistry formed between Johan, who was twenty-two years old, and me. We met briefly several times during his stay in Israel and we toured Jerusalem together. It was a first love, innocent and real; a Platonic love that never came to fruition. He confessed in his letters. He missed me and wanted to see me again. I asked him what his parents would say if I came to his village in Tyrol as a Jew. For an entire month he did not reply, until finally he wrote: "I don't think that would be a good idea. I talked to my father, and he doesn't want to see you. He had a bad experience with the Jews in the past." Thus, he hinted that our relationship had ended. I was angry at this reply and wondered at his decision. How could someone break their vow of love? I could not imagine that standing in the background of the relationship between Johan and me, there was a Nazi with a mustache. I had not yet heard of Mauthausen and the other camps scattered around the area. Who was his father? What had he done? Twenty years later, when I delved deeper into this subject, I was shocked: In a joint study with a colleague from Vienna University, we discovered abominable rituals from the Middle Ages that were performed in the camp before executions. To this day, these rituals are performed each year as entertainment in village festivals throughout Tyrol and are also shamelessly aired on television. I was horrified. Was that the atmosphere in which Johan was raised?! The bleeding wound caused by a forbidden love, and the desertion and unfairness of the situation, haunted my life and career for many years. Even though we lived next to the Mount of Remembrance at Yad Vashem, and despite conducting my research there, I never went to the archive to check on his father, I was afraid of what I would find. On the other hand, my need to learn about the Holocaust grew stronger, as its fringes had now touched me too.

How is it possible to both love and hate at the same time, I asked myself? In the final analysis, I had fallen in love with the son of a Nazi, who rejected me in favor of his heritage—some kind of love. This incident became the cornerstone of my research, which revolved around the relations between Nazis and Jews in the Holocaust, and relations of trust between Gentiles and Jews (*Judenräte* (*Ältestenrat*) and *kapo*). I saw my experience reflected in others and I asked myself, "What would I have done in their place?" My personal experience became a trademark of my research and was also expressed in my poetry. That same year, the first collection of my poems was published. Its main motif, shared by all my poems since then, was touched by the agony of the Holocaust, coping with loss, desertion, and the betrayal of trust.

Immediately after finishing my army service, I felt that if I became familiar with German language and culture, I would be able to better understand the monster. Without a penny in my pocket, I invested the little I had in German lessons at Beit Ha'am in Jerusalem. The teacher was an Austrian and to this day when I am in Germany, people ask me which part of Austria I'm from. Two trilogies—*Saul and Joanna* by Naomi Fraenkel and the Trilogy by Lion Feuchtwanger (*Success, The Oppermann Siblings*, and *Exile*)—which I found in the YMCA library, provided me with the context of the zeitgeist, Germany, and the Germans. I identified with the protagonists in Fraenkel's book: Emile, the German boyfriend who was radicalized and joined the Nazis, and Edith, the Jewish lover he abandoned, were to me the mirror image of my "this could have happened to me" scenario.

Approaching Holocaust Research through Film

For the next ten years I found the subject too painful to approach, other than reading Holocaust literature and watching the occasional film that Israeli television was kind enough to offer. I studied at David Yellin College, acquiring two undergraduate degrees—one in education and communication and another in education and the history of the Jewish people. But the

Holocaust narrative was always there. To avoid the subject, my two research papers—on the Hitler Youth and the Lebensborn Children—dealt with the Second World War rather than the Holocaust but still took a deep look into German society. I got to know the monster on its home turf. However, I felt I did not know how to approach the study of the Holocaust itself and I pretty much failed whenever I tried. A paper assigned by a lecturer in a course on the Majdanek trials received a low grade. I was unable to write critically about the trials. I didn't think I could judge and evaluate what had happened. I felt I was out of my league, that I had no right. But the subject fascinated me, and I kept coming back to it.

At the same time, at the beginning of the 1990s, I was teaching at a high school for underprivileged children in Jerusalem, most of them from Mizrahi families. As a first-year home room teacher, I had planned with my teacher colleagues to take the children on a field trip to Yad Vashem. To my surprise, some of the children objected and refused to come, arguing that it did not concern them and that it was "a holiday for Ashkenazim." For the first time in my life, I became aware of the fact that part of the Israeli populace does not cherish the memory of the Holocaust as does most of the country, and even resent the substantial attention accorded to the subject. I discovered that there are rabbis, both Ashkenazi and Sephardi, who repress the issue and object to Holocaust remembrance as practiced in our nation. At this point I realized that bridges must be built between worlds in order to facilitate dialogue between them, or else the rift will only grow wider. Not everyone has had the "opportunity" to experience these memories and understand their significance. And indeed, the rift between the "First" Israel (the Ashkenazi insiders) and the "Second" Israel (the Mizrahi outsiders) is evident to this day in all its severity, and not only because of the Holocaust narrative, which had sidelined the Mizrahim, as they see it. In fact, quite the opposite—when the second generation, the new generation of Israeli Mizrahim, discovered that its parents were part of the extermination campaign and had experienced it personally, it rebelled against the silencing by the Ashkenazi hegemony. This issue burned within me for a decade, but it was only after I came to academia, found my research topic, and received academic recognition for the unusual combination of Holocaust and film that I began to write about it.

My master's thesis was supervised by Prof. Shlomo Zand at Tel Aviv University, who was a pioneer in writing in Hebrew about history and film. I was enchanted by the possibility of connecting the subjects. I moved away from the study of Europe, Israel, and Judaism and focused on US studies, specifically, the history of American law and Hollywood movies. The mutual influences fascinated me. I found that in recent centuries, the imagination and values of an entire nation had been shaped, for the most part, by cinema and the media. It appeared that my world of content was consolidating and my interest in the Holocaust had waned. My PhD at the University of Haifa focused on the death penalty in US history and its representation in film.[1]

Everything was moving along smoothly until the Holocaust once again grabbed me by the throat.

My research developed and naturally reached the next stage in the research of the death penalty, which falls under the purview of military law in the United States. The main findings, which linked the courts, witnesses, and audio-visual testimony, led me to international military tribunals, and specifically to the Nuremberg trials, which was the largest legal event to utilize photographs and films instead of live witnesses. In January 1946, the Allies chose to promote and hasten the trials of the senior Nazi figures through a clear and unequivocal instrument: the films of the liberation of the camps, produced by Hollywood's senior directors, cinematographers, and scriptwriters, in addition to materials collected by the Russians when they liberated Auschwitz-Birkenau. The films were brought in place of the testimonies of the liberating soldiers and the survivors. The prosecutors, led by American judge Robert Jackson, thought that under the circumstances and due to the intensity of the event, the tribunal should be presented with the results of the Nazis' crimes rather than deal individually with witnesses and testimonies. The language of filmic images was international: One picture was worth a thousand words and made it possible to explain and powerfully experience the nature of the war and the Holocaust. On behalf of all the victims—and in their stead—the significant power of film and the camera was used as a critic and as witness to the court. Film and camera informed the audience and validated and confirmed the prosecution's claims. They provided proof of the atrocities by filming first hand in the camps and through photographic documentation of the German's themselves, which was used as proof of their own acts. Above all, they granted insight into the horror of the war and its outcome and conceptualized how these events occurred.

I assimilated this knowledge in my post-doctoral research, titled "The Shaping of the Holocaust Visual Image by the Nuremberg Trials: The Impact of the *Nazi Concentration Camp* Movies" conducted at the Yad Vashem International Institute for Holocaust Research, with the support and encouragement of Prof. Dan Michman.

Applying a quantitative method, I found that the majority of the research participants' Holocaust consciousness was affected by films and television in the main. This finding, together with history, culture, and sociology studies, led me to conclude that the Holocaust consciousness in terms of "how things looked in the camps and ghettos" was shaped mostly through the filmic image. In fact, as an imitation of reality, through the sensory experience of hearing and viewing, films affect viewers cognitively and emotionally; as a result, they identify with events on the screen and feel part of them to the extent that they make ad hoc judgments as if they were there themselves. This is a major advantage but also a disadvantage as film is highly malleable and can be used to change and distort the Authentic historical narrative. Our task as Holocaust researchers is to sound the alert in such cases.

Throughout my studies, I have been fascinated by the ability of audio-visual media to enhance people's knowledge and understanding of the essence of the Holocaust. Thus, for example, the filmic of the liberated camps succeeded in demonstrating what a hungry person looks and feels like through a plethora of facial expressions and refined miming. Furthermore, the films "imported" sights from the camps and brought them before the viewers' very eyes: from the depiction of the *Musselmänner* in the liberation films as an iconic image of suffering, through scenes overflowing with meaning and subtext: No words are required to convey the horrifying insights displayed on screen. I found that the filmic experience can traverse cultural constructs and express universal concepts.

The assistance of Lawrence Baron and Frank Stern (both experts in film and Holocaust researchers) helped secure acceptance from the conservative academic establishment in Israel, which previously had viewed my research topic as not historical "enough." Nonetheless, the articles I wrote in ensuing years proved the importance of my research in understanding several issues, such as French and Italian attitudes and values toward their involvement in the Holocaust as depicted in film, representations in Polish TV series of that nation's repression of the past, and even the implied shirking of responsibility in contemporary German movies and series.

The intersection of history, the Holocaust, and film was very convenient for me. I felt more at ease with the mediation of films, which served as a partition between me and the Holocaust. I no longer had to apologize over and over again to those inquiring—both Ashkenazim and Mizrahim—"Why are you studying the Holocaust?" Films brought a compromise: not the Holocaust but related to the Holocaust.

From my point of view, films and television became a litmus test from which one could learn about European cultural attitudes toward the Holocaust during it, after it, and in the present day. Also, by publishing articles with other researchers such as Sonja M. Hedgepeth (gender and literature) and Rochelle Saidel (history and gender), we succeeded in providing an academic platform for issues that had previously been silenced, such as the sexual abuse of women and children during the Holocaust and the phenomena representation in the cinema. I spoke at numerous conferences and felt that I had found peace, at last.

"Yes, I Can": Approaching the Holocaust and Antisemitism Among Mizrahi Jews

Although my academic career seemed to be taking shape finally, there remained one controversial issue that had been largely ignored by Israeli society but which continued to beckon me: The Holocaust of North African Jewry.

Until recently, Holocaust recognition and research in Israel focused solely on European Jewry. The Israeli establishment and society refused to accept the fact that North Africa was part of the extermination plan and rejected the right of North African communities to be counted among those who suffered at the hands of the Nazis and their collaborators. I got the idea to research this topic from students of North African descent who wanted to learn more about their past. I looked for the reasons behind this omission from Israeli discourse even though North-African Jews constitute 40 percent of Israeli society. My findings were by no means flattering to either the Zionist institutions, which failed to acknowledge and appreciate the experiences of an entire population in the camps in the Sahara, or to the North African communities themselves and especially their secular leadership. Mizrahi politicians and intellectuals did nothing to preserve their communal and religious-traditional history. Moreover, their religious leadership acted to extinguish age-old traditions as well as recent memories of experiences in the Second World War. As my research progressed, I was astounded to find that the experiences of Mizrahi Jews during the 1939–45 conflict are not mentioned in any noticeable way in either Israeli media or in France and Italy, the two colonial powers that ruled over the North African countries in which Jews suffered from the Nazis as much as they did in Europe. Hence, North African Jews are absent from Holocaust consciousness as shaped by the media in the West: What is not seen is forgotten.

Although I identified with the findings, here too I was ambivalent about my personal connection to the subject of my research. Iranian Jewry was not involved in the war, and the cultural commonalities I shared with North African Jewry were coincidental; the language was different as well. The fact that I was studying the subject through a glass lens made the work easier for me. I wrote two books about the holocaust of North African Jews.[2] The first deals with their representation in Israeli media as a platform in which the discourse of memories was held. The second book engaged with how the colonial powers dealt with the events of the war and memories of this period in audio-visual media, as well as the representation of Jews and Israel in Arab countries. For me, these issues connected with the story of my family.

My grandmother and father often told me about their antisemitic experiences in Iran, hers as a teacher and a deputy principal of the Alliance School in Hamadan, and his as a rebellious student. I heard about the beatings he endured in public school from the teacher because he was Jewish and the lengthy periods of time he was forced to stand barefoot in the snow with his hands above his head. This happened quite often, with all sorts of excuses. In fact, Shiite Iran was never fond of its Jews, and my grandmother had numerous stories about how her own grandparents had to deal with the edicts of the local religious authorities. Their cruelty knew no limits, and the term "to skin a person alive" can be attributed in actual fact to their aggression towards Jews.

My expanded visual consciousness could now relate more easily to my mother's experiences of being beaten by her Muslim peers. From my point of view, my parents were just like Saul and Johanna, the protagonists of Fraenkel's book *Saul and Joanna* in the chapters before the war. Now I was also able to understand what brought them to Israel and their faithfulness to the land they admired. This circle was now closed and the picture became clear. I felt closer to my work and at peace with it: I had permission to study the Holocaust. Clearly, the hatred that reached its peak in the Holocaust was not solely the problem of European Jewry—Holocaust research concerned all Jews. All Jews must internalize its lessons and study with every tool at their disposal.

Approaching the Holocaust in a Global Context

Since writing my MA, I have taught courses and seminars on the subject in various academic institutions in Israel. Over time, variations on these courses were added, such as "Holocaust and genocide, and other holocausts." I understood from my students that their ability to understand the Holocaust had been undermined by incorrect usage and overuse. Accordingly, I constructed a scale by matching and linking (rather than comparing) other genocides to the Holocaust. This is a legal-ethical scale (based on international law) which includes, in order of severity, international human rights instruments and fundamental definitions of war crimes (Geneva Conventions), ethnic cleansing, and genocide, and an ideological scale (based on scientific racism and antisemitism) that draws from the content worlds of other nations (Rwanda, Yugoslavia, and others) and is part of teaching the colossal Holocaust of the Jews. Films served excellently here, as they are visual and palpable, varied, multi-faceted, with multiple narratives. Accessibility to films has improved: We have gone from videotapes to digitalization and YouTube. Everything is in the palms of our hands, on our smartphones, accessible to the students, providing a plethora of readily available sources for research papers. All of this is informed by historical material, newspaper articles, and other audio-visual media.

Afterword: Approaching the Future

Researching the Holocaust through the lens of film became a central, palpable element of my life, enabling me to find my own personal path to the events of the Holocaust and to study them without hesitation and with the greatest respect. Through the cinematic prism, I learned to analyze abstract situations and discover the new terminology that shaped our Holocaust consciousness.

Writing this essay has been both a burden and a vexing journey. Laying out the story of my life on the computer screen, and seeing the nuances in each point in my life and how they affected it, has shaken me. It has already been said that the ways of the Lord are wondrous. How did my destiny lead me here? I have understood this through writing these words today, and for that I am grateful. What will tomorrow bring? I suppose I will find out in the next chapter of my life.

Notes

1 I authored two books following this research: *God Have Mercy on Your Soul: History, Law and Cinema* (Tel Aviv: Resling, 2010, in Hebrew); *The Death Penalty in American Cinema: Criminality and Retribution in Hollywood Film* (London-New York: Tauris 2014).

2 Yvonne Kozlovsky Golan, *Forgotten from the Frame: The Absence of the Holocaust Experiences of Mizrahim in Visual Arts and Media in Israel* (Jerusalem: Resling, 2017, in Hebrew); Yvonne Kozlovsky Golan, *Site of Amnesia: The Lost Historical Consciousness of Mizrahi Jewry* (Leiden, The Netherlands: Brill, Series in Jewish Studies, 2019).

18

Voicing the Unvoiced

Liliane Steiner

Childhood Seeds

I heard about the Holocaust for the first time when I was twelve years old, a new immigrant in the ulpan of Mevasseret Zion. This knowledge was doubled a week later by Israel's Memorial Day and Independence Day. Since then, the three special days of the year bear a very strong feeling of sanctity for me. For me, the Holocaust is strongly related to Zionism. It underscores the miracle of the Israeli state. Moreover, the victims, who were trapped in Europe, left us a legacy: To bear witness in order not to be forgotten and to build a society based on tolerance, acceptance, and growth in response to death and destruction. The sacrifice of fallen soldiers permits a safe place for the Jews and demands that we be worthy of their sacrifice. My way to Holocaust research has been paved by small and large incidents that continued to shape my interest in this research.

I was born in Fes, Morocco, where I lived until the age of eleven. My childhood there was marred by few antisemitic events, though I was never allowed to walk around by myself; my sisters, brothers, cousins, or parents accompanied me. Under the façade of the relatively quiet life Jews led in Fes, especially compared with the lives of their counterparts in Casablanca that was fraught with daily violent attacks, I remember the fear when we saw a group of young Arabs walking down the street. As a rule, Jewish children never went to school unescorted by adults or older peers. We always went in groups, ready to face the Arab children's attacks. My own experience resonated with the pogrom of Fes that wreaked havoc on the Jewish population in 1912 and which I heard about from my grandmother, a great storyteller. She was my first encounter with first-hand testimony. She told us, her grandchildren, about this terrible event that had deprived her of her parents, siblings, and financial resources. She was a young child at the time and suffered from health problems due to immense shock she experienced then. I couldn't understand her fully at the time since she spoke Moroccan Arabic, but I grasped the terror from the way she recounted her experience. Her grandchildren used to sit and listen to her accounts for hours. In 2012, Paul Fenton's book *Le Pogrom de Fes ou le Tritle* (*The Pogrom of Fes*)[1] affirmed this childhood experience as documented history. She was a survivor, a fact that had never crossed my mind until I started to read memoirs of Holocaust survivors. My feeling of insecurity originated in her story, rampant, sometimes tacit, but always present. I grew up in a home where the word *tritle* (pogrom) was used as a synonym for chaos and where Jerusalem, my grandparents' metonymy for Israel, was the safe, desired destination; all our decisions were made in response to it. Years later, when I learned more about the Holocaust, I could comprehend the anxiety and the helplessness of the Jews in Europe. Today, I know that my grandmother's stories taught me the importance of remembering the victims and talking about them without hesitation.

Meeting a Holocaust Survivor

The Fes pogrom affected my family profoundly. From the 1920s to 1973, most of us emigrated to Israel. My parents, sisters, and I arrived in Israel on October 3, 1973, thrilled to be "at home" at last. Three days later, war broke out. We were frightened but knew we were in our country, protected by the Israel Defense Force. Some soldiers were in Mevasseret Zion. Their presence increased our feelings of security and gratitude to be in Israel. Six months later, for the first time in my life, I heard about the Holocaust on the Holocaust Remembrance Day.

I came home bewildered by the facts. My parents told me that the Jews of Morocco were lucky to be spared the same fate as their European brothers and sisters at the last minute. My father told me that he was assigned to prepare—and indeed began work on—a detailed list of the Jews' possessions in Fes. It was frightening information. I appreciated even more my life in Israel. Two years later, on a school trip to Jerusalem, we visited the Israel National Museum. On my way out, an venerable man stared at me, perplexed, and rooted to the spot. At first, I was surprised, not understanding the situation, but since he didn't move and I was becoming embarrassed, I ventured to ask him: "Can I help you?" He moved restlessly and then said hastily "you look so much like her," before moving away. Confused and puzzled, I described this incident to our tour guide, who happened to be a student at the Hebrew University. He told me it was pretty likely that this man was a Holocaust survivor who had lost his family; incidents like this happened a lot. This encounter confronted me with loss and its aftermath, which became the focus of my later research.

Silence and the Holocaust

In the twelfth grade, I joined my school's youth delegation which travelled to Belgium, France, and Germany in a twinning program. We met with young people from France and Germany. In their countries, we were hosted by non-Jewish families. The mother of the family in Germany waited for us at the Andernach town hall; luckily, two of us were staying with this particular family. My friend and I had to cope with the German woman, who understood English but could not speak it. Drinking coffee, we waited for her daughter Ulrike to arrive. The mother then broke the heavy silence and started to speak German. Since I spoke French and English and my friend spoke only Hebrew, I assumed the role of spokesperson and answered her questions in English. We talked for half an hour until Ulrike finally arrived. We were all relieved! We introduced ourselves to Ulrike and started to chat with her. Suddenly, Ulrike asked me: "Where did you learn German?" Surprised, I told her that I didn't know any. She answered: "My mother told me that you understood her and answered her questions." I laughed and replied that I had no idea my answers were accurate; I was just trying to be polite and have a conversation. Later, while traveling round in Germany, I understood the language and assumed that my knowledge of French and English helped me do so. During our trip, I told my friend that I felt very uneasy because maybe we were walking on the graves of Jews murdered by the Nazis. I hated the clean streets. They were in stark contrast with the terrible pictures of *Kristallnacht* and other Holocaust images that we had seen in history books and films. I decided to ask Ulrike about the history of her town and the region. She immediately understood my question and brushed it away: "Please," she said, "let's not talk about the past. We are different." I had heard this answer before, though in different versions from the other young Germans with us. We Israelis felt uncomfortable and didn't press the point, but I was furious at the silence imposed by the new German generation. I told my friend: "It's too easy to move on and avoid the topic!" I talked about it to the teachers who accompanied us; the answer was that it was indeed a very delicate topic. I couldn't believe my ears! So they, too, were asking the same thing? How could Israeli silence be the polite answer to history? Why do we have to consider the Germans' feelings while the victims' blood cried from the ground? It contradicted my beliefs of justice and growing sense of fighting back, an Israeli attitude I adopted from my first days living there. The issue of silence about the Holocaust would mark my future path. I made a vow to break this silence.

"The Lost Shore"

I enrolled in academic studies at Bar-Ilan University after completing my national service. I was submerged in the aftermath of the Second World War on linguistics, literature, philosophy, and culture. In the third year of my first degree, I took a seminar on the subject of the Holocaust. My seminar paper focused on Anna Langfus' novel *The Lost Shore*.[2] I spent days and nights discovering the life of this survivor. When writing a paper that dealt with the theme of stone and petrification, I tried very hard to do justice to her novel and mainly to her experience. I read psychology books to understand the defense mechanisms and coping strategies she used in the post-war reality. "One day, maybe, I will no longer have to hide, one day I may become similar to a smooth and cold pebble, forgotten on a beach, having finally found the perfect shape to escape time" (236). In order not to succumb to her past, like the stone, Anna detaches herself from its reality. She repudiates every penetration, scratch, or decay. This work introduced me to the multifaceted world of survivors' coping strategies.

Choosing Silence

Survivors coped with a wide variety of mechanisms and adaptations. As a non-survivor, I felt I had no right to question them. Then I met a student from a different department at the university who later became my husband. He is the son of survivors, but he never talked about the Holocaust. All I knew was that his father died at a young age, thirty-five, because of the death camps. He grew up as an orphan from the tender age of three. It was a past he didn't want to deal with—or rather, preferred not to. Instead, he focused on the post- Holocaust present, his parents' Israeli past, and the Israeli future. He rarely talked about the impact of the Holocaust on his life. On Lag BaOmer days, he shared his concern about his mother. He told me that for her, it was a nightmare to see so many fires (lit in honor of the holiday) round and about. The aftermath of the Holocaust drifted and would surface on some days, only to be repressed the next. Several months after our relationship grew serious, I was introduced to his mother. She had no tattoo on her arm although she had been in Auschwitz, a fact that maybe helped her maintain her silence. She, too, never talked about her past except for referring to a very rich family. I somehow complied with the code of silence implicitly imposed on me. When we were married and had our family, I understood the importance of our children for my husband's family, an additional significance drawn in a painful past. For me, it was my revenge, my triumph over the Nazis. I was happy to play an important role in this triumph. Only years later, when our sons grew up and joined the army, did

I dare to express this triumph more openly. I was very proud of the fact that my sons fought in the IDF.

Voicing the Unvoiced

After completing my doctoral studies, I started to teach in a religious high school. While plotting out a lesson plan for the Holocaust Remembrance Day, I decided to teach the Holocaust through the life stories of twelve children (the number of the tribes of Israel) who survived the Holocaust. The pupils had to learn about their childhood, their parents, and families as well as their countries and history. The project was a success; the pupils became very interested in the children's stories and the darkest period of the Jewish people. Through the survivors' stories, they learned about the ghettos and the concentration camps along with the brighter sides of humanity and the Jewish people's strength, courage, and resilience. This teaching experience taught *me* a great lesson: using an indirect route to teach very important subjects and reach the souls of students. First-person accounts and stories made history less dreadful and distant, but more real. If at the beginning of the lessons, the pupils were not keen to hear about the Holocaust, once they started to learn about real children, real families, they wanted to know more. The reluctance faded away. Three years later, I started to teach in a religious teachers' college. I offered to lead a seminar class about gender, women's writing, and the Holocaust. I believed that Jewish educators should be versed in the Holocaust to comprehend the privilege of educating Jewish children. I believe that every Jewish child is a miracle and therefore educators should try their hardest to enhance their intellectual and emotional development and lead them to success.

My goal was to expose my students to the Holocaust from a feminist point of view. I emphasized women's experiences that had been neglected in history books. I believed that through this aspect female students will relate to these painful parts of history. I spent eight months preparing this course. The narratives of female survivors were a bridge to the Holocaust experience of men and children. I was thrilled to teach my seminar and considered it as a precious mission. The more I read and learned about the Holocaust, the more I was persuaded that I made a good choice.

Edith's Talk

At the beginning of the year my students were reluctant to engage with the Holocaust, claiming that it was emotionally too hard for them to read about the atrocities perpetrated on the Jews; it was too difficult to read about the children in the ghettos and those who were brutally taken from their mothers' arms by the Nazis.³ I tried to explain that as Jewish educators, we must learn about the Holocaust. I seemed to be the only one in the room to really believe that, though. At the end of class, I felt quite confused and disappointed. I almost gave up and started to think about a new topic for the seminar. While driving back home, I had an idea: Only a survivor could convince my students to change their attitude. I had a few days to find one, and to convince her to come to my class and tell her story. When I shared my plans with my husband, he told me that his father's cousin, Edith Feigenbaum, could be a perfect match. Indeed, she was an ideal choice. Since she was a teacher, she gave a wonderful talk, the type I could only have dreamed about. Edith started by giving the full details of the German invasion of Hungary, then described the life of the Jews in her city before the invasion and after, including her school and schoolmates; she also told us about her family's experiences during the Holocaust. Throughout the talk, she was joyful and pleasant. She had nothing of the powerlessness they expected to encounter. On the contrary, she displayed a remarkable strength and resilience. At the end of the talk, Edith stressed how important it was for educators to learn about the Holocaust. My students were swept away by both her personality and her talk. They asked her many questions and she answered eagerly and honestly, keeping the students' concerns at bay. After meeting her, they were all keen to learn more about the Holocaust and Jewish women's experiences. I, too, was reassured that I was taking the right path and from this moment on made it my mission to voice the unvoiced and bring the words of the victims as well as of the survivors to as many people as possible. I expected my students to carry the torch and told them so. They were flattered and understood the importance of this vital mission.

A Voice from the Holocaust

Two years later, I confronted a similar reluctance in the first class of this seminar. But this time, I was stronger in my beliefs and convictions. I couldn't rely on Edith's testimony since her health was deteriorated. I introduced the class to the diary of a fourteen-year-old Jewish girl, Rutka Laskier, that had been discovered four years prior, *Rutka's Notebook*.⁴ I came across this diary one summer holiday while looking for new memoirs on Yad Vashem's website. The diary immediately drew my attention. Maybe it was Rutka's portrait on the cover and her eyes and their expression. To this day, I don't know why I felt immediately obligated to her, but I did everything in my power to let her voice be heard and known in Israel after it had been silenced for so many years. I bought Rutka's diary from Yad Vashem and waited impatiently for it. When it finally arrived, I read it and resolved to let this voice from the Holocaust be heard. Her intelligence and her writing talent impressed me a great deal. I wanted her to live in the hearts of many people.

The introduction explained that the diary had survived the Holocaust and made its way to Dr. Zahava Scherz, Rutka's half-sister, who was born in Israel and lived in Rehovot. I found her phone number and called, but got no answer. I kept trying, at different times of day, but to no avail. A month passed; I assumed I had a wrong number. I tried again over the next three months, but to no avail. By the end of the summer, desperate but determined not to give up, I left a new message in the hope of an answer. Three weeks later, late in the evening I checked my voicemail and could not believe my ears: A long-awaited message banished my despair. Zahava Scherz told me that she had been abroad for a long period and had just arrived home. I was more than thrilled to hear her message and waited until the morning to call her back. We had a long conversation and scheduled a meeting. In the fall semester, when I assigned the diary, I told my students about my meeting with Rutka's half-sister. Underscoring Zahava Scherz's career at the Davidson Institute in Rehovot, I stressed the relevance of the diary, of the voice of an intelligent teenager whose hopes and dreams were crushed by the Nazis, and of history to Israeli educators and Jewish women.

From Bedzin to Dimona

Rutka's story inspired me to create an international program that encompasses history, culture, and literature. I included a creative element to make it relevant to the pupils and enable them to explore the theme in their creative writing and artwork. I shared my plans with Zahava Scherz. She was thrilled at the prospect and gave me the email address of Anita Palimaka, a history teacher in Bedzin, the town from which Rutka was taken to Auschwitz. Anita taught Rutka's diary in her history class and was very enthusiastic about cooperating. I was overjoyed. One of my students agreed to teach the diary in her class and coordinated it with a friend from a different school in Dimona. I had built a program with three teachers from three elementary schools in Poland and in Israel who were keen to work together. All I needed was books. I needed sixty diaries for the Israeli pupils. The school principals had no budget for this project. We tried to find funds for it but found only one-third of the needed sum. I was frustrated. I decided to donate the rest from my own pocket. Zahava Scherz launched the program and signed the diaries distributed to the Israeli students. In the same week, she met with Bedzin students via video conference. The students of both countries were asked to write about their dreams and ambitions and to perform parts of the diary in the ceremony of the Holocaust Remembrance Day in their respective schools.

In Israel, my student spoke to the teacher, who was responsible for the ceremonies in her school. The latter read the diary and was instantly fascinated by it. She shared her fascination with a friend, who was the stage director in the municipal theater. They needed a scriptwriter and had found a very talented one. Rutka's voice came to life in a play in which the pupils of the project together with other children of the municipal group theatre acted. On Holocaust Remembrance Day, Rutka's voice was first heard in Israel by 450 citizens of Dimona. Zahava Scherz was invited to talk about Rutka's diary and about the way it had been discovered sixty-four years after it was written. Two years later, the play was included in the Beer-Sheva Yom Hashoah Memorial. Rutka's diary has take on a life of its own. Teachers in southern Israel heard about the program and joined it. My students taught it in their classes. Two years ago, just before the coronavirus pandemic began, Zahava told me that Rutka's diary was about to be staged on Broadway. It was good news. Rutka's diary needed a succession of small acts and perseverance to reach the hearts of many people.

A Chain of Memory

Over the years, my commitment to the victims and the survivors increased. The more I learned and read, the more I was determined to bring the silenced voices to the public. It has never been an easy task. I had to combat not only reluctance, but sometimes also sheer adversity. One year, I had a student in my seminar who expressed her dissatisfaction in almost every class. One day she told me: "Do you know that even my parents are angry at you?" Stunned, I asked her why. The answer was: "Because when I read the memoir I have chosen, I cry. They see me cry and they blame you for that!" I told her that her sensitivity was a good starting point from which to make the world a better place. To do it, we need to learn and hear the voices of the victims of injustice, intolerance, and racism. She was skeptical but found some good reason to continue reading the memoir. When she submitted her seminar paper at the end of the course she thanked me, telling me that working on the memoir had been the most meaningful research she had ever done. She was so transformed that I preferred not to remind her of her earlier negative attitude. For me, it was a small victory. I knew that she understood the importance of knowing Jewish history. I also knew that for her, too, future Holocaust Remembrance Days will be much more meaningful than they had been previously it had been.

    This student made me find other ways to touch the souls of my students. I wrote to Ruth Sender, a Holocaust survivor who lives in America. She has written three memoirs: *The Cage*, *To Life*, and *The Holocaust Lady*. I asked her to write a letter to my students. The following year, I started the seminar with Ruth Sender's missive to them:[5]

Dear Lilian and students,
    My name is Ruth Minsky Sender. The author of THE CAGE, TO LIFE, THE HOLOCAUST LADY.

I am a mother, a grandmother, a great grandmother, a Jewish educator, I am a Holocaust survivor, a miracle.

Each survivor is a miracle.

The personal stories of survivors speak of courage, pain and hope.

My mother perished but she left a legacy that helped me hold on to life when it was easier to give up. I still hold on to this legacy,

AS LONG AS THERE IS LIFE, THERE IS HOPE.

We do not know how much hidden courage we have until we need it. We must remember our past so history cannot repeat itself.

We must remember the Holocaust. We must learn. We must teach.

Readers ask me "did you take revenge"?

I survived, I brought forth a new Jewish generation, I teach Jewish children. The children were not to be born, still there are here and I, a Holocaust survivor, teach new Jewish generations to be proud of the Jewish heritage.

As long as there is life, there is hope.

Ruth Minsky Sender.

They were stunned to get a message from a survivor and felt committed to the topic. She convinced them of the importance of history/ her story. Good seminar papers on Ruth Sender's trilogy or on one of her memoirs are sent to her. It is not only a tribute, but also a legacy. Usually, students gain a great deal from working on the memoirs of survivors; they grow as a result of writing their papers. Two years ago, I faced very strong opposition from one student. She was in her late forties. She told me that her mother had survived the Holocaust. She was her only child and that in fact she was now her family's sole survivor, since her mother died several years ago. She explained about her loneliness, having no family. Since she was an Orthodox Jewish woman who wore a wig, I knew she was married, but I didn't dare to ask her about children and instead tried my best to comfort her. She chose to write her seminar paper on *The Choice: Embracing the Impossible* by Edith Eva Eger.[6] Before reading the memoir, she watched some videos about Eva Eger. Her personality and her resilience affected my student deeply. She was eager to write her seminar paper, but the coronavirus disrupted her plans. She suffered from fatigue and other symptoms several months.

When she finally submitted her paper, she wrote me a letter in which she told me that the paper had helped her overcome a long-running anger she had felt for many years towards her family—including her mother—because she had been left all alone in the world. When writing her paper, she realized that she had unfinished business with her mother that blurred her understanding of the challenge of being her family's sole survivor. She had come to realize that her children were survivors too, and that she was not alone after all. I read her letter with tears in my eyes, knowing the great impact Eva Eger had had on the life of my student and her family. This moment was one of many for me when I understood that my persistence has been entirely worthwhile. Knowing that this student had made peace with her past (and mainly with her late mother) while working on her seminar paper strengthened my beliefs in the importance of broadening the chain of memory and enlarging the circle of Holocaust witness-bearers via research on Holocaust survivors' memoirs.

Conclusion

My own experience has taught me that Holocaust survivors' memoirs affect readers deeply. The power of the testimony, coupled with the personality of the author/ survivor expressed in the memoir, turns the reader into a co-bearer of the witness. Holocaust Studies in Israel should be broadened to enhance values such as tolerance, acceptance, authenticity, and responsibility and to promote self-actualization among the youth as a Jewish counter-response to loss and crushed hopes and dreams.

Notes

1 Paul, Fenton, *Le pogrom de Fes ou* le *Tritle* (Jerusalem, Ben Zvi Institute 2012).
2 Anna, Langfus, *Les bagages de sables* (*The Lost Shore*), (Paris, Gallimard, 1962).
3 I must admit that after years of teaching this seminar, I am still offended by this type of reluctance. Almost every year, I confront it at the beginning of the year and find myself almost in tears while explaining to my students that 6 million Jews were annihilated in silence because of the indifference of the people in the world. The voices of the victims and the survivors should never be silenced once again.
4 Rutka Laskier, Rutka's Notebook- A voice from the Holocaust, (Time), 2008.
5 Sometimes I send to her some questions my students ask me about the resilience of the inmates in the camps. I choose to bring the answers from first- hand testimony.
6 Edith, Eva Eger, *The Choice, Embrace the impossible*, (New York: Scribner Book Company, 2017.

19

How Literature Chose Me

Bela Ruth Samuel Tenenholtz

Introduction

I was sitting across the table from Tova, an 87-year-old survivor, whose life path had taken her on an impossible route from a pampered childhood in Lithuania to Israel by way of Siberia, Poland, Cyprus, and Atlit, and finally to a kibbutz where she arrived when she was fourteen and all alone in the world. Perhaps insisting on writing down her life story is a culmination of everything that affected my life as a second-generation child of Shoah survivors. It also brought me to write this autobiographical chapter with my doctorate in English literature tapping me on the shoulder to come clean about what exactly I had done with all those years of study.

My parents did not talk about the Shoah, but it whispered inside the walls and carpets of our home. There were portraits of people staring at me with disapproval from every surface. I was the child born in The Netherlands, in 1946, a birth intended to make everything right again, and here I was, not listening to my parents, tearing my dresses, and falling off my bicycle, so full of life that my parents could not keep up with me. The strongest memory of my childhood as the only Jewish child in our village school, was probably my nine-year-old self, picking up a package of kosher meat which had arrived by train, and which I brought home on the back of my bike, dripping blood. If not that one, then, perhaps, the times I stood, shamefaced, and told my teacher why I had not been in school during the first and last two days of Passover, or Succoth (the Feast of Tabernacles). My mother told me to say we had had two extra Sundays that week. The children giggled, and the teacher, not quite comprehending, waved me to my seat.

Perhaps I should not be so surprised that by the time I became a freshman at the University of Haifa, at the age of forty-eight, I knew that my guiding principle would be to use academia to allow me to go back to that nine-year-old girl and study and analyze the events that had left my family the only surviving Jewish family in a pastoral Dutch village that had once had a Jewish community. I would unravel the mystery of how growing up in the shadow of the Shoah had affected my life, and in doing so, forgive my parents.

History Catching Up

Of course, throughout my childhood and youth, I had already seen the curtain over the Shoah rent a little here and there, but I did not get a very clear picture of our ancestry beyond our isolated Jewishness until an American crew came to the Netherlands to film the diary of Anne Frank. My parents' attempts to "put it all behind us and pretend we are fine" disintegrated. The film seemed a public admission of guilt by the powers that be. I was allowed to borrow the diary from the library and, with growing consternation, read that my parents had not been the only ones to save themselves by *onderduik*, the Dutch word for going underground, literally diving under. I wanted to read more, but our rural library had nothing on the persecution of the Jews, and so I learned nothing new until the Eichmann trial, which was broadcast in the Netherlands. While still too young to truly understand the magnitude of this event, and lacking both Hebrew and English, I could only stare at the face of evil in its bulletproof glass booth, at the man who had sent my relatives to their horrible death. I silently apologized to my dead grandparents, to my aunts and uncle. The words "Shoah" or "Holocaust" were as yet unknown to me. In the Jewish Netherlands, this period was referred to as "the Catastrophe" or "the Persecution" (if mentioned at all), but mostly people simply spoke of "the war."

In retrospect, as an observant Jew I felt that everything that happened afterwards was like a prophecy coming true: that G-d would not forget the Remnant of the Jewish People. Even in our isolated corner of the Netherlands, the Israeli emissary who had come to revive Bnei Akiva, the religious and Zionist youth movement, eventually discovered us, and when a clubhouse was established in Deventer, I joined in with its activities. Every Sunday I took three buses to get there, and as I was one of the oldest children, quickly became active in the running of our meetings. My reward was that at the age of sixteen, I was chosen to take part in a one-month international Bnei Akiva seminar; there I would meet Jewish youths from all over Europe and study both the Bible and Jewish history. Eager to practice my English, I exaggerated my language skills and was allowed to study with the British group. We had classes about the persecution in Europe, and for the first time I heard the word Holocaust. When I asked what the word meant, there was a horrified silence. In my ignorance, I had assumed this was a word I simply had not yet learned in my eleventh-grade English class. The argument that followed was well beyond my comprehension, but in general I understood that important information had been kept from me, and from all the Jewish children I knew. What had happened in the Netherlands was not a simple catastrophe, a terrible time, a persecution, confined to one country. It had been a plague on Europe orchestrated by one man. I understood that I needed to do some serious reading, but where would I find the books?

Achieving the Rudiments of Literacy

I finished high school and, with an all-expense-paid scholarship, came to Jerusalem for a year at the Institute for Youth Leaders from Abroad. I loved the Americans with their perfect teeth and skin, their strange Bermuda shorts, and spaghetti straps. They were so, well, normal. They had no problem with their dual identity as Jews and Americans. Both seemed equally significant in their lives. I was totally flabbergasted when they sat on the ground and cried for days when JFK was assassinated. How could this man mean so much to them? In my home, we mostly ignored the royal family and we never flew the flag on the queen's birthday. I decided to concentrate on making Aliyah and becoming Israeli: Then there would be no question of dual identity, and it would be easy to define who I was.

In Jerusalem, I learned about the connection between the murder of six million Jews in Europe and the establishment of the Jewish state. We were taken on guided tours of the Yad Vashem Holocaust museum in Jerusalem. I was hooked. My childhood was a riddle I could solve and integrate into my identity. A light had been turned on in the dark hallway of my childhood, and the portraits hanging there were coming more alive. They nodded their approval as I read and read. This was 1963–4, and most material available today was not yet out there, but I read books by Primo Levi and Eli Wiesel. I wanted to find out about the death marches, because my mother's brother, Louis Yaacov, had perished on one of those. I wanted to read about Sobibor because most of my family had been murdered there. I tried to read Hannah Arendt's treatise about Eichmann and the Banality of Evil, but it was beyond me. Still, whispered conversations in my home about the local police, people who betrayed Jews, beatings, and arrests, were beginning to make sense, and I realized that my parents had only narrowly escaped, as had my two older sisters. I failed to equate my father, neatly dressed in his expensive tailored suit and silk tie, and my mother with her designer clothes and not a hair out of place, with those desperate people who had run for their lives. And where had my over-protective parents found the courage to hand over their small daughters to unknown arms? For the first time I realized that my birth in March 1946 was significant. I was living proof of my parents' will to live. I even understood the bloody packages of meat I brought home every week: My mother and father had made a conscious decision to cling to their

Jewishness, and to rebuild their lives as Jews. I read about the Warsaw Uprising and knew that my parents had staged their own revolt simply by surviving and raising their children as Jews. I imagined my mother as Hannah Senesh, unafraid and determined. I imagined my father breaking curfew to save his family. They were victims, but they were also heroes, and they had won!

Aliyah

The magical year in Jerusalem ended with my engagement to a nice American boy I had met during the year; we married and settled in New York, planning to return to Israel once his education was complete. It took us nearly five years but in 1969, now a family of four, we came back to Israel as new immigrants. It was the era following the Six-Day War; Jerusalem was united, and we could touch the Wailing Wall. In Hebron, we entered the Cave of the Patriarchs, and paid our respects to the Matriarch Sarah at her final resting place. It was overwhelming. My earth mother was buried here, the woman whose story I knew from the sacred texts. I could leave a stone on her grave. It was an indescribable experience of belonging. Over the next twenty years, we built our family, and in the end were the proud parents of six children, including four sabras born in the ancient homeland. We had succeeded! I had succeeded! In Israel everyone bought challah on Friday, wished each other *Shabbath Shalom*, a pleasant Sabbath; on Hanukkah there were candles in every window, and on Rosh Hashanah and other Festivals people called out appropriate greetings. I forgot when Christmas came around. I did not remember to wish my Dutch family happy new year on January 1. It was all about living among Jews like me.

However, I quickly learned that one income was not going to support us, and taking advantage of my fluent English, I found government courses that would train me as an English teacher. At first, I taught the subject in elementary school, and over the years moved up to teach high school. Life had assumed a comfortable rhythm.

Haifa University, 1994

By the early 1990s, I was a grandmother several times over and while I basked in my new status, it also brought home what Hitler had taken from me before I was even born. For more than twenty-five years, the story of the Shoah had stagnated in my awareness as my focus had shifted to the mundane tasks of raising a large family and holding down a job. The tools to further integrate the murder of the generation before my time remained hidden behind my grandparents' portraits, which I had brought from my parents' house. Like in my childhood, I passed them by with averted eyes.

My catalyst appeared in the form of a school inspector of English, who handed me the key to understanding without either of us realizing it. She observed me as I discussed a Bernard Malamud story with my students and asked me to come into the office for some feedback. "The lesson was fine," she started, but went on to say that my lack of college training had become an obstacle to staying on as a high-school teacher. When I had first been hired, English teachers were scarce and my certification was outweighed by my fluent English, but now this was changing. If I expected to be kept on, I would have to upgrade my license.

The next day—yes, the next day—I called the English Department at the University of Haifa, passed the initial interview, took the entrance exam, was accepted, and started my first college course a few weeks later. I took my SATs while already enrolled. I was forty-eight but felt sixteen. As soon as I entered the enormous library, I knew why I was there: to learn my history; to integrate what had happened before I was born; to make sense of my childhood. I was a single major student in the English language and literature department, but the university nevertheless required me to take enrichment courses outside the department. I chose the history department's package of the history of the Jewish People. Being a late starter was becoming an advantage: I knew exactly what I wanted to learn. History spilled over into my English courses. Whenever possible, I convinced my professors that there were Jewish aspect in the syllabus I could pursue, such as Shakespeare's *The Merchant of Venice* in a course about Spencer, or Longfellow's poem "The Jewish Cemetery at Newport" in the American literature course. I questioned Mark Twain's familiarity with Jews and wondered how the founding fathers had treated them. I saw Jews everywhere, and twisted my teachers' arms to be allowed to expand my focus. I was learning to unforget, to lift the veil my parents had lowered over the Shoah.

I was raised in a family that believed in G-d and lived by the rules and precepts of Judaism, just as my parents had also been raised. Being Jewish was central to our lives, and this sense of being part of a greater whole—the Jewish People—and having a Higher Power who will guide us, has never left me. After all, in my heart I knew He had kept my parents and two older sisters safe against all odds! Therefore, I also believe that G-d sends help when it is really needed, and He did: In my history course on American Jewry I had to write a seminar paper, but my professor knew a lot about the Netherlands, and even understood Dutch. I approached her and asked if I could write about Anneke Beekman, a Jewish toddler who had been abducted by the Catholic Church in the aftermath of the Second World War and had vanished. When asked how this topic connected to American Jewry, I suggested that I could easily prove that had Anneke's family moved to America, this tragedy would not have taken place. She laughed and allowed me to write the paper. She even introduced me to an American researcher who had also written about the case, and this seminar paper turned into one of my first published articles after I earned my PhD. I became a missionary, feeling that too much

Shoah material focused on Poland, and not enough on Western Europe, the Netherlands in particular. Oftentimes people that Hitler had conquered the latter and had murdered 75 percent of its Jews. So decimated was the community I was born into that it would take two generations for Jewish weddings and also funerals to become a normal part of my world, and yet another before family life with grandparents, aunts and uncles, returned to the DNA from which I had come.

As a teacher, I was entitled to a scholarship funded by the Ministry of Education, and after earning my BA *cum laude*, I applied to graduate school. By then I was knee-deep in Primo Levi and also read Jacob (Jacques) Presser's *Ondergang*, the classical corpus of the destruction of Dutch Jewry. I found a book by Elma Verhey, *Om het Joodse Kind (Concerning the Jewish Child)*, which examines the way the Netherlands treated the Jewish orphans after 1945. The book accuses certain people who were at the forefront of attempts to save Jewish children of having had ulterior motives to "rescue" the children's souls rather than return them to their biological families. I read A. J .J. Meershoek's *Dienaren van het Gezag (Servants of the Authorities)*, which examined the involvement of the Dutch police in the murders, and understood why my father would not walk into a police station. A real eye-opener was Isaac Lipschitz's *De Kleine Sjoa (The Little Shoah)*, which dealt with life after the "Terrible Times" in the Netherlands and, to a large extent, echoed my own experience.

It was clear to me that my thesis would discuss the influence of Shoah on the next generation, and in doing so, I would honor the memory of my murdered relatives. However, I still had to educate myself about the lives of the survivors. I devoured Nehama Tec's *Dry Tears*, about her wartime experiences, and *In the Lion's Den*, her biography of Oscar Rufeisen, aka Father Daniel. For a while I lived at my sister's home in Jerusalem and read everything available at the Center for the Research of Dutch Jewry at the Hebrew University. I discovered *Le'Ezrath Ha'Am (In Aid of the (Jewish) People)*, a newspaper produced between the winter 1944 and summer 1945, and distributed to liberated areas as the Allied Army made its way north through the Netherlands. Jewish soldiers took the newspapers with them and gave them to the Jews they liberated. In the April 1945 edition I found my father's name, with the address listed as that of the family where he and my mother had been hidden during their *onderduik*, in Nijverdal. My father was listed as the contact person for anyone looking for survivors. I always thought how sad that was, as not a single member of my parents' immediate family returned, but as I was working on this chapter I found out that immediately after the liberation of the village, my father walked everywhere to find families with whom Jews had been hiding.

Henk Pontsteen, a native of Nijverdal, and son of parents who hid Jews during the war, is writing a book together with Dinand Webbink to commemorate his parents' heroism during that time with the help of a diary his father kept and correspondence between his mother and one of the

Jewish children the family rescued. The book's subtitle is *Mador lechasidei oemot haolam (The Department of the Righteous Gentiles)*. The book has an entry about my father, dated April 1945. "Mr. Samuel is registering the Jews hidden in the municipality, and I will go to visit him this afternoon with Hansje." Hansje was Jochanan, Joop Sanders, rescued by the Pontsteens. The quote ends by saying that "so far, [Samuel] already has the names of 120 Jews hidden here." I understood that my poor, broken father had gone to work immediately upon liberation, returning to his leadership role, and had used *Le'Ezrath Ha'Am* to help survivors find each other. No wonder my father loved Nijverdal: So many people had been "good" during the war. The village's Jewish community had numbered only twenty-five, but during the war at least 120 Jews had been hidden there.

When some of my fellow students chose to write about witches in literature, or Shakespearean allusions in Byron, and suggested that my focus was too narrow, I shrugged it off. I was a student at a university in Israel, had access to one of the best libraries in the country, and was no longer limited to one single copy of Anne Frank's diary in a rural library where I was the only Jewish girl to borrow books. I was a Shoah zealot by then, but in a good way. Once again, I believe that it was divine providence that helped me to find an MA (and later PhD) advisor whose mother had lost her husband and child during the war and who had built a new life afterwards. Dr. Sarah Gilead was a fellow second-generation survivor and encouraged me to hold on to my determination.

My MA thesis focused on Jewish writers and the Shoah, and I settled on writing about so-called marginal writers whose works had never quite made it into the mainstream because of their use of Shoah metaphors and symbolism. The thesis earned me high honors, and I graduated in the top 10 percent of the 800 MA students that year. I drew on the autobiography of Cardiff native, Danny Abse—*Ash on a Young Man's Sleeve*, the very title of which is an allusion to T. S. Elliot's *Ash on an Old Man's Sleeve*—but Abse takes us to a London underground train filled with skeletons wearing striped uniforms and a drinking buddy called Gassy, who wears a mask because he cannot breathe in a countryside filled with smoke-belching towers. I had Primo Levi in my court, the Dutch writer Clara Asher Pinkhoff's *Sterrekinderen*—Starchildren, the children destined for death in Westerbork, the camp in the Netherlands—and Eli Wiesel's *Night* and *Beggar in Jerusalem*. I could hear them clapping. My thesis showed that the Shoah was the prism through which the literature under study came to life.

PhD

Haifa University asked me to expand my thesis into a full-blown dissertation, and I asked Dr. Gilead to guide me through the process. "Use your voice," she kept saying, "and know that people will either love your chosen topic or hate it. Be prepared for that." I was and felt confident enough in my strong Shoah studies background to challenge myself. This time, I looked for famous writers whose works had not previously been the focus of the kind of scrutiny I planned to give them. Encouraged by Norman Ravvin's *A House of Words: Jewish Writing, Identity, and Memory*, I looked for what he called a portal in the cave to look out onto the landscape of the post-Shoah world. Jews were dispossessed and murdered wherever they settled, and so, unlike other American immigrants, they had no old country to return to. At best there would be a monument or a neglected graveyard. Therefore, in Ravvin's view, Jews had to preserve their history in words, and because of that, their stories were not part of the Platonic cave of literature; instead, a portal had to be found, somewhere high up, and out there would be the house of words. The old house. It was a graphic image I immediately connected with. In order to learn how the authors of my choice had created their own portal in the vault of the corpus of literature, I needed to know how they felt about the Shoah. It was only logical to look for those who had written autobiographies or whose works clearly reflected identity and the influence of the Shoah. They needed to be people who were neither survivors nor second-generation Jews.

I found Arthur Miller, the quintessential American playwright, lauded for his many American plays, and read *Timebends*. He wrote that two events shaped his life: the Great Depression; and the Shoah. This would be my hypothesis: Miller had used those two events as the background for his oeuvre and both would come shining through. I looked for his early material, written when the Second World War was still very much a presence in the world. I took Miller's decision to write plays with a more universal appeal, and to turn away from overtly Jewish material as a challenge. I settled on *All My Sons* (1947) and *Death of a Salesman* (1948). With his autobiography as a guideline, I hypothesized that the Shoah might be a subconscious connection: His play *All My Sons*, aside from being a protest against profiteering during the war, also worked as an allegory of the Nuremberg trials, with the setting, use of numbers, and physical description of Joe Keller echoing that of Hermann Goering. Miller also makes sure that Keller cannot be mistaken for a Jew and gives him a son called Chris.

I was first struck by the fact that the setting is not Europe, and that there is no mention of the Shoah in this war play. This strange omission spoke volumes to me, and, of course, there was a subtle Jewish connection to the war in the Jewish neighbor who knows about Keller's war crimes but is too broken, perhaps afraid, to do anything about it. Miller's later play, *Death of a Salesman*, has *klezmer* music playing in the background; the Loman house is a small hut-like structure surrounded by towers belching smoke, and a fearful angry orange light flickers above the high buildings. The latter disappears only after Willy Loman dies. Miller's orange light is a metaphor for the belching towers of the crematoria of Auschwitz. Miller apparently liked this metaphor so much that he used it again in *Playing for Time*, the translation of Fanya Fenelon's Shoah memoir originally written in French. In her book she describes red fire in the sky of Auschwitz-Birkenau, but Miller, thirty years after writing *Death of a Salesman*, returns to his orange glow even though the original memoir never does. This proved that Miller meant the light in the sky above the Loman house to be an allusion to the crematoria. Other phrases in the play support this notion, and the link had been established. I was also able to connect Miller to the aftermath of the Shoah and the Nuremberg trials. He wrote a scathing essay entitled "The Nazi trials and the German Heart," in which he blasts the entire German nation for their silence and blames even the "German housewife [...] who weeps" when she hears the testimony, but who for ten years has never protested against Nazism.

Philip Roth's *The Ghost Writer* served to support my close reading of Jewish identity and ethnicity and the way memory is perceived. After my advisor approved all 228 pages, Haifa University sent it to two outside readers for evaluation, one in America and one in England, although British universities were boycotting our institutions of higher learning at the time. They would decide whether I deserved to be a PhD. The person who received my dissertation there was a world-famous Arthur Miller scholar, and he did not like my premise. He wrote, "Let us put aside, for the moment, the notion that the Jews are a separate ethnic group," and added that because Arthur Miller was not a religious Jew, he was unaffected by the events of the Shoah. "When he wished, he would engage with the Holocaust, and at other times, he chose not to do so," continued this reader. He did praise me for my erudition as a reader of Shoah literature and—although he liked my treatment of Philip Roth—finished by saying that a candidate cannot write whatever he or she wants but has to base it on the material. "In my world," he concluded, "this would not fly." In other words, he failed me. Normally speaking, a fail means the end of the road for a PhD candidate, but the specifics of his letter worked as a red flag, especially when the second reader suggested that my dissertation should be awarded a *summa cum laude*. The university realized that not considering the political climate might have affected the response received from England and after some deliberation on their part, and nail-biting on mine, sent my dissertation to a third reader. He liked it. It was Dr. Samuel Tenenholtz.

* * *

The PhD ceremony was overwhelming. When I was called to receive my new title, I shook hands with everyone, including the famous person who acted as MC. "You are very emotional," he said. "Don't cry." But they were tears of completion; tears of having brought back something that was almost lost beyond repair. I dedicated my dissertation to my dead ancestors by name. I even legally changed my last name to include my maiden name, so that my father would be included in the honor. "A lot of names," said the MC when he called me to come forward. Perhaps, but they all deserved their place in the pages of my history, and they had all played a role in bringing me to that point in my life.

I am a member of the tribe that is known as the second generation. It has made me who I am. It has led me unto my path, forced me to search for roots and a achieve a sense of belonging.

One of my greatest joy is a book about that I was able to write about my family's history. It was originally written in Hebrew and published by my college, Shaanan. I also wrote a Dutch version, *Land van vele bruggen: het verhaal van mijn vader* which was published in November 2020. In Israel the book did well, and an English translation of *Land of Many Bridges: My Father's Story* came out in 2022. I also wrote a second book, which was published in 2021. Its English title is *My Sister, My Self* and deals with a second-generation character who goes on a quest to fix a terrible injustice perpetrated on her family before she was born. It seems that being a second-generation child has taught me that the most important gesture I can make to honor my grandparents, aunts, and uncle, is to remember them, and to bring their stories into the public eye.

Autobiography is a flawed oeuvre. It has neither beginning nor end, for we cannot truly describe life before we entered it, or remember the early, crucial years, nor can we describe our death and what comes after that. I realize that I am closer to the latter, and so I hope that I have left enough of a stamp on my world to arm my children, grandchildren, and great-grandchildren with the strength to build their lives around their Jewishness, to be proud of their country, and to know they have a homeland here in Israel. Coming back to the memoir Tova is writing with my help, when I told her that I mentioned our project in my own, she said, "that is not all! I was in Germany and France too. And my maiden name was Perlov. You have to add that." I promised I would. Perhaps our children will then continue to carry the memory of all those who were denied even the decency of a funeral in their souls, the way the Children of Israel carried the bones of Joseph to the Promised Land.

Contributors

Victoria Aarons is Mitchell Distinguished Professor of Literature at Trinity University, San Antonio, TX, where she teaches courses on American Jewish and Holocaust literatures. In addition to numerous scholarly articles and book chapters, she is author or editor of eleven books, including *The Cambridge Companion to Saul Bellow* (2017); *Third-Generation Holocaust Representation: Trauma, History, and Memory* (co-authored with Alan L. Berger, 2017); *Third-Generation Holocaust Narratives: Memory in Memoir and Fiction* (2019); *The New Jewish American Literary Studies* (2019); *Holocaust Graphic Narratives: Generation, Trauma, and Memory* (2020); and *The Palgrave Handbook of Holocaust Literature and Culture* (co-edited with Phyllis Lassner, 2020). She is on the editorial board of *Philip Roth Studies*, *Studies in American Jewish Literature*, and *Women in Judaism*, and she is series editor for Lexington Studies in Jewish Literature. She serves on the San Antonio Holocaust Memorial Museum Commission and chairs the Holocaust Education Committee.

Prof. Thierry J. Alcoloumbre is an Associate Professor at Bar-Ilan Department of Comparative Literature (chair 2009–13). *Ancien élève* (alumnus) of the École normale supérieure de la rue d'Ulm (Paris), he received his PhD in Ancient Philosophy from the University of Paris 1 Panthéon-Sorbonne. His research focuses on the dialogue between Hellenism and Judaism in Western thought and literature and, in particular, in French thought and literature. He has published in the field of medieval and modern Jewish thought, as well as in the field of French poetry, specializing in the writings of Mallarmé, Edmond Jabès, and (last but not least) Claude Vigée. His recent research focuses on the Maharal of Prague (1520–1609) and his influence on French Jewish contemporary thought. Since 2010, he has served as Chairman of The Simone Veil Chair in Literature and Resistance, Bar-Ilan University. As of 2022, he is also the co-director of *Perspectives*, Journal of the Hebrew University of Jerusalem (Magnes Press).

Prof. Karen Alkalay-Gut is a retired professor of English Literature at Tel Aviv University, and chairs the Israel Association for Writers in English. Born on the night of the last buzz bomb (V1 flying rocket) in London, England, to refugees from Lithuania, Alkalay-Gut's first publications were in Yiddish at the age of eleven. Alkalay-Gut was raised in Rochester, New

York, and moved to Israel in 1972. Her publications include *Alone in the Dawn: The Life of Adelaide Crapsey* (1988, 2008), *Ignorant Armies* (1994), *So Far, So Good* (2004), *Danza del ventre a tel aviv* (2010), *Layers* (2012), *Yerusha* (2018), *Surviving Her Story: Poems of the Holocaust/ Survivre à son histoire* (2020) and *Egypt: An Israelite Returns* (2020). Her most recent work, *Inheritance*—poems in Yiddish and English translation—was published in October 2021 by Leyvik Press, and discusses the need to relay the voices of the generation that disappeared in the Holocaust.

Lawrence Baron held the Nasatir Chair of Modern Jewish History at San Diego State University from 1988 until 2012 and directed its Jewish Studies Program until 2006. He received his PhD from the University of Wisconsin, where he studied with George L. Mosse. He taught at St. Lawrence University from 1975 until 1988. He has authored and edited four books, including *The Modern Jewish Experience in World Cinema* (2011) and *Projecting the Holocaust into the Present: The Changing Focus of Contemporary Holocaust Cinema* (2005). He served as the historian and an interviewer for Sam and Pearl Oliner's *The Altruistic Personality: Rescuers of Jews in Nazi Europe* (1988). In the fall semester of 2015, he served as the Ida King Distinguished Visiting Professor of Holocaust and Genocide Studies at the Richard Stockton University of New Jersey.

Prof. Judith Tydor Baumel-Schwartz was born in New York in 1959 and immigrated to Israel with her Holocaust survivor father and American-born mother in 1974. She completed her undergraduate and graduate degrees at Bar-Ilan University and specializes in Holocaust Studies and Israel Studies with emphasis on rescue, religion, gender, commemoration, and descendants of Holocaust survivors. She has written and edited numerous books and articles about these subjects. Today she directs the Arnold and Leona Finkler Institute of Holocaust Research at Bar-Ilan University, where she is a Professor of Modern Jewish History. She is married to Prof. Joshua Schwartz and together they have a blended family of children and grandchildren.

Prof. Michal Ben-Horin is the head of the Department of Comparative Literature at Bar-Ilan University. She received her PhD in Cultural Studies from Tel Aviv University. She published extensively on the poetic and esthetic representation of the Holocaust and the catastrophe of the Second World War in German, Jewish, and modern Hebrew literature. She is the author of *Musical Biographies: The Music of Memory in Post-1945 German Literature* (2016) and *Reading the Voices: Musical Poetics between German and Hebrew* (forthcoming). She is co-editor with Galili Shahar of *Natural History of Destruction: W. G. Sebald between Literature and History* (2009), and has published articles on Thomas Mann, Arnold Schoenberg, Ingeborg Bachmann, Paul Celan, and Tuvia Ruebner, among others.

Rachel Feldhay Brenner was the Max and Frieda Weinstein-Bascom Professor of Jewish Studies at the Center for Jewish Studies at the University of Wisconsin-Madison. She published widely on responses to the Holocaust in Canadian Jewish literature, Israeli literature, and Polish literature. Her book length Holocaust literature studies include: *Writing as Resistance: Four Women Confronting the Holocaust: Edith Stein, Simone Weil, Anne Frank, and Etty Hillesum* (1997), *The Ethics of Witnessing: The Holocaust in Polish Writers' Diaries from Warsaw, 1939–1945* (2014), which was awarded The University of Southern California Book Prize in Literary and Cultural Studies and *Polish Literature and the Holocaust: Eyewitness Testimonies, 1942–1947* (2019). Among other fellowships, Brenner's work was recognized by The Jack, Joseph and Morton Center for Advanced Studies in The US Memorial Holocaust Museum where she was awarded several fellowships. Among her awards were the Canadian Studies Research Grant awarded by Social Sciences and Humanities Research Council of Canada, NEH Fellowship, and the WARF named professorship. Prof. Brenner passed away in February 2021 as this book was being prepared.

Margarete Myers Feinstein is Clinical Assistant Professor in Jewish Studies at Loyola Marymount University. Interested in the legacies of Nazism, Feinstein has written about postwar German national identity and Jewish displaced persons. She is the author of *State Symbols* (2002) and *Holocaust Survivors in Postwar Germany* (2010). Feinstein's current project uses survivor narratives to investigate retribution against Germans after the Holocaust.

Dr. Keren Goldfrad received her PhD from Bar-Ilan University with highest distinction in the field of Holocaust Literature. She is also the recipient of the Nahum, Sarah, and Baruch Eisenstein Foundation Prize from Yad Vashem. Keren has taught English in the EFL Unit at Bar-Ilan University since 1993 and chaired the unit between 2015-2021. In addition, Keren is the Head of the Teaching Enhancement Center, which is charged with promoting excellence in teaching and assisting faculty with individual consultations and workshops. She has taught a number of Holocaust Literature courses on the TASP program at Bar-Ilan University and Orot Israel College, and was a member of the Mofet Institute's Holocaust Consortium. She has been on the editorial board of *PRISM: An Interdisciplinary Journal for Holocaust Educators* since 2009. Among her publications, Keren is co-editor of *The Call of Memory: Learning about the Holocaust through Narrative: An Anthology & A Teachers' Guide*.

Prof. Yvonne Kozlovsky-Golan is Head and founder of the MA Interdisciplinary Program for Culture and Film Studies in the University of Haifa's Faculty of Humanities. Her interdisciplinary research addresses the encounter between history, legal history and their representation in film and media. Her research focuses on the audio-visual representations of the Holocaust, and their impact on viewers throughout the twentieth and twenty-first centuries. Prof. Kozlovsky-Golan is the author of five books on film and history, three of which process American legal history, focusing on representations of law and order, the Holocaust, and ethics in diverse American media, while two focus on the misrepresentation of North African Jewry's experiences of the Second World War in Israeli, Arab, and European media and cinema.

Dr. Roy Horovitz is a graduate of the Nisan Nativ Acting Studio, and holds a BA and MA (with Distinction) from Tel-Aviv University. He gained his PhD from the Department of Comparative Literature at Bar-Ilan University, where he is currently a senior faculty member. Horovitz has performed many roles for various theaters and was awarded Best Actor at the 1997 International Haifa Festival. He also won awarded Best Director for his work on *Pollard's Trial* (The Cameri Theatre, Tel-Aviv). Film roles include *The Body*, with Antonio Banderas. Horovitz has directed a succession of critically acclaimed productions (including Tennessee Williams' *Not About Nightingales* and David Lindsay-Abaire's *Rabbit Hole*). He was artistic director of the Mara theatre in Kiryat Shmona, dramaturge of Beer-Sheba Theatre and a visiting professor at the University of Texas at Austin and the American University in Washington, DC. His book, *World of Innocents: The Dramatic Afterlife of the Bible in Yaakov Shabtai's Plays*, was published in 2021.

Dr. Joshua Lander is an independent researcher currently working as a secondary-school teacher. He has published on Philip Roth, Judith Kerr, and Eva Tucker, and has recently had his first piece of fiction published in *New Writing Scotland*. His current research is focused on how the Holocaust emerges across British-Jewish literature.

Phyllis Lassner is Professor Emerita in The Crown Center for Jewish and Israel Studies, Gender Studies, and Writing Program at Northwestern University. She has published widely on the interwar period, the Second World War, and mid-century women writers, including two books on Elizabeth Bowen, *British Women Writers of World War II*, *Colonial Strangers: Women Writing the End of the British Empire*, *Anglo-Jewish Women Writing the Holocaust*, and essays on Holocaust representation in literature, film, theater, and art. She co-edited the volume *Philosemitism and Antisemitism in the Twentieth and Twenty-first Centuries*, the new edition of Gisella Perl's memoir, *I Was a Doctor in Auschwitz*, and the *Palgrave Handbook of Holocaust Literature and Representation*. Her most recent book is *Espionage and Exile: Fascism and Anti-Fascism in British Spy Fiction and Film*. She was the recipient of the three-year International Diamond Jubilee Fellowship at

Southampton University, UK, for her work on Holocaust representation and co-editorship of the special journal issue of *The Space Between: Literature and Culture 1914–1945* on the subject of "Espionage as Cultural Artifact." She serves on the Education and Exhibition Committees of the Illinois Holocaust Museum. Her current research concerns intermarriage in the Third Reich and mid-century fictions of the Holocaust.

David Patterson holds the Hillel A. Feinberg Distinguished Chair in Holocaust Studies at the University of Texas at Dallas and is a Senior Research Fellow for the Institute for the Study of Global Antisemitism and Policy. He is a member of the Executive Board of the Annual Scholars' Conference on the Holocaust and the Churches. He has lectured at universities on six continents and throughout the United States. A winner of the National Jewish Book Award, the Koret Jewish Book Award, the Hadassah Myrtle Wreath Award, and the Holocaust Scholars' Conference Eternal Flame Award, he has published forty books and more than 240 articles, essays, and book chapters on antisemitism, the Holocaust, and Jewish studies. His most recent books are *Judaism, Antisemitism, Holocaust: Making the Connections* (2022), *Shoah and Torah* (2022), *Portraits: Elie Wiesel's Hasidic Legacy* (2021), *The Holocaust and the Non-Representable* (2018), and *Anti-Semitism and Its Metaphysical Origins* (2015).

Dr. Joanne Pettitt is a lecturer in Comparative Literature at the University of Kent. She is the secretary of the British Association of Holocaust Studies and a member of the executive board of the European Association of Holocaust Studies. She is also co-editor-in-chief of *Holocaust Studies: A Journal of Culture and History*. Joanne's work focuses on representations of Holocaust perpetrators in literature and her first monograph—*Perpetrators in Narratives of the Holocaust: Encountering the Nazi Beast*—was published by Palgrave Macmillan in 2017. She is currently working on a comparative study on the uses of Nazism in representations of the British far right.

Alexis Pogorelskin chaired the History Department at the University of Minnesota-Duluth for nineteen years. After receiving her PhD from Yale, she was Rhodes Visiting Fellow at St. Hilda's College, Oxford. She has published with Cambridge University Press, *Oxford Slavonic Papers*, and numerous other journals in Slavic Studies. She was the founding editor of *The NEP Era. Soviet History, 1921–1928*. She has guest-edited *Canadian American Slavic Studies* and co-edited *The Space Between. Literature and Culture, 1914–1945*.

Ravenel Richardson is a lecturer at Case Western Reserve University in Cleveland, Ohio. Her research and teaching focuses on women's personal narratives of war and genocide, specifically examining how the historical traumas of war intersect with life-writing and literature. She has published articles on women's writing in journals including *Contemporary Literary Criticism* and *The International Journal of Military History*, and is currently completing a monograph, *Trauma and Representation in Women's Diaries of the Second World War*, which explores the potential of women's diary writing in representing the trauma that occurred in Europe during the Second World War and the Holocaust.

Dr. Liliane Steiner has a BA in French and Arabic, an MA in French and a PhD *summa cum laude* in Comparative Literature from Bar-Ilan University. She is a senior lecturer at Hemdat Hadarom Academic College and currently serves as Head of the M.Teach Program and as the Secretary Academic Affairs at the college. She is a children's literature author. Her two first books, *Hila's Choice* (Hebrew) and *Bittersweet Chocolate*, deal with self-awareness, independence, acceptance of others, and the uniqueness of every child. Her third book, *Two Little Overseers of the Synagogue*, is her own initiative to commemorate IDF soldiers through children's books based on the biographical details of soldiers' childhoods. She ran a project of collecting life stories of Holocaust survivors in the southern part of Israel. In 2011 she initiated a project and wrote an international program centered on *Rutka's Notebook*, the diary of a fourteen-year-old Jewish girl for the three months before she was taken to her death in Auschwitz. Dr. Steiner's article, "Broken wor(l)ds," helps teachers in Israel and throughout the world to teach the diary.

Dr. Bela Ruth Samuel Tenenholtz is a Spiegel Fellow at the Finkler Institute of Holocaust Research at Bar-Ilan University. Born in the Netherlands, she is a daughter and sister of Shoah survivors. After marrying an American Jew and living in New York for almost five years, where her two sons were born, she moved to Israel in 1969 and had four daughters. At age forty-eight she was accepted to the Department of English Language and Literature at the University of Haifa, and completed all her degrees in ten years. After twenty-five years as an English teacher in religious state schools, she moved on to teach English literature, language, and translation studies at Gordon and Shaanan education colleges in Haifa, where she taught Shoah literature and Jewish identity in literature. During this time, she published articles and books connected to her field of expertise and personal history. She is still involved in translation.

INDEX OF PEOPLE

Abse, Danny 227
Adam 71
Adorno, Theodor W. 119, 145
Almog, Ruth 38, 168
Alter, Robert 15
Améry, Jean 40
Amichai, Yehuda 166
Amir, Michlean 95, 96
Amis, Martin 129, 134
Antelme, Robert 94
Appelfeld, Aharon 66, 172
Aschheim, Steven E. 46
Askenazi, Léon 142, 142, 144, 146, 147
Avisar, Ilan 27, 33

Bachmann, Ingeborg 95, 168, 232
Bailey, Blake 107
Bakhtin, Mikhail 128, 134
Banderas, Antonio 192, 233
Barabash, Benny 191, 197
Baron, Lawrence 3, 23, 32, 33, 34, 206, 232
Bassman, Rivka 152
Bateman, Lew 52, 53
Beekman, Anneke 225
Bejski, Moshe 178
Bellow, Saul 15, 17, 18, 19, 22, 231
Ben Haim, Mula 152, 153
Berenzyk, Basya 156
Berg, Scott 87, 89
Bergen, Doris L. 47, 50, 96
Berlin, Isaiah 32, 34
Bernhard, Thomas 168
Binder, Elisheva 40, 41
Blum, John Morton 81
Borowski, Tadeusz 128
Bos, Pascale R. 49, 55

Bottome, Phyllis 85, 86, 87, 88
Boyne, John 130, 131, 134, 185
Brauner, David 135
Brecht, Berthold (Bertolt) 149, 190
Brenner, Rachel 7, 35, 97
Brod, Max 164, 166, 167
Brodsky, Joseph 93
Brooks, Linda 92, 97
Browning, Christopher 83, 84, 88
Bubis, Ignatz 167
Burns, Bryan 127

Camus, Albert 59, 60, 133, 142
Carey, C.J. 132
Carlson, Marvin 194, 197
Cayrol, Jean 134
Celan, Paul 95, 131, 166, 172, 232
Cesarani, David 29, 33
Churchill, Winston 80
Cixous, Hélène 93, 94, 95, 98, 101
Clancy, Dan 192, 197
Clark, D. Worth 85
Claudel, Paul 142
Cohen, Beth 53
Cohen, Boaz 179, 184, 185
Conrad, Joseph 64, 125

Dawidowicz, Lucy 25, 32
Defonseca, Misha 130
Deighton, Len 132
Delbo, Charlotte 62, 131
De-Nur, Eliyah 74
De-Nur, Yehiel 73, 74
Dietrich, Marlene 149
Diner, Dan 182, 185, 186
Diner, Hasia 29
Dinnerstein, Leonard 88, 89
Doneson, Judith 27, 28, 29, 33

Dostoevsky, Fyodor M. 16, 69, 128
Du Bois, W.E.B. 129
Duras, Marguerite 93, 94, 95, 98, 100, 101

Ecksteins, Modris 84, 88
Eger, Eva Edith 219, 220
Egoyan, Atom 31, 34
Eichmann, Adolf 19, 24, 222, 223
Elisha, Ron 195, 197

Faust, Drew Gilpin 99, 101
Feigenbaum, Edith 216
Feinstein, Rabbi Morley T. 50
Feldman, Gerald D. 49
Fenelon, Fanya 229
Fenton, Paul 212, 220
Fermaglich, Kirsten 29
Frank, Anne 32, 39, 40, 92, 119, 120, 190, 200, 222, 227
Fink, Ida 64, 66, 67, 96, 180, 182, 183, 185, 186
Finkelstein, Israel 144, 145
Finlay, Joseph 134
Fleischmann, Lea 46
Fleischner, Eva 178
Floyd, George 100
Fourrier, Charles 72
Frank, Anne 23, 32, 39, 40, 92, 119, 120, 190, 200, 222, 227
Franklin, Sidney 79

Gerron, Kurt 8, 139, 149, 150, 151, 151, 153, 155
Gertzovsky, Henie 159
Gilead, Sarah 227
Goldberg, Leah 38
Goldhagen, Daniel J. 83, 84, 88, 123, 124
Golding, William 125
Gorbachev, Mikhail 81
Gordon, Victor 195, 197
Gouri, Haim 73
Govrin, Michael 38
Grade, Chaim 30, 33
Grant, Linda 107, 131, 134
Grass, Günter 168
Greenberg, Eliezer 15, 22

Greenblatt, Stephen 15
Grese, Irma 127
Gross, Benjamin (Beno) 143, 144, 145, 147
Gross, Yoram 31, 34
Grossman, David 19, 22

Haber, Fritz 46
Hagen, William W. 52
Hájková, Anna 96
Hannam, Charles 126
Harari, Yuval Noah 190, 197
Hareven, Shulamit 37
Harmel, Kristin 130, 131
Hauptman, Martha 70
Hegel, G. W. F. 72
Heineman, Elizabeth 96
Hellbeck, Jochen 98, 101
Herzog, Chaim 196
Hill, Geoffrey 129, 135
Hillesum, Etty 39, 95
Hirsch, Marianne 109, 114
Hitler, Adolf 11, 24, 31, 34, 35, 36, 43, 48, 77, 83, 87, 88, 89, 99, 106, 117, 120, 122, 123, 124. 149, 153, 154, 158, 189, 201, 204, 224, 226
Hoder-Salmon, Marilyn 85, 88
Hoffmann, Yoel 168
Hokin, Catherine 130
Holstein, Bernard 130
Holtschneider, Hannah 133, 135
Horowitz, Sara 7, 57, 96
Horvath, Rita 179, 184
Howe, Irving 15, 33
Hussein, Saddam 36
Husserl, Edmund 26, 32

Indersthyn, Lyuba 159
Insdorf, Annette 27, 33

Jacob 69, 141
Jacobi, Derek 192
Jacobson, Howard 107, 108, 133, 134, 135
Jakobson, Hamutal 96
Jameson, Storm 133
Jannings, Emil 149
Jefferson, Thomas 100

INDEX OF PEOPLE

Jerzak, Katarzyna 92, 93, 96
Jesus 39, 144, 188
Jones-Rogers, Stephanie 99

Kafka, Franz 58, 99, 109, 133, 142, 146
Kant, Immanuel 72
Kaplan, Chaim 130
Karpf, Anne 107, 114
Kaye, Danny 149
Kenaz, Yehoshua 168
Keneally, Thomas 127
Kermode, Frank 182, 186
Kerr, Judith 108, 120, 126, 234
Koenig-Stolper, Lia 194, 195, 196
Kofman, Sarah 93
Kovner, Abba 157
Kravetz, Maliye 158, 159
Kravitz, Malca 153, 156, 158, 159, 160
Kravitz, Sonya 191
Kruk, Hermann 190
Kulka, Otto Dov 109, 110, 114

Langer, Lawrence L. 8, 9, 48, 49, 55, 62, 64
Langfus, Anna 214, 220
Lanzmann, Claude 27, 33, 130
Laqueur, Renata 96, 97, 98, 101
Laskier, Ruth 216, 220
Lassner, Phyllis 1, 84, 85, 86, 88, 97, 98, 231, 234
Lee, Robert E. 100
Leech, Margaret 80
Lessing, Theodor 26, 32
Levenbuk, Miriam 159
Levi, Primo 19, 223, 226, 227
Levick, Carmen 127
Levin, Hanoch 190, 193
Lévinas, Emmanuel 75, 142, 143, 144, 146
Levitsky, Holli 53
Levi-Valensi, Eliane Amado 142, 143, 144, 146, 147
Lévy-Hass, Hanna 98
Lindbergh, Charles 87, 89
Lindbergh, Reeve 87
Linn, Ted 27

Lipschitz, Isaac 226
Liverpool, Lord Russell of 126
Lower, Wendy 99
Lowry, Lois 30, 33
Lowry, Malcolm 128

Malamud, Bernard 14, 15, 16, 17, 18, 22, 225
Man, Paul de 3
Mann, Thomas 93, 168, 232
Marx, Karl 72
Mayer, L.B. 86, 87
Mechlowitz, Chaim Simcha 178
Meershoek, A.J.J. 226
Michman, Dan 205
Mickiewicz, Adam 41
Milch-Sheriff, Ella 185
Miller, Arthur 228, 229
Mitterrand, François 94
Morris, Heather 128
Mosse, George 25, 84, 232
Mühsam, Erich 25, 32

Nachman of Breslov, Rabbi 13
Neher, André 142, 143, 144, 145, 147
Nietzsche, Friedrich 72
Novick, Peter 23, 24, 28, 29, 32, 83, 88

Oberski, Jona 128
Oliner, Samuel 26, 32, 33, 232
Ozick, Cynthia 17, 18, 96

Pagrach, Louis Yaacov 223
Paley, Grace 14, 15, 22, 27
Palimaka, Anita 217
Paul 26
Pauly, Max 151
Pearson, Sue 129
Peretz, I. L. 16, 69
Perlov-Keret, Tova 221, 230
Petropoulos, Jonathan 51
Pinkhof, Clara Asher, 227
Plain, Gill 95
Pogorelskin, Alexis 7, 79, 88, 89, 97, 235
Pollock, Griselda 129, 134
Popper, Robert 126
Preminger, Otto 24, 32
Presser, Jacob (Jacques) 226

Proudhon, Pierre-Joseph 72
Pyle, Ernie 80

Rabi Hanina 177, 184
Rashkes, Roi 190
Ravikovitch, Dahlia 165
Ravvin, Norman 228
Rawicz, Piotr 62, 127
Regev, Miri 196
Reim, Hanoch 190
Resnais, Alain 126, 129
Reubeni, David 167
Ricœur, Paul 143
Roosevelt, Franklin 80, 81
Rosenberg, Alfred 72
Rosenfeld, Alvin 76
Rosenstone, Robert 27, 28, 33
Rosenthal, Jack 126
Roth, Freya 80, 87
Roth, Henry 15
Roth, John 66, 96
Roth, Philip 15, 17, 18, 22, 107, 108, 111, 134, 229, 231, 234
Rothberg, Michael 31, 34
Rubinlicht (Rubinlikht), Leyb 150, 153, 160
Ruebner, Galila 165
Ruebner, Tuvia 170, 172
Rufeisen, Oscar (Father Daniel) 226

Sachs, Nelly 95
Sand, Shlomo 144, 145
Sanders, Joop 227
Sansom, C.J. 132
Sasaki, Sadako 190
Schenck, Nicholas 85
Scherz, Zahava 217, 218
Schlesinger, Arthur 80
Schlink, Bernhard 185
Schönberg, Arnold 170, 232
Schönberner, Gerhard 126
Sebald, Georg Winfried 93, 171, 232
Sebba, Shalom 149, 160
Seidler, Naomi 53
Seiffert, Rachel 132
Seipp, Adam R. 54
Sellers, Susan 95
Semel, Nava 185

Sender, Ruth 218, 219
Sforim, Mendele Mocher 16
Shaham, Nathan 168
Shakespeare, William 16, 120, 225
Shawn, Karen 177, 178, 184, 184
Sheffield, University of 125, 127, 129
Sholom Aleichem 13, 15, 16
Sienkiewicz, Henryk 41
Silverman, Max 129, 134
Simon, Paul 77
Singer, Bryan 30, 34
Sinn, Andrea 54
Skibell, Joseph 21, 22
Słowacki, Julian 41
Smith, Ali 131, 132
Sobol, Joshua 189, 190, 197
Spender, Stephen 24
Spiegleman, Art 120
Stepanova, Maria 113, 114
Stern, Frank 206
Stern, Fritz R. 46
Stoppard, Tom 132

Tec, Nehama 185, 226
Tekoah, Yosef 199, 202
Tolstoy, Leo 16, 34, 69
Tomer, Ben-Zion 190
Toussenel, Alphonse 72
Tucker, Eva 108, 234
Turner, Henry 81, 82, 88, 89, 108

Vajda, Georges 144
Vardi, Dina 37, 43
Verhey, Elma, 226
Verhoeven, Michael 30, 34
Vishniac, Roman 178, 184

Wagner, Richard 72, 195, 196, 197
Wallant, Edward Lewis 19, 20
Walser, Martin 167
Walters, Joel 179, 184
Webbink, Dinand, 226
Weiss, Zev 82
West, Claudine 86, 87
Wiesel, Elie 1, 53, 55, 60, 61, 69, 70, 71, 73, 92, 127, 134, 234
Wiesenthal, Simon 178, 184
Wilkerson, Isabel 98

Wilkomirski, Binjamin 129, 130
Wilson, Katharina 92
Winterson, Jeanette 93
Wolfgang von Goethe, Johann 120, 165
Wordsworth, William 125

Yolen, Jane 30, 33
Yudof, Mark 84

Zand, Shlomo 204
Zohar, Miriam 194

INDEX OF PLACES

Alsace 83
Andernach 213
Aschau 179
Auschwitz-Birkenau 39, 72, 73, 74, 76, 110, 127, 129, 134, 143, 149, 150, 151, 156, 176, 178, 183, 184, 205, 214, 217, 229, 235, 236

Będzin 217
Beit She'an Valley 163
Bergen-Belsen 40, 97, 98, 101, 128, 152
Berlin 53, 92, 149, 154, 155, 163, 166, 167, 169, 189
Bletchley Park 85
Britain 8, 17, 81, 82, 84, 87, 103, 107, 108, 110, 118, 125, 126, 129, 131, 132, 133, 134, 135
Brussels 110, 111
Bug River 46

Canada 26, 191
Channel Islands 133
Charlottesville, Virginia 95
Chełmno 132
Chernobyl 73
Chernowitz 172
Cleveland, Ohio 96, 235
Czechoslovakia 26, 176

Danzig 154, 155, 158
Dimona 217, 218

East Galicia 179
Ellis Island 155
Emek Yizre'el 164, 165
England 109, 116, 133, 154, 155, 158, 191, 229, 231

Fez 8
France 81, 82, 84, 94, 115, 141, 142, 143, 144, 170, 207, 213, 230

Gainesville 169
Galicia 173, 179
Germany 7, 24, 25, 26, 30, 34, 45, 46, 51, 54, 62, 75, 82, 84, 92, 108, 110, 112, 131, 132, 133, 143, 146, 155, 164, 166, 168, 169, 170, 171, 184, 189, 190, 191, 193, 203, 23, 230, 133
Givat Shaul 201
Glasgow 105, 106

Holland 8, 155
Hollywood 7, 87, 121, 122, 204, 205
Hull 132
Hungary 109, 216

Israel 7, 8, 29, 36, 37, 38, 39, 41, 64, 66, 73, 100, 137, 140, 141, 142, 144, 145, 149, 149, 153, 164, 166, 168, 170, 172, 185, 187, 188, 189, 190, 193, 194, 195, 196, 197, 202, 204, 206, 207, 208, 209, 212, 215, 216, 217, 218, 220, 221, 224, 227, 230, 231, 232, 233, 234, 236

Jerusalem 36, 50, 60, 66, 78, 101, 142, 144, 146, 147, 156, 167, 168, 169, 171, 197, 201, 202, 203, 204, 209, 212, 220, 223, 224, 226, 227

Kibbutz Hamaapil 152
Krakow 163, 173

Lida 156
Łódź 131, 132

London 87, 132, 191, 227, 231
Lviv 173

Majdanek 73, 74, 86, 156, 204
Mevasseret-Zion 211, 212
Mexico 128
Mount Sinai 75, 76, 179, 185

Netherlands 26, 33, 255, 191, 221, 222, 223, 225, 226, 227, 236
Nijverdal 226, 227

Oranienburg 25
Osnabrück, Germany 95, 101
Ozorków 131, 132

Paris, France 42, 97, 141, 142, 143, 144, 231
Philadelphia 169, 170
Poland 31, 38, 41, 52, 73, 74, 83, 93, 131, 155, 163, 164, 169, 173, 176, 217, 221, 226
Prague 129, 147, 231

Rzeszow 163, 173

Skokie 24

Sobibor 223
South Carolina 91, 99
Soviet Union 24, 36, 38, 43
Stanisławów, 40
Stuthoff 151

Tel Aviv 36, 164, 165, 168, 171, 191, 195, 204, 231, 232, 233
Theresienstadt 149, 155
Tiberius 178
Tibet 119
Toronto 36, 67
Treblinka 36, 73
Turkey 31
Tyrol, Austria 202, 203

Vichy France 140, 143
Vienna 108, 202
Vlissengen 155

Warsaw 36, 38, 41, 42, 156, 170, 224
Warsaw Ghetto 93, 96, 129, 130
Washington D.C. 24, 51, 80, 91, 92, 95, 234
Westerbork 39, 227

Zhetel 158, 159, 160

INDEX OF ORGANIZATIONS

Academy of Motion Picture Arts and Sciences Margaret Herrick Library 76
Academy of Music (Buchmann-Mehta School of Music) Tel Aviv University 165
American Historical Association 52
American University in Washington 234
Annual Scholars' Conference on the Holocaust and the Churches 234

Bar-Ilan University 171, 179, 181, 196, 214, 231, 232, 233, 235, 236
Beit Leyvik, the Association of Yiddish Writers 152
Bnei Akiva 222
Boston University 70
Bricha 153
British Library 86, 87, 88
Bryn Mawr College 80

California State University ot Northridge 53
Cambridge University Press 52
Cameri Theatre of Tel-Aviv 233
Case Western Reserve University 235
Center for Advanced Judaic Studies 170
Center for Research on Antisemitism 167
Center for the Research of Dutch Jewry at Hebrew University 226
Center for the Study of the Holocaust, Genocide, and Human Rights 51
Claremont McKenna College 51
Columbia University 46, 59

David Yellin College 203

Edinburgh Festival 193

Fringe Theatre Festival, Edmonton 193

German Academic Exchange Service 46
German Studies Association 52

Habima National Theatre 190
Haifa Festival 233
Haifa Municipal Theatre 192
Hebrew University in Jerusalem 168, 171, 212, 226, 231
Hemdat Hadarom Academic College 235
Holocaust Education Foundation 82

Imperial War Museum 129, 135
Indiana University South Bend 50

Jewish American and Holocaust Literature Association 53

Lenin Brigade 157, 159
Lipinsky Institute for Judaic Studies 27
Loyola Marymount University 51, 233

Middlebury College 192
Museum of Jewish Heritage 195

Nissan Nativ Acting Studio 190
Northwestern University 82, 96, 234

Oklahoma State University 71
Orot Israel College 233

Palmach 166

Reed College 46
Richard Stockton University of New Jersey 232
Rosenzweig Center 168

St. Hilda's College, Oxford 235
St. Lawrence University 25, 26, 232
San Diego State University 232, 272
Shaanan College 230
Shoah Foundation Visual History Archive 51
Southampton University 235
Staatsbibliothek 167

Tel Aviv University 164, 165, 171, 191, 204, 231, 232, 233
Tmuna Theatre 192
Trinity University, San Antonio 231
Tzavta Theatre 190

UCLA Center for Jewish Studies 51
UCLA Center for the Study of Women 51
United Nations 199
United States Holocaust Memorial Museum 48, 91, 178, 184
University of California 15
University of California at Davis 46
University of Florida 169

University of Georgia 92
University of Haifa 168, 200, 204, 221, 224, 225, 227, 229, 236
University of Illinois 24
University of Kent 118, 234
University of Memphis 70, 71
University of Minnesota–Duluth 81, 84, 235
University of Notre Dame 50
University of Oregon 69
University of Paris I Panthéon-Sorbonne 231
University of Portsmouth 97
University of Sheffield 125, 127
University of Southern California 51
University of St. Andrews 93
University of Strasbourg 143
University of Texas at Austin 192, 234
University of Texas at Dallas 70, 234
University of Virginia 92, 95
University of Warwick 119
University of Wisconsin 25, 232

Vienna University 202

Yad Vashem 50, 156, 159, 160, 197, 202, 203, 204, 205, 216, 223, 233
York University 66

www.ingramcontent.com/pod-product-compliance
Lightning Source LLC
Chambersburg PA
CBHW062135300426
44115CB00012BA/1929